Exploring Health Communication

Routledge Introductions to Applied Linguistics is a series of introductory level textbooks covering the core topics in Applied Linguistics, primarily designed for those beginning postgraduate studies, or taking an introductory MA course as well as advanced undergraduates. Titles in the series are also ideal for language professionals returning to academic study.

The books take an innovative 'practice to theory' approach, with a 'back-to-front' structure. This leads the reader from real-world problems and issues, through a discussion of intervention and how to engage with these concerns, before finally relating these practical issues to theoretical foundations. Additional features include tasks with commentaries, a glossary of key terms, and an annotated further reading section.

Exploring Health Communication brings together many of the various linguistic strands in health communication, while maintaining an interdisciplinary focus on method and theory.

The authors critically explore and discuss a number of underlying themes that constitute the broad field of health communication including spoken, written and electronic health communication. The rise of the internet has led to an explosion of interactive online health resources which have profoundly affected the way in which healthcare is delivered, and with this, have brought about changes in the relationship between provider and patient. This textbook uses examples of real-life health language data throughout, in order to fully explore the topics covered.

Exploring Health Communication is essential reading for postgraduate and upper undergraduate students of applied linguistics and health communication.

Kevin Harvey is Lecturer in Sociolinguistics and Co-ordinator of the Health Language Research Group, School of English Studies at the University of Nottingham.

Nelya Koteyko is Lecturer in Media and Communication at the University of Leicester.

Routledge Introductions to Applied Linguistics

Series editors:

Ronald Carter, *Professor of Modern English Language,*
University of Nottingham, UK

Guy Cook, *Chair of Language in Education,*
King's College London, UK

Routledge Introductions to Applied Linguistics is a series of introductory level textbooks covering the core topics in Applied Linguistics, primarily designed for those beginning postgraduate studies, or taking an introductory MA course as well as advanced undergraduates. Titles in the series are also ideal for language professionals returning to academic study.

The books take an innovative 'practice to theory' approach, with a 'back-to-front' structure. This leads the reader from real-world problems and issues, through a discussion of intervention and how to engage with these concerns, before finally relating these practical issues to theoretical foundations. Additional features include tasks with commentaries, a glossary of key terms, and an annotated further reading section.

Exploring English Language Teaching
Language in Action
Graham Hall

Exploring Classroom Discourse
Language in Action
Steve Walsh

Exploring Corpus Linguistics
Language in Action
Winnie Cheng

Exploring World Englishes
Language in a Global Context
Philip Seargeant

Exploring Health Communication
Language in Action
Kevin Harvey and Nelya Koteyko

Exploring Professional Communication
Language in Action
Stephanie Schnurr

'The innovative approach devised by the series editors will make this series very attractive to students, teacher educators, and even to a general readership, wanting to explore and understand the field of applied linguistics. The volumes in this series take as their starting point the everyday professional problems and issues that applied linguists seek to illuminate. The volumes are authoritatively written, using an engaging 'back-to-front' structure that moves from practical interests to the conceptual bases and theories that underpin applications of practice.'

Anne Burns, *Aston University, UK,*
University of New South Wales, Australia

Exploring Health Communication

Language in Action

Kevin Harvey and
Nelya Koteyko

Routledge
Taylor & Francis Group

LONDON AND NEW YORK

First published 2013
by Routledge
2 Park Square, Milton Park, Abingdon, Oxon OX14 4RN

Simultaneously published in the USA and Canada
by Routledge
711 Third Avenue, New York, NY 10017

Routledge is an imprint of the Taylor & Francis Group, an informa business

British Library Cataloguing in Publication Data
A catalogue record for this book is available from the British Library

Library of Congress Cataloging in Publication Data
Exploring health communication : language in action / Kevin Harvey and Nelya
Koteyko.
p. cm. -- (Routledge introductions to applied linguistics)
Includes bibliographical references and index.
1. Medicine--Information services. 2. Medical informatics. 3. Communication in
medicine. I. Koteyko, Nelya. II. Title.
R858.H3357 2012
610.285--dc23
2012010260

ISBN: 978-0-415-59721-0 (hbk)
ISBN: 978-0-415-59722-7 (pbk)
ISBN: 978-0-203-09643-7 (ebk)

Typeset in Sabon
by Saxon Graphics Ltd, Derby

MIX
Paper from
responsible sources
FSC
www.fsc.org   FSC® C004839

Printed and bound in Great Britain by the MPG Books Group

Kevin Harvey
For my parents, Malcolm and Elaine

Nelya Koteyko
For my parents, Vladimir and Nadiya

Contents

Acknowledgements

We would like to thank the series editors, Ron Carter and Guy Cook, for their encouragement, support and feedback throughout the planning and writing of this book. It was Ron Carter who first presented us with the irresistible proposition of putting together a book on health communication, and we are grateful for his giving us the opportunity to pursue such an exciting venture.

We would also like to thank Sophie Jaques and Louisa Semlyen at Routledge for their enthusiastic backing of this book and for all their practical guidance in helping it to come together so splendidly.

Finally, we wish to acknowledge the help (technical, practical, emotional) that the following people, all in their inimitable, selfless ways, have provided us: Stephen Mckibbin, Rebecca Peck, Catherine Smith, Patrick Allen and Ana Jolly.

Permissions

The authors would like to thank the following copyright holders for permission to reprint the following materials:

Figure 6.1 Patient information leaflet for paracetamol tablets: courtesy of Wockhardt UK Ltd.

Figure 8.1 Homepage of *Teenage Health Freak* website: courtesy of Aidan Macfarlane (Teenage Health Websites).

Series editors' introduction

The Introductions to Applied Linguistics series

This series provides clear, authoritative, up-to-date overviews of the major areas of applied linguistics. The books are designed particularly for students embarking on masters-level or teacher-education courses, as well as students in the closing stages of undergraduate study. The practical focus will make the books particularly useful and relevant to those returning to academic study after a period of professional practice, and also to those about to leave the academic world for the challenges of language-related work. For students who have not previously studied applied linguistics, including those who are unfamiliar with current academic study in English speaking universities, the books can act as one-step introductions. For those with more academic experience, they can also provide a way of surveying, updating and organising existing knowledge.

The view of applied linguistics in this series follows a famous definition of the field by Christopher Brumfit as:

> The theoretical and empirical investigation of real-world problems in which language is a central issue.

> (Brumfit 1995: 27)

In keeping with this broad problem-oriented view, the series will cover a range of topics of relevance to a variety of language-related professions. While language teaching and learning rightly remain prominent and will be the central preoccupation of many readers, our conception of the discipline is by no means limited to these areas. Our view is that while each reader of the series will have their own needs, specialities and interests, there is also much to be gained from a broader view of the discipline as a whole. We believe there is much in common between all enquiries into language-related problems in the real world, and much to be gained from a comparison of the insights from one area of applied linguistics with another. Our hope therefore is that readers and course designers will not choose only those volumes relating to their own particular interests, but use this series to construct a wider knowledge and understanding of the field, and the many crossovers and resonances between its various areas. Thus the topics to be covered are wide in range, embracing an exciting mixture of established and new areas of applied linguistic enquiry.

The perspective on applied linguistics in this series

In line with this problem-oriented definition of the field, and to address the concerns of readers who are interested in how academic study can inform their own professional practice, each book follows a structure in marked contrast to the usual movement *from* theory *to* practice. In this series, this usual progression is presented back to front. The argument moves *from* Problems, *through* Intervention, and *only* finally to Theory. Thus each topic begins with a survey of everyday professional problems in the area under consideration, ones which the reader is likely to have encountered. From there it proceeds to a discussion of intervention and engagement with these problems. Only in a final section (either of the chapter or the book as a whole) does the author reflect upon the implications of this engagement for a general understanding of language, drawing out the theoretical implications. We believe this to be a truly *applied* linguistics perspective, in line with the definition given above, and one in which engagement with real-world problems is the distinctive feature, and in which professional practice can both inform and draw upon academic understanding.

Support to the Reader

Although it is not the intention that the text should be in any way activity-driven, the pedagogic process is supported by measured guidance to the reader in the form of suggested activities and tasks that raise questions, prompt reflection and seek to integrate theory and practice. Each book also contains a helpful glossary of key terms.

The series complements and reflects the *Routledge Handbook of Applied Linguistics,* edited by James Simpson, which conceives and categorises the scope of applied linguistics in a broadly similar way.

Ronald Carter
Guy Cook

Reference

Brumfit, C. J. (1995). 'Teacher Professionalism and Research', in G. Cook and B. Seidlhofer (eds) *Principle and Practice in Applied Linguistics.* Oxford, UK: Oxford University Press, pp 27–42

Note

There is a section of commentaries on a number of the tasks, at the back of the book. The (TC) symbol in the margin indicates that there is a commentary on that task.

Introduction

Although health and illness have long been social and political concerns, recent times have witnessed an increasing preoccupation with monitoring and promoting physical and emotional well-being. For example, people are being increasingly subjected to the clinical gaze, that is, to unprecedented levels of medical scrutiny. Governments, health providers and charities continually exhort us to monitor and enhance our physical and emotional well-being, specifically, among other injunctions: to take daily exercise; to limit alcohol intakes and consume more fruit and vegetables; to regulate body weights; and to take part in screenings for various diseases and conditions such as cancer, depression, diabetes and heart disease.

And if we're not being subjected to governmental or institutional sanctions about lifestyles, then we're actively taking greater personal responsibility for maintaining our own health. In contemporary modes of health promotion, individuals are addressed on the assumption that they wish to be healthy (Rose, 1999: 86). Expectations of healthy living and self-fulfilment are demandingly high, with doctors being confronted by rising numbers of the 'worried well' and placed, as a consequence, under ever increasing pressure to offer personalised and often unnecessary services (Greenhalgh and Wessely, 2004).

Alongside these and other developments in healthcare, we are presently witnessing seismic shifts in the realignment of healthcare systems. For instance, at the time of writing (November, 2011), the British Government is in the process of seeing its Health and Social Care Bill through the House of Lords. The bill aims to further open up the National Health Service (NHS) to market forces, allowing private companies to compete for service provision. In the UK and many other countries around the world, free access to healthcare no longer seems to be an inviolable right of citizens, but a commodity for consumers to purchase. For healthcare, then, these are testing, pivotal times which require greater critical attention.

What does all this contextual preamble have to do with language and communication? Well, a central premise of this book is that language plays a significant role in healthcare delivery and mediating people's experiences of, and beliefs about, health and illness. Applied linguistics has a long tradition of investigating the domains of personal, social and cultural life. The domain of healthcare is no exception. Over the last thirty years or so there has been a proliferation of discourse-based research into health communication, research which, excitingly, continues to grow apace.

The linguistic analysis of medical discourse reveals much about the practical realities of healthcare, and this book contains many examples of linguistic analyses which aim to illustrate the connection between discourse processes and contemporary medicine. This is not to claim that healthcare issues can simply be reduced to, and explained in terms of, linguistic behaviour alone. Applied linguistics is only one of a number of approaches that are able to shed light on medicine and society. However, it is our contention that scrutinising language in use offers a means of making sense of some of the complexities of healthcare: exposing beliefs and practices that might be taken for granted or overlooked altogether.

Health communication is a broad field that encompasses the analysis of a variety of spoken, written and computer-mediated texts and processes. It is essentially an inter- and multi-disciplinary field that goes beyond the core disciplines of communication and medicine to include such fields and sub-disciplines as media studies, sociology, philosophy, social psychology and informatics. In the interdisciplinary spirit of applied linguistics we draw on a range of these approaches throughout this book – although language is always at the forefront of our consideration. Such a multifaceted approach to communication and health, we suggest, is well suited to contribute to our understanding of health provision and health promotion, not to mention other aspects of medical culture.

Health communication research takes place in and across a number of contexts, including (1) relations between health professionals and patients (2) individuals' use of and search for health information, (3) the construction of public health messages and campaigns, (4) the dissemination of individual and population health risk information, that is, risk communication, (5) images of health and illness in the mass media and the culture at large and (6) the development of e-health tools and applications (Jackson and Duffy, 1998; see also Healthy People 2010, 2010).

In order to capture this multiplicity of themes we have resolved this book into three sections: (I) Spoken health communication, (II) Written health communication and (III) Computer-mediated health communication. This tripartite structure allows us to present readers with a broad overview of the various health communication concerns that take place across these three semiotic modes. In Part I we review the practitioner–patient relationship, exploring the interactional routines of a variety of health professionals. Although we give substantial attention to the doctor–patient consultation, we also focus on practitioners who have featured less frequently in health communication research. As Iedema (2007: 4) observes, clinical work involves the contributions of many professionals and focussing exclusively on the work of the doctor runs the risk of obscuring the fact that patient care relies on many personnel beside physicians.

The final chapter of Part I examines the powerful role of narrative in shaping people's understanding and experience of health and illness. Again, as well as aiming to do justice to some of the main research themes, we have sought to represent areas of research that have received relatively little scholarly attention, such as narratives of mental health. Distressed individuals commonly experience difficulty discussing their emotional turmoil with others. Yet, as we will see, forms of narrative provide a resource for people seeking to express and make sense of their problems.

Part II widens our focus to incorporate written texts. Here we review the patient case record, a text that is pivotal in patient care. We examine the ways in which patients are represented in the document, and how, accordingly, interrogating the written forms of the patient record can inform our understanding of clinical routines and inter-professional communication. This part of the book also looks at media representations of health and illness, with specific emphasis on infectious disease outbreaks. We pay particular attention to metaphor: how it is used to not only represent medical knowledge but also create a sense of urgency and dramatise events. Interrogating media accounts of infectious outbreaks such as SARS and the swine flu pandemic, we argue, enhances our understanding of the ways health and illness discourses that circulate in society are formulated and reproduced, and how they operate persuasively. The final chapter reviews research into the patient information leaflet. We consider the difficulties that text producers have in presenting cogent and accessible health information, and how such information is processed by readers.

The final part of the book reviews research into computer-mediated health communication. We consider how the Internet, the rise of which has led to an explosion of online health forums, affords people a means of advice and support which they might otherwise have difficulty obtaining. We explore the types of advice-seeking routines which occur online, examining, for example, how peers provide emotional support and advice to one another, as well as how individuals communicate problems to health professionals. We also examine the expressive potential of electronic discourse, and how professionals, in the absence of face-to-face contact, fashion online expert identities for themselves.

Although the book serves as a wide-ranging introduction to health communication, there are a number of areas that, inevitably, we have been unable to cover. Health communication is an impossibly broad subject to represent sufficiently in one volume and, given further print, we would have liked to have devoted space to, among other areas, genetic counselling, telemedicine, palliative care, and emergency medicine.

However, despite these gaps, we hope that this volume serves as a stimulating invitation to the continually fascinating subject which is health communication, equipping aspiring investigators with a range of linguistic theories and frameworks for conducting their own work in this increasingly significant field of research.

Part I

Spoken health communication

1 The practitioner–patient relationship

Doctor–patient encounters

Introduction: spoken discourse in clinical settings

A significant amount of medical practice takes place through verbal interchange. Indeed it is no exaggeration to claim that, over the last three millennia, healthcare has principally been conducted through some kind of face-to-face encounter between patient and health expert (Brown *et al.*, 2006: 81). Yet it is only relatively recently – with the advent of sophisticated tape and video recording (technical advancements that allow researchers to capture naturally occurring spontaneous talk with exceptional degrees of precision) that the patient-provider exchange has been studied in any significant linguistic detail. With the availability of detailed transcripts that faithfully account for not only the content of conversation, but also the precise way in which such content is articulated (including details such as pitch, speed, pauses, false starts, repetitions, overlaps and interruptions), researchers have brought to bear a range of broadly discourse-based approaches on the medical consultation, resulting in a proliferation of studies that have contributed to our understanding of the patient-provider exchange.

In tandem with the aforesaid technological advances, the twentieth century has witnessed what has commonly been described as a 'linguistic turn', that is, a concern for 'the modalities of language use' that has preoccupied disciplines from sociology and anthropology through to literature and philosophy (Silverman, 1987: 19). The linguistic turn has led to researchers focussing on observable communication in a range of everyday and institutional settings. In particular, the medical setting has become an important research site for investigation, with micro-analytic attention to the discourse of the clinic offering a more precise study of the 'human social world' (Brown *et al.,* 2006: 81) than that afforded by other forms of sociological analysis. Although the clinical setting encompasses a range of communicative practices that involve a variety of medical and non-medical personnel, applied linguistic research has favoured doctor–patient interaction, and it is this specific encounter between professional and patient that we explore extensively this chapter.

Putting the doctor–patient encounter in context: themes and issues

Research into doctor–patient interaction to date has been extensive and still continues to grow apace, hence it is impossible to do justice to all the rich variety of work in the area. Nonetheless, there are several broadly applied linguistic research themes that have dictated enquiry into the doctor–patient encounter, chief among them typological/structural concerns, that is, attempts to identify and explicate recurring sequences of talk that make up the consultation process, and issues relating to the enactment of authority and control in the consultation. Since arguably the most outstanding characteristic of the doctor–patient encounter is, at least from an interactional perspective, 'the unequal nature of the power relationship' (Gwyn, 2002: 63), we shall devote most of this chapter to exploring the connection between authority and the linguistic resources on which participants draw to enact and negotiate power relations during the consultation.

Among the wide range of practitioner–patient exchanges that routinely take place in clinical settings, the doctor–patient relation has been described as the most interpersonally complex (Ong et al., 1995: 903). Part of this complexity lies in the multi-purpose function of the consultation. For example, three distinct yet connected purposes of doctor–patient communication can be readily identified, namely building a good inter-personal relationship, exchanging information and making decisions about treatment (Ong et al., 1995: 903-4). Moreover, these discursive activities take place in an institutional context where the participants are situated in unequal positions, with patients 'investing their trust and faith' (Lupton, 2003: 114) in the clinical proficiency of the doctor. Thus, as Gwyn (2002: 62) observes, asymmetries between doctor and patient can be seen to arise, to some extent, as a consequence of the format of the consultation itself (an issue to which we will return later in this chapter).

As ten Have (1991: 138) observes, medical interviews are tightly organised interactional events, and the doctor–patient consultation is no exception. Given the relatively unvarying format of the exchange, researchers have been able to identify a number of recurring phases of action that take place within it. Two influential typologies are those proposed by Byrne and Long (1976) and ten Have (1989). Byrne and Long, who were among the first researchers to systematically interrogate the structure of the consultation, describe six characteristic sequences of action:

I   Greeting and relating to the patient
II   Ascertaining the reasons for the patient's attendance
III Conducting a verbal or physical examination or both

IV   Considering the patient's condition
V   Outlining further treatment
VI   Terminating the consultation.

(Byrne and Long, 1976: 132)

From the doctor's perspective, the value of this structural template is that it forms a model sequence, a logical order, deviation from which, in some instances, can potentially to lead to problems for the participants. For example, the sequence I-II-III-V-III-I-VI is identified by Byrne and Long as being particularly indicative of a problematic encounter. This can be seen in the following extract in which the patient, a labourer who has a long history of back troubles, is returning to his GP following a hospital referral. At the start of the sequence, the doctor has already greeted the patient (Phase I) but still has, as the exchanges demonstrate, to fully discover the reasons for his attendance.

1   D: (Phase III) What is your job?
2   P: Well, I'm on a quarry job, carting clay, as a slagger – it's a very rough job – that's the trouble… well I've been seriously thinking about getting a lighter job if I could and I'm travelling to Denton but it would be out on the moors type of thing.
3   D: (V) Oh, well that's no good to you…and this business of turning your head round most of the time, you see you're putting a strain on your neck.
4   P: I have to move back into the yards.
5   D: Oh that's no good to you. It's enough trouble if you've got your neck normal. It would be better if you could find a job – this is a fairly new job, isn't it? Were you on long distance before that?
6   P: Well, I was on middle distance actually, it wasn't as strenuous.
7   D: It might be better to look for something lighter. (III) How old are you now?
8   P: Fifty-three.
9   D: (V) It's not the time of life to start looking for another job, is it?

(Byrne and Long, 1976: 134)

Throughout these exchanges, the doctor shifts between the activities of conducting a verbal examination of the patient (Phase III) and outlining further treatment for his problems (V), missing out Phase IV (considering the patient's condition). According to Byrne and Long, the doctor's leaping back and forth between these two phases betrays the 'mess' in which he finds himself. Although already possessing much information about the patient's prior clinical treatment and personal biography, the doctor continues to elicit this same information from the patient, details of which he should of course be readily aware. The doctor's reverting to Phase III of the consultation is, Byrne and Long suggest, a means of 'keeping control over of what he is doing' (1976: 135), imposing order on the seemingly erratic development of the interaction.

Byrne and Long's six phases of the consultation serve as what they call 'a checklist' with which doctors might 'facilitate their self-learning' (1976: 132). As Brown *et al.* observe, this typology (and others similar to it) is thus pedagogically motivated, designed to equip medical students with frameworks 'within which to learn and diligently reproduce the lists, typologies and forms of knowledge that would gain them the best marks' (2006: 86). This emphasises the fact that a number of structural typologies (Byrne and Long's included) are designed from the perspective of, and intended for, the medical practitioner. This inevitably downplays the role of the patient in the consultation: consultations are two-way exchanges in which patients, to varying degrees, jointly verbally negotiate clinical outcomes with their doctor. A more sensitive structural typology of the consultation – or at least one that emphasises negotiated speech activities between the participants – is that outlined by ten Have (1989), who describes what he calls the 'Ideal Sequence'. Consultations that feature the Ideal Sequence are resolved into six phases of action which unfold in a predictable order:

1 opening
2 complaint
3 examination or test
4 diagnosis
5 treatment or advice
6 closing

These six phases overlap with Byrne and Long's model typology. However, ten Have is at pains to point out that the sequential structure he describes is only 'ideal' in the sense that there will inevitably be deviations from it, although such departures are still likely to remain acceptable to the participants. For example, both doctors and patients well advanced into the consultation might well return to an earlier phase, particularly if further issues have arisen (ten Have, 1989: 118). Ten Have's approach to the consultation also emphasises the interactive nature of the exchanges between doctor and patient. Phases 2 to 5 of the consultation, for instance, are likely to involve both sets of participants jointly engaged in 'some sort of 'discussion' of what is proposed or done' (ten Have, 1989: 118), even if it is the doctor who typically initiates the phases and the patient who follows. The following examples are testament to this variety. Both extracts are taken from the early stages of the consultations of which they are part. (For details of the transcription code we use here and throughout the rest of the book, please see Appendix.)

I

34   D: well we will take a look it can simply be that that she has
            a little blood shortage she is [nine years
35   M: [yes that's what I also
36   D: the ages
            …
45   D: I don't know if it's something but we can just prick

II

27   P: well (1.2) yes there we are again there we are again yes
28   P: I have two more things that uh you have to take a look at
29   D: and that is?
30   P: first uh at my throat and then at this knee
31   D: okay (.) and how are you doing besides that?
                                (adapted from ten Have, 1989: 119)

In the first extract the doctor (D) is discussing the problem of a child who has been brought to the surgery by her mother (M). The doctor initiates the examination sequence, proposing – 'we will take a look' – a 'test' (ten Have, 1989: 119) and then (at line 12) referring to the physical undertaking of this procedure more specifically: 'we can just prick'. The mother contributes minimally to this sequence of talk (her single utterance, which offers an agreement of the doctor's assessment, is incomplete, terminating mid-clause). The doctor ignores the mother's statement, an action which, ten Have remarks, preserves the established distribution of medical knowledge between the participants and the Ideal Sequence in which this distribution is articulated (1989: 120).

In the second extract, however, there is a greater degree of sequential variation, a departure from the Ideal Sequence. In this example, the patient, ten Have observes, appears more 'forceful' about his or her medical concerns, introducing (without being prompted by the doctor) two further problems and thereby setting the complaint agenda. The doctor allows the patient to formulate these extra concerns ('and that is'), but insists on first having a general discussion concerning the patient's health: 'and how are you doing besides that'. Thus the doctor forestalls entry into the examination phase of the consultation, further extending the complaint phase before attending to the patient's knee and throat concerns directly.

What these two extracts demonstrate is that rather than doctors solely leading patients through an agenda, participants tell or show each other what they are doing or what they want the other to do (ten Have, 1989: 119). The various phases of the consultation are typically advanced by the doctor, but as the second extract reveals, patients can (and do) themselves commence sequences, manipulating the structure of the consultation to set the complaint agenda. Thus the notion of the Ideal Sequence affords researchers a useful resource for interrogating the structure of medical interviews, not least its ability to account for sequential variation and the joint negotiation between doctors and patients that gives rise to such variation in the consultation.

(TC)

Task 1.1 Identifying phases of the consultation

The following short, yet (surprisingly) complete, consultation features a patient who has repeatedly visited her doctor with a persistent problem. On prior occasions she has been given a certain prescription and has been happy to receive it. On this occasion, however, the doctor seeks to persuade the patient to come off this medication and to try a different treatment.

Read through the transcript and then see if you can answer the following questions:

- How many of the six phases described by Byrne and Long and ten Have appear in this consultation?
- In what order and whereabouts do the phases appear and which participant initiates them?
- Does any phase feature less prominently than any of the others?

1	D:	Come in. Hello. How are you?
2	P:	I feel shocking. You know, when I came to see you last week and you knocked those capsules off – well, every morning when I get up, and my head – Doctor you could have amputated it. It was a terrible headache and it was as if someone was dragging my eyeballs out. So I took more tablets, I haven't had anything since…swollen, I've had bags under my eyes and all snuffly and watery, and at the moment, all the top of my head here feels as though there's pressure on it and I feel this stuff going down the back of my throat.
3	D:	Are you coughing any of it out?
4	P:	No, I can't cough it out as…when I blow my nose it's clear.
5	D:	Is your nose blocked? Lie your head back and I'll have a look.

6	P:	Just here and inside of my throat is always very tender and all under here...and with both my hands tucked underneath my ribs and my head feels as if it's going to fall off.
7	D:	Well, I'll give you a change of tablets for that and when you're over this I'll start you back on the capsules.
8	P:	Well, all the aches and pains have gone, apart from under my ribs.
9	D:	Well, leave it a week and come and see me again. It sounds as if it's the cold that's affecting your sinuses. Right, so a week from today.
10	P:	Bye-bye, now.

(Byrne and Long, 1976: 132-3)

Getting critical: unpacking asymmetry in the doctor–patient consultation

The notion that the doctor–patient relationship is characteristically an inequitable one is well established (Pilnick and Dingwall, 2011). A number of early approaches to the healthcare encounter began with the premise that there was something wrong with the conversation between doctors and patients (West, 1984). Doctors, specifically general practitioners (GPs), were described as verbally dominating the consultation process and not sufficiently listening to their patients (Rowen, 1977 cited in West, 1984). At that time, however, little was known about the precise means through which verbal dominance was linguistically enacted. Despite their emphasis on communication difficulties, these assessments of the consultation, conducted from both lay and scholarly perspectives (including assessments by practitioners themselves), were not concerned with systematically explicating and describing the interactional dynamics of the interview. Rather than empirically studying the clinical interview, their focus was more on medical praxis, assigning, for example, functional meanings to utterances and, through the use of coding schemes, resolving utterances into functional categories (Ainsworth-Vaughn, 2001: 453).

Furthermore, although the aforesaid research often described the imbalance of power between doctor and patient, it was typically conducted without drawing on linguistic theories and insights, and was predicated on the assumption that language is straightforwardly 'a transparent vehicle' (Ainsworth-Vaughn, 2001: 453), that is, something that merely reflects participants' agendas and in no way shapes or determines them. It was only during the 1980s that an emerging body of broadly applied linguistic work provided detailed textual evidence for the asymmetrical relationship between doctors and patients, drawing on contemporary theories of language in use and exploring the situated and sequential nature of spoken discourse.

One of the factors recognised as potentially contributing to restricting the patient's verbal contributions in the consultation is time. Or lack of it. As West (1984: 2) puts it, 'talking with patients takes time'. Yet doctors commonly want to arrive at diagnoses as quickly as possible (Wodak, 1997: 177). Conversely, patients are likely to want to explain their personal circumstances as extensively as possible and to know the implications of their complaints and illnesses (ibid.). This conflict of interests is, understandably, liable to give rise to inter-personal difficulties in the consultation.

The average time of the consultation with a primary care physician is, in the United Kingdom at least, estimated to be on average 13 minutes (Royal College of General Practitioners, 2004). General practitioners typically interview around 177 patients a week and manage 90% of the problems presented in the consultation without referral to other services (Brown *et al.*, 2006). All of these factors unavoidably put pressure on practitioners to be maximally verbally efficient when investigating their patients' problems, factors that potentially contribute to the conversational asymmetry that is characteristic of much doctor–patient talk.

In order to demonstrate how systematic attention to linguistic detail can expose power and dominance in the consultation, we shall consider a sample of doctor–patient analysis conducted by Fairclough, a leading proponent of critical discourse analysis. Critical discourse analysis (often abbreviated as CDA) is a mode of discourse analysis dedicated to exposing how language is influenced by power relations and ideologies, neither of which is likely to be apparent to language users themselves (Fairclough, 1992: 12). But not only does CDA expose the use and abuse of power in discourse, it also condemns such discursive practices, seeing the exercise of power through discourse as being reflective of, and contributing to, broader social inequalities.

The following analysis, which is based on clinical data first presented and discussed by Mishler (1984) in his pioneering work *Discourse of Medicine: Dialectics of Medical Interviews,* serves as an excellent example of a CDA approach to discourse analysis, revealing some of the tensions that can surface in communication between doctors and patients. In this particular encounter the doctor (D) is male, the patient (P) female.

```
1   D:   Hm hm (.3) now what do you mean by a sour stomach?
2   P:   (1.1) What's a sour stomach? A heartburn
3        like a heartburn or someth[ ing.
4   D:                              [ Does it burn over here?
5   P:                                                   Yeah
6        It li- I think- I think it like- If you take a needle
7        and stick [ ya right [ ....there's a pain right here [
```

```
 8   D:                [ Hm hm  [ Hm hm                    [ Hm hm
 9   P:    and and then it goes from here on this side to this side.
10   D:    Hm hm does it [go into the back?
11   P:                     [It's a:ll up here. No. It's all right
12          [Up here in the front.
13   D:    [Yeah              And when do you get that?
14   P:    (1.3) Wel:l when I eat something wrong
15   D:    How- how soon after you eat it?
16   P:    Wel:l probably an hour maybe [ less.
17   D:                                 [ About an hour?
18   P:    Maybe less I've cheated and I've been
19          drinking which I shouldn't have done.
20   D:    Does drinking make it worse?
21   P:    Ho ho uh ooh Yes (1.0) especially the carbonation and
            the alcohol.
22   D:    Hm hm how much do you drink?
23   P:    (1.5) I don't know enough to make me
24          sleep at night and that's quite a bit.
25   D:    One or two drinks a day?
26   P:    O:h no no no humph it's more like ten [at night
27   D:                                           [How many drinks
            – a night.
28   P:    At night.
29   D:    Whaddya ta- What type of drinks? I [ ((unclear))
30   P:                                        [ Oh vodka yeah
31          vodka and ginger ale.
32   D:    How long have you been drinking that heavily?
33   P:    (1.4) Since I've been married.
34   D:    How long is that?
35   P:    ((giggle)) Four years. ((giggle))
```

As Fairclough (1992: 140-4) observes in his commentary on these verbal exchanges, the encounter is clearly organised around the doctor's questions to which the patient then responds. The doctor controls the organisation of the talk by opening and closing each interactional phase of the consultation while acknowledging the patient's answers. (Although this is not always the case, for in some instances the patient's contributions are not acknowledged at all. For example, the doctor's question in line 4, though topically connected to the patient's prior utterance, does not acknowledge the formulation offered by the patient.) The patient's turns at talk, therefore, are limited since she talks only when the doctor elicits a response from her, principally by his asking questions. The doctor, conversely, is not granted turns at talk by another party but initiates them himself, taking them when the patient has finished her answers or when she has provided sufficient information to satisfy the doctor's query.

Another linguistic feature of the interview which evinces the doctor's authority and control is the introduction, maintaining and changing of topic. In this instance, it is the doctor who sets the topical agenda since, typically, it is he who introduces new subjects and chooses whether to ignore the pursuit of new topics introduced by the patient. For instance, at line 18, the patient discloses that she has 'cheated' – that she's been 'drinking', which she 'shouldn't have done'. The doctor, however, does not follow up this potentially revealing and significant personal admission, instead pursuing a strict line of questioning directed at eliciting medical details relating to her use of alcohol. Fairclough suggests that, given his narrow focus on medical aspects (as opposed to the patient's social and personal concerns), the doctor is limiting topics in accordance with a predetermined clinical agenda which the patient is prevented from disrupting (1992: 141).

Moreover, as well as severely restricting the patient's access to new topics, the doctor further limits her turns through the regular use of polar questions. Such questions (for example, 'Does it burn over here?' and 'Does it go into the back?') produce only information-limited 'yes/ no' responses and do not allow the patient to take the floor in the same way that a request for information such as 'Tell me about your concern' would do. Yet, for all that, the doctor does employ a number of more open questions which should, in principle, provide more substantial access to the conversational floor: 'How many drinks a night?', 'What type of drinks?'. But again these questions are closely focussed on specific details (e.g. the kind and quantity of alcohol) in relation to the patient's drinking and do not encourage her (as her subsequent responses demonstrate) to introduce new topics germane to the personal and social context of her medical complaint. As a result, the patient seems to be a rather passive entity who merely responds to 'the stimuli of a physician's queries' (Mishler, 1984: 10).

It is also telling how a number of the doctor's questions (as in lines 4, 17, 23) overlap the patient's as yet to be completed turns. These overlapping instances possibly appear to indicate occurrences where the doctor has received all the information he considers necessary from the patient's replies to his questions and that therefore he is simply cleaving to the pre-set agenda or routine mentioned above, an agenda through which he passes swiftly and efficiently (efficiently in the sense of time and verbal economy). This rapid routine might well be experienced by the patient as a series of what Fairclough refers to as disjointed and unpredictable questions, a strategy of interrogation which might well account for the hesitations before the patient produces a number of her answers (as in lines 2, 14, 23, 33). (However, these pauses might also be due to other factors, such as the high degree of self-monitoring required by the patient in response to the sensitive subject matter broached by the doctor (Vershueren, 2001: 78.))

This example of linguistic analysis is, as Fairclough himself concedes, one-sided in its focus on interactional authority and control. Furthermore, some of the claims that Fairclough makes concerning the use of certain linguistic forms (such as questions) and their coercive function are, arguably, not fully borne out by the exchanges examined in the extract above. The number of questions that participants ask in medical consultations is indeed an important index of interactional control since 'to ask a question is to claim power over emerging talk' (Ainsworth-Vaughn, 1998: 462). However, this is not to say that every occurrence of a question or series of questions is necessarily emblematic of interactional dominance on the part of the questioner. As Verschueren (2001: 77) argues, respondents' answers to questions might exert similar levels of organisational control over an interaction. Although answers are likely to be constrained by questions that, necessarily, require them to be 'conversationally appropriate next action[s]' (Treichler et al., 1984: 68), speakers who respond to questions are not automatically (and on every occasion) powerless: the answers they produce, in turn, are liable to determine the type of turn that follows, thereby contributing to the shape and organisation of the interaction as it develops. A linguistic form itself, such as a question, is not indubitably emblematic of control. When assessing conversational asymmetry, one must consider how participants jointly operate and negotiate meaning in interactions.

Nonetheless, in closely explicating linguistic activity as Fairclough does, the foregoing commentary demonstrates how the doctor, using a number of discursive strategies, dominates the medical encounter, restricting the conversational resources of the patient in order to adhere to a pre-determined medical agenda. The doctor's authority is manifested in linguistic features (such as turn-taking, topic shifts, interruptions and so on) which collectively evince a clear degree of interactional control. The medical agenda which the doctor pursues requires his attending to clinical and technical matters, rather than his adopting a different approach, a different voice, such as his exploring the personal and social context of the patient's complaint. Indeed, adopting such an attitude would be counterproductive to the speed and efficiency of the interview.

Task 1.2 Towards a more egalitarian medical encounter?   (TC)

As noted, Fairclough's commentary on the language of the doctor–patient consultation depicts an inequitable relationship between the participants. However, in this analysis, he does not explicitly outline what characterises a more equitable relationship, and nor does he offer any express linguistic recommendations for addressing the conversational asymmetry he identifies. What recommendations would you make? See if you can answer the following questions:

- How would you characterise (if such a thing is possible) an egalitarian relationship between doctor and patient?
- From a linguistic perspective, what would be its key features?

Conflicting interests? The voice of medicine and the voice of the lifeworld

Research suggests that when doctors and patients communicate, they adopt different perspectives from which to view and make sense of the patient's complaint (Mishler, 1984; Todd, 1989; Fisher, 1991). The doctor is seen to exhibit an almost exclusive concern for medical topics at the expense of the social and biographical context of the patient's life (Fisher, 1991: 158). According to Fisher, the doctor–patient relationship rests on a medical model which sees illness as the organic pathology of the individual patient. Thus the problem for the doctor to solve rests in the patient's body: non-organic issues, such as the social context of the patient's life, do not readily fit into this medical model (ibid.). Or to put it another way, doctors manifest the 'voice of medicine', whereas patients embrace the 'voice of the lifeworld', that is, the ordinary experience and the natural attitude 'of everyday life' (Mishler, 1984: 14).

'Voice' in this sense has a special meaning beyond its more familiar literal definition. Voice is taken to mean 'the relationships between talk and the speakers' underlying frameworks of meaning' (Mishler, 1984: 14). In the stretch of doctor–patient dialogue examined above, the dominant voice was that of medicine, a voice of medical authority and technical expertise, a voice oriented to by the doctor. The doctor appeared to pursue a time-efficient, pre-set diagnostic agenda, overriding, as a result, the everyday, non-expert voice through which the patient sought to make sense of her problems. The extract revealed how the doctor institutionally adhered to the practices of official medicine. The doctor responded to the scientific, clinical aspects of the patient's complaint, without exploring her condition in the context of other aspects of her personal, social life (such as the reasons for her drinking). Effectively, the doctor reconstructed the patient's 'practical interests into technical ones' (Mishler, 1984: 127).

Mishler's voices of medicine and the lifeworld are effective concepts for making sense of the dynamic tensions at the heart of the doctor–patient consultation. (Moreover, as we shall see throughout this book, the concept of these two voices yields invaluable insights into other modes of health communication, particularly written documentation, such as patient records/medical case histories.) Although Mishler's (1984) original research from which the concept of the two voices is derived is somewhat dated now, exploring the consequences of doctors' and patients' orientations to these ways of meaning-making has continued to afford medical discourse analysts a promising means of evaluating participant behaviours in the consultation. For example, Barry *et al.* (2001) analysed the discourse of 35 British general practice consultations, looking for communicative patterns across this broad range of interviews. Unlike Mishler's study, in which all the doctor participants were white males, the encounters analysed in this more recent study comprised an equal number of male and female participants, and three Asian physicians. From this diverse collection of doctor–patient consultations the researchers identified four types of encounter, each of which featured assorted combinations of the medicine and lifeworld voices, the categories being: 'Strictly Medicine', 'Lifeworld Blocked', 'Lifeworld Ignored' and 'Mutual Lifeworld'.

What is perhaps most notable about this research into the doctor–patient encounter is that it identifies two types of consultation which are qualitatively distinct from those identified by Mishler in his original, pioneering work. Mishler described what he calls the 'Unremarkable Interview', a baseline or default doctor–patient dyad, the kind of encounter we have previously considered in which the doctor conducts the consultation exclusively in the voice of medicine, using discursive strategies to maintain control of the unfolding spoken exchanges. Although the voice of the lifeworld is sometimes introduced by the patient, the doctor blocks its full emergence. A number of the consultations that Barry *et al.* examined were similar to this kind of voice-of-medicine-dominant encounter. Yet the 'Lifeworld Ignored' and 'Mutual Lifeworld' interviews constitute a different type of consultation, each possessing unique linguistic behaviours.

To illustrate their distinct interactional properties, let us consider extracts from each. First: an example of the 'Lifeworld Ignored', an encounter in which the patient, Steve, a 24-year-old accountant, is presenting with the problem of pilonidal cysts between his buttocks, a chronic problem that causes him extreme pain, discomfort which is aggravated by his having to drive long distances as part of his job.

L=voice of the lifeworld (in bold); M=voice of medicine

1	L	P:	**Er during the night er er, I don't know how-**
2			**what you say, it burst or something**
3		D:	Right. [Right
4	L	P:	[**I've got a hole in my back and it was**
			pouring out with blood and=

5		D:	[Right. Right. Right.
6	L	P:	[(unintelligible) and I'm in quite a lot of pain
7	M	D:	Right. Just getting the timescale [sorted out
8		P:	[yeah
9	M	D:	so it's been over nine months?

–	M		*Exchange continued in voice of medicine by doctor and patient*

10	L	P:	**I can't do any sports, I do a lot of travelling with work**
11		D:	Sure. Yeah.
12	L	P:	**and I just don't know where I am from [one day to the next.**
13	M	D:	[Did you go you up to the outpatient clinic following on from that at all. Were you actually referred?

–	M		*Exchange continued in voice of medicine by doctor and patient*

14	L	P:	**but with the [travelling I d- I do eight- over**
15		D:	[Yeah. Sure sure.
16	L	P:	**And that's just going to work and then if I have to travel from work**
17	M	D:	Can I just take a look?

(adapted from Barry et al., 2001: 496)

In these exchanges Steve presents his problem almost entirely in the voice of the lifeworld. He consistently translates his medical (physical) problem into concerns about his personally managing his daily-life activities, such as how his condition chronically impedes his occupational and social life. As he says himself, 'I can't do any sports', 'I do a lot of travelling with work', 'I just don't know where I am from one day to the next'. These lifeworld statements are not merely glimpsed but substantially recur, as can be seen above, throughout the consultation. Steve is evidently determined to highlight to the doctor the extent to which his condition affects his everyday routine. Yet his personal fears and anxieties are overlooked by the doctor, who fails to pick up on, develop and show apparent empathy for his lifeworld concerns, preferring to maintain a close focus on clinical and procedural matters. For instance, the doctor, through the use of backchannelling tokens such as 'Right', 'Yeah', 'Sure', exhibits active listening, but this apparent 'involvement behaviour' is in fact, according to Barry *et al.*, little more than selective listening, used 'more as a way of vetting information in order to dismiss the lifeworld and seek voice of medicine information with which to continue the consultation' (2001: 495).

The rapid cluster of interjections which the GP produces at line 5 – 'Right. Right. Right' – appear to have a checking, verifying function rather than encouraging the patient to continue with his current topic, and the fact that these three interjections appear one after the other potentially indicates that the doctor has heard all that she wants to hear about the topic and is impatient to take the floor again and change the topical direction of the exchange, presumably in a more biomedical direction.

This foregoing extract reveals the lengths to which some patients go in order to articulate their lifeworld agendas, resisting, in doing so, the doctor's interactional control of the consultation. The fact that Steve repeatedly presents his concerns in the voice of the lifeworld suggests that he is not satisfactorily able to convey his problem in the way he wishes, making for what Barry *et al.* consider to be a poor-outcome consultation (in the sense that the doctor fails to address the concerns that the patient persistently seeks to disclose).

This de-personalising 'Lifeworld Ignored' type of encounter between GP and patient illustrates how the consultation should ideally be a 'dialectical process' (Berger and Mohr, 1976: 74), a contest but also a negotiation between two voices. In order to appreciate the patient's condition fully (an appreciation that involves responding sensitively to contextualised lifeworld accounts), the doctor 'must first recognise the patient as a person' (ibid.). Recognising and treating the patient as a person is a characteristic feature of the 'Mutual Lifeworld' strain of interview. In contrast to the 'Lifeworld Ignored' encounter, the 'Mutual Lifeworld' consultation involves both sets of participants routinely employing the voice of the lifeworld. This type of encounter provides an intriguing picture of what a more patient-centred doctor–patient relationship looks like, the type of humanistic encounter that Mishler advocates where the patient is treated as a whole person and the doctor picks up on social-psychological issues rather than dogmatically cleaving to clinical matters.

The following 'Mutual Lifeworld' interview neatly evinces the linguistic means by which both doctor and patient jointly collaborate in producing lifeworld interaction. In this extract, Jeremy, a retired senior manager, is presenting with heartburn but is concerned that this complaint is a symptom of a more serious underlying condition. In addition, Jeremy has been experiencing considerable stress regarding his daughter who has been recovering from a serious illness. The GP, Ben, is in his late forties. The letters L and M in the second column represent the voices of medicine and the lifeworld respectively.

1	L	P:	Hello Ben
2	L	D:	Hello
3	L	P:	[How are you

4	L	D:	[How are- er how- ((laughs))
5	L	P:	((laughs))
6	L	D:	I'm okay
7	L	P:	Okay?
–	L		*Doctor and patient chat about the patient's previous GP who the doctor knows*
8	L	D:	Right. (0.9) Right. What are we talking about?
9	L	P:	What are we talking about today I don't know. I just feel slightly (0.3) a bit like a fraud I suppose. But I thought I'd have a word with you.
10	L	D:	Yeah.

(Barry *et al.*, 2001: 498-9)

The opening exchange here appears to be one of mutuality and relaxed intimacy. Indeed we might even excuse ourselves for believing that we are witnessing the beginnings of an interchange between intimates rather than the unfolding exchanges of a clinical interview. As Barry *et al.* (2001: 497) remark, there is a 'relaxed feel' to these exchanges, an impression which is supported by the fact that the participants are principally engaged in the interactive business of establishing and maintaining interpersonal relations instead of engaging in the transactional processes of eliciting and disclosing medical information. The doctor's inclusive use of the personal pronoun 'we' in line 4 – 'What are we talking about?' – further indicates that the agenda between practitioner and patient is jointly produced. Humour also plays a part in these opening exchanges, with the participants engaging in laughter together (lines 4 and 5), an interpersonal episode which further contributes to convergence between professional and patient (Grainger, 2002). So far, then, the consultation has been conducted purely in the voice of the lifeworld. The encounter continues:

11	L	P:	**Erm (0.3) I'm feeling fine. In in every respect except one.**
	M		And that is I am getting chronic I suppose for the sake of a better word heartburn
12	M	D:	Mhm.
–	M	P:	*Patient discusses symptoms of heartburn which occur when he consumes hot and cold liquid and feels as though he's been hit in the chest*
13	M	P:	And I thought I'd just check it out with you.
14	M	D:	Sure. Are you getting any erm water – what's called waterbrush? Are you getting any reflux of acid or
	L		**any frothy stuff coming up into your mouth?**
–	M		Doctor asks patient where he experiences pain
15	M	D:	Right. How long has it been a problem?

16	M	P:	(0.3) Oh I don't know. Six weeks.
17	M	D:	Right
18	M	P:	Hoping it's going to go away but it's not.
19	L	D:	Has anything changed in your life over the last five or six weeks? Anything sort of putting you under any undue pressure? Or-
20	L	P:	Well I had a problem earlier in the year.
21	L	D:	Yeah.
22	L	P:	But I think that's er getting- that's okay. Er you know my daughter was [ill
23	L	D:	[Mm. Yeah.
24	L	P:	Er but I mean that's er- [it-
25	L	D:	[Is that- How's that sort-
26	L	P:	Yeah that's sorting itself out. I mean it's er er- but I mean that did put us- you know this is a year and Carol's coming up for its anniversary.
27	L	D:	Mhm.
28	L	P:	Erm it was just after Easter [that happened.
29	L	D:	[I think anniver- I think anniversaries are a constant source of fascination to me. Erm it is con- staggering how often people will start to become unwell
30	L	P:	[At the time-
31	L	D:	[round about the time of an anniversary and will have completely forgotten that's it an anniversary.
32	L	P:	Yeah.
33	L	D:	Erm I've seen this happen often.

(Barry et al., 2001: 498-9)

In the above exchanges the patient first adopts, though briefly, the voice of medicine in order to relay his complaint (heartburn) to the doctor (lines 11-13). The doctor, in response to the patient's disclosure, also adopts the voice of medicine but is evidently careful not to overuse technical terminology to elicit further responses from Jeremy, providing, for instance, a more familiar gloss for the medical term 'waterbrush' ('any frothy stuff coming up into your mouth?'). Thereafter, following a brief discussion about the duration of Jeremy's heartburn, both participants jointly conduct the interaction almost entirely in the voice of the lifeworld. This is achieved through the use of a range of discursive strategies including the doctor's open-ended and lifeworld-probing questions ('Has anything changed in your life over the last five or six weeks? Anything sort of putting you under pressure?'); active listening (use, for example, of the continuers 'Mhm' and 'Mm' which encourage the patient to continue elaborating his problems); and acknowledging the patient's predicament and reassuring him ('I've seen this happen often'). Collectively these discursive strategies contribute to the patient's being 'treated as an equal partner', a participant who, being allowed (even encouraged) by the doctor to bring his own expertise to the consultation, takes an active part in his diagnosis and treatment (Barry *et al.*, 2001: 497).

Although only a series of extracts from a larger encounter, the above 'Mutual Lifeworld' sequence provides us with an impression of how a medical consultation conducted within the lifeworld might, to an extent, play out. Due to the characteristic conversational unfolding of the exchanges, and the apparent detachment from a strict pre-formulated medical agenda, the patient emerges from the interview as a unique person, someone actively involved, jointly with the doctor, in seeking to contextually understand his problems; problems which are explored from both physical and psychological perspectives. Embracing 'the natural attitude to everyday life' (Mishler, 1984: 14), the 'Mutual Lifeworld' consultation is an example of the kind of humane clinical practice that Mishler advocates in favour of the exclusively voice of medicine interview.

So far we have assumed that imbalances of power in the consultation arise from a clash of distinct perspectives. The concept of the ideal, patient-centred consultation proposed by Mishler rests on the assumption that the two voices of medicine and the lifeworld are discrete and irreconcilable, and that one (medicine) takes preference over and interrupts the other (lifeworld). The voice of medicine is equated with and enacted through response-constraining, interrogative forms of discourse (such as question and answer formats, and the assessment and evaluation of patients' replies), whereas the voice of the lifeworld is realised in forms of everyday ordinary conversation. Yet some health communication researchers claim that this voice division is too divisive. Surely, Silverman argues, the voices of medicine and the lifeworld intersect and overlap each other rather than their being in constant contest and opposition: the 'issue is always the relation between voices rather than establishment of the single authentic voice' (1987: 196). Doctors and patients do not necessarily adopt one particular voice (as we noted in the 'Mutual Lifeworld' encounter above). Consultations are made up of an interplay of voices: participants 'can and do speak in both medical and social voices' (Fisher, 1991: 160).

It is also somewhat problematic to equate the voices of medicine and the lifeworld with particular forms of language. Why, for instance, is ordinary conversation the appropriate medium to communicate the voice of the lifeworld? What essential connection is there between ordinary conversation and the lifeworld and the articulation of lifeworld concerns? Mishler advocates ordinary conversation as the template for the medical consultation, but forms of everyday conversation in themselves are not inherently democratic and equitable, nor are they shorn of coercive potential. There is no reason why defining features of natural conversation, such as open-ended questions, joint topic development and active and open listening (Barry *et al.*, 2001), can't be manipulated by speakers to coerce fellow participants and steer the course of an interaction in a particular direction.

There is, moreover, a more fundamental challenge to Mishler's advocating ordinary conversation as the baseline of the consultation. Why shouldn't response-constraining language be the principal form of interaction? The medical interview is, after all, a unique type of encounter that has a particular function. Patients (for the most part) expect advice and solutions from their doctors and therefore being subjected to questioning 'is an eminently suitable way of establishing clinical facts' (Gwyn, 2002: 73). Given this expectation, patients might feel uneasy about taking part in a clinical encounter that harnesses seemingly equitable conversational forms of language (Silverman, 1987: 196). Just because a consultation fails to embrace forms of ordinary conversation does not mean that is wrong or inhumane (Gwyn, 2002: 73).

Despite these criticisms, the notion of the voices of medicine and the lifeworld still offer health communication researchers an important resource for interrogating and making sense of the language of medical interviews. Mishler was one of the first (and has certainly been the most influential) scrutineers of the doctor–patient relationship to give close, systematic attention to naturally occurring talk in the consultation and thereby evaluate the communicative significance of language to the participants. For only by focussing on the precise nuances of verbal exchanges is it possible, so Mishler argues, 'to make explicit how conversationalists themselves make sense of what they are saying to each other' (1984: 47), an endeavour which, in turn, affords us a greater understanding of medical practice.

Personal reflection

Pilnick and Dingwall (2011) suggest that medical authority and patient deference are an inescapable part of doctor–patient interaction. Despite advances in clinical communication skills training that promote patient-centred care, asymmetry continues to persist in the consultation. Indeed, unless there is some major reorganisation of medical practice, according to Pilnick and Dingwall, it is almost certain that medical consultations will never be patient led.

Do you agree with this assessment? Or do you see modern medicine moving closer to embracing patient-centred care?

Beyond primary care: exploring encounters in mental health settings

In this chapter so far we have considered doctor–patient interaction solely in the context of general medical care. Yet many of the issues concerning tension and authority in the consultation similarly, if not more urgently, obtain in the discourse of psychiatry and therapy. Language is vitally connected to the domain of mental health: the elicitation and presentation of psychiatric symptoms, and the diagnosis and treatment of many psychological problems are all eminently discursive activities. Language is a crucial aspect of psychiatric practice, and the enactment of power and control through linguistic means can have, as we shall soon see, profound consequences for patients, not least, in some cases, the losing of their liberty. Thus, in the psychiatric setting, the issue of power takes on a special significance.

A key issue for applied linguists investigating interaction in the context of mental health has been the exploration of the link between communication and the outcome of psychiatric interventions. Or to put it another way: does it make a difference how doctors interact with their patients? (Hassan *et al.*, 2007: 150). Relatively little is known about the linguistic routines that occur in psychiatric settings (Buus, 2008) and this fact makes the psychiatric intake interview a particularly significant site of investigation. The purpose of this encounter is to evaluate whether patients, interrogated by psychiatrists, should be committed to hospital on the basis of their responses, or what Jorg Bergmann describes as their 'observable behaviour', during the interview (1992: 137).

In his study of mental health communication, Bergmann identifies a number of manipulative linguistic strategies that psychiatrists employ to conduct psychiatric intake interviews. For example, as well as using questions to formally assess the mental well-being of patients, psychiatrists also frequently present interviewees with personal information in order to elicit further responses from them. This type of verbal probing is sometimes referred to as 'fishing' (Pomerantz, 1980), an interactional phenomenon whereby a speaker, in this case the psychiatrist, does not present the patient with a direct question but ventures a statement describing the patient's personal state of affairs (for example, their health, mood and outlook). But, according to Bergmann, such statements are tentative since the psychiatrist, as an outside observer, only has limited access to these details and cannot be certain of their validity. Thus fishing, somewhat artfully, invites patients to talk about their private affairs – their feelings and troubles (Bergmann, 1992: 155). One of the consequences of this type of rhetorical strategy is that, among other things, it helps obscure any overt exercise of power and authority on the part of the psychiatrist:

rather than interrogating patients directly and compelling them to answer, patients are gently solicited to provide accounts of themselves – to talk about issues which they would have otherwise been reluctant to broach.

As interactional strategy, then, fishing is an insidious practice, trapping patients in what Bergmann describes as a 'double-bind'. For example, if patients provide information voluntarily, then this is to accept what the doctor is insinuating in these (characteristically negative) assertions about their personal predicaments. Yet to reject the psychiatrist's assertion is an act of resistance, with the patient risking their psychological state being negatively evaluated and, as a result, being subject to continuing psychiatric treatment. The following extract powerfully illustrates the argument.

Dr. F:	You feel angry about being committed by Doctor Kluge
Patient:	No I don't feel angry about being committed by Doctor Kluge. But that you somehow –
	(1.0)
Dr. F:	What?
	(0.6)
Patient:	<u>hhh</u>
	(3.0)
Patient:	Mhh hh please.
	((patient sweeps the doctor's papers with a wave of the hand off the table))
Patient:	I can't stand you Doctor Fischer.

(source: Bergmann, 1992: 157)

Doctor Fischer's exploratory utterance 'You feel angry about being committed by Doctor Kluge' takes the form a declarative statement. But its underlying function (its illocutionary force) is that of a question, provoking an answer from the patient. The psychiatrist's statement contains a negative proposition which tacitly accuses her of being angry about, and therefore resisting, an act of professional decision-making. Thus aggravated, the patient immediately rejects the implication and then produces a 'fatal' reaction, a response that exhibits unusual and aggressive behaviour liable to be viewed as being indicative of psychological disturbance. Seeking to induce patients to disclose their feelings and opinions in this way, psychiatrists' exploratory utterances put patients in an invidious position. It is not surprising then, as Bergmann points out, that many patients chose to reject psychiatrists' insinuations and round on their interrogators – as this example dramatically illustrates.

These tensions that surface in the intake interview reflect broader problems and contradictions in the institution of psychiatry itself.

According to Bergmann, psychiatry as an institution is 'caught and twisted between medicine and morality' (1992: 159). In other words, psychiatry has to manage the contrary requirements of practicing medicine, which involves dealing with mental illness in an impartial, detached way, while at the same time practicing morality, which involves dealing with individuals whose behaviour is evaluated as morally deviant in some way (Hassan *et al.*, 2007: 150). This contradiction, however, is not self-evident. It has, to some extent, become obscured and naturalised. Yet, as Bergmann demonstrates, and we have witnessed, this fundamental, if extremely subtle, tension exhibits itself at the micro level of discourse, in the verbal texture of the intake interview itself. The appeal of this applied linguistic critique rests not only in its exposing the turn-by-turn enactment of control by psychiatrists over individual patients, but also its connecting such intricate linguistic behaviour to more fundamental problems in psychiatric care. Intriguingly, other exercises in psychiatric discourse analysis have revealed similar problems at the heart of psychiatric care, some of which we investigate in the following section.

The psychiatric discharge interview: the consequences of footing

If the psychiatric intake interview commences the patient's journey through the mental healthcare system, the discharge interview concludes it or at least heralds its conclusion. Considered together, these two discursive events offer revealing insights into the treatment of psychiatric patients. As with the intake assessment, the discharge interview involves doctors evaluating the well-being and communicative performance of patients. However, whereas the intake interview is geared towards diagnosis and the service requirements of the patient, the purpose of the discharge interview is to ascertain the patient's suitability for release from hospital. The discharge interview marks not only the patient's release from hospital but also their transition from patient to person (Ribeiro, 1996: 181).

Throughout our exploration of various kinds of doctor–patient encounter in this chapter, we have focussed in some detail on the turn-taking and questioning strategies employed by doctors to achieve certain aims and objectives. Another way of making sense of participants' behaviours in medical encounters is to consider how doctors and patients align themselves to one another as their verbal exchanges unfold. The process of alignment between speakers and listeners is known as 'footing' (Goffman, 1981). Footing relates to participants' stances, postures and projections of themselves during evolving interaction (1981: 128). Broadly speaking, footings are the various social roles that speakers and listeners continually step in and out of during conversation (Ribeiro, 1996: 181). In the psychiatric discharge interview, participants can choose from a range of official and non-official social attributes, adopting the ones that most appropriately meet the communicative situation in which they find themselves (ibid.).

As a form of medical consultation, the psychiatric discharge interview (as with other types of psychiatric exchange, such as the intake interview) is structured in a predictable way and directed to specific ends, with the participants principally displaying their official roles of doctor and patient throughout the encounter (Ribeiro, 1996: 181). Yet, as Ribeiro observes, there can arise during the interview subtle clashes of footing between the participants, specifically, mismatches in expectations concerning their roles, ways of interacting with each other, topics for discussion and the management of topics they discuss (ibid.). For instance, patients often interrupt the voice of medicine with their own private repertoire or informal footings which are acutely germane to their own personal experience and understanding but do not relate to the institutional agenda.

Let us see how footings can play out in, and help us to make sense of, psychiatric discourse. The following extract from a discharge interview features Mrs Cordozo, a patient (P) who has been institutionalised due to a severe psychotic crisis, and a treating psychiatrist, Dr (D), who is conducting the interview.

1	D:	you were born on what date?
2	P:	(.) on January 11th
3	D:	(.) of what year?
4	P:	of 1921 (.) ((patient nods)) I am sixty-one= ((nods and smiles))
5	D:	((nods)) =you have a son, [don't you?
6	P:	[I have a son. ((nods and smiles))
7	D:	what's his name?
8	P:	Francisco Ferreira de Souza.
9	D:	and he is how old now?
10	P:	he's about forty-two. ((looks away, looks at doctor and smiles))
11	D:	mmm (.) you also have a granddaughter, don't you?=
12	P:	=I've got a (little) sixteen-year old granddaughter.
13	P:	(1.4) ((raises head and smiles))
14	D:	mmm
15	P:	she's my life ((raises head, looks up, big smile))
16	D:	do you- really?=
17	P:	=really. I am crazy (about her).
18	P:	I like (her) ((smiling)) [ve-
19	D:	[do you take care of her?=

```
20    P:    =I don't take care of her because my daughter-in-law
21    P:    takes very good care, y'know (.) ((short smile))
22    P:    I just see her and all that. (I don't )
23    D:    do you always keep in touch with them?
24    P:    oh, yes, always (.) ((nods))
25    P:    well as much as possible I do, y'know doctor (.)
26    P:    ((nods and smiles, looks at doctor))
27    D:    where do you live, Mrs Cardozo?
28    P:    what? ((lips tighten and frowns))
```
                                            (source: Ribeiro, 1996: 185-6)

At the beginning of this interview, Ribeiro notes, the patient adopts an institutional footing, clearly and straightforwardly occupying the role of patient. This is borne out by her responses to the doctor's questions: up until line 10 she articulates no more than what is required of her. These early exchanges between the participants clearly establish the roles of doctor and patient, with the psychiatrist controlling the institutional agenda through a series of precisely focussed, topically constraining questions. However, from line 12, the patient becomes increasingly expressive, providing more information than the essential minimum required to answer the questions sufficiently. She offers, for example, evaluative personal information concerning her granddaughter (note her nodding and smiling (lines 13, 15, 18), her production of value-laden remarks ('she's my life'), and her repeated use of the discourse marker 'you know', a feature of talk which could be considered an involvement strategy redolent of normal, everyday interaction). During this expressive sequence of the interview the patient-interviewee footing drifts into the background, giving way to the footing of a gentle grandmother addressing a friendly, personally interested listener (Ribeiro, 1996: 186).

Yet rather disconcertingly, at line 27, the doctor's footing suddenly shifts: she redirects the topic of the interview by abruptly steering it back to eliciting factual responses from her interviewee ('where do you live, Mrs Cardozo?'). Thus, without warning or any other kind of intimation, the doctor disruptively reinstates the roles of doctor and patient, producing, understandably, a reaction of disquiet from Mrs Cardozo:

```
28    P:    what? (lips tighten and frowns))
```

This abrupt jink in footing illustrates how this crucial stage in the interview is oriented to differently by the participants: the doctor evidently views the exchange as a medical encounter, whereas the patient construes it as personal talk. Tension clearly results from the participants' struggle to adopt their preferred footings, and this mismatch of expectations between them reveals how Mrs Cordozo is caught in a double-bind situation.

As Ribeiro explains, in order to terminate her stay as an inpatient and commence her transition to ex–patient, Mrs Cordozo has to play the official (and passive) role of patient during the interview (discharging her social identities of mother, grandmother, etc.). On the other hand, in order to become a person, she has to reclaim her social roles to be considered suitable for release. As the interview unfolds, the patient's talk, as we noted, becomes more expressive and involved, reflecting the social roles that, as a person, she has to recover in order to display connection with the outside world. Yet the psychiatrist resists the patient's personal framing of the encounter, refusing to interact with her for any length of time on a personal footing. The psychiatrist repeatedly confines the patient to the 'single and limiting role of patient' (1996: 190). Thus, whether she is aware of this restriction or not, the psychiatrist's prevailing interactional strategy is at odds with the rehabilitative purpose of psychiatric treatment; treatment which, crucially, should not only permit, but also support the patient's adoption of a personal footing.

The point, then, is that if the doctor had displayed greater sensitivity to footings, there would inevitably emerge during the interview the woman behind the patient – namely, that sense of personal identity and social competence which Mrs Cordozo is expected to demonstrate if she is to be discharged from hospital (Ribeiro, 1996: 190). Yet given the interactional constraints upon her she is, paradoxically, unable to demonstrate this essential competence and thereby expedite her release from the institution.

Task 1.3 A further look at footings in the consultation   (TC)

As the foregoing analysis demonstrates, identifying changes in footings (and the consequences of such changes) is an effective means of charting the interpersonal contours and enactments of power in psychiatric discourse. However, changes in footing, of course, are not just present in psychiatric encounters: they regularly occur in various kinds of spoken interaction. Unlike the disruptive footings shift we have just witnessed, changes in alignment can be, and often are, relatively innocuous (if not natural and expected). Indeed, if there were no changes in alignment during interaction, participants would have a troublesome time realising their transactional goals.

We have considered footings in psychiatrist–patient encounters, but consider the following:

- What footing shifts do you think commonly occur between GPs and patients in routine primary care consultations?
- What are the consequences of such changes in footing?

What's wrong with authority? Theorising power in the consultation

Readers would be forgiven for thinking that in our foregoing exploration of the doctor–patient consultation we have construed the exercise of power as an inherently negative operation, a process that leads to nothing but adverse clinical outcomes for the patient. We are, as are a number of health communication researchers, critical of verbal practices that give rise to misunderstandings and breakdowns in interaction – the often extremely subtle disruptions and confusions that only linguistic and other micro-level analyses of doctor–patient talk can apprehend. But, of course, the exercise of some degree of linguistic power is unavoidable, indeed is necessary, in medical encounters, and the doctor–patient exchange is no exception. For example, without recourse to agenda-constraining verbal activities, doctors would be unable to elicit vital information from patients and proceed with appropriate treatment.

Power is a complex issue that is worth exploring further, particularly as there are various ways of making sense of it, and determining the extent to which its effects can be judged as harmful or beneficial. Treichler *et al.* (1984: 63) rightly argue that there is 'no independent or uncompromised stance from which power can be viewed or interpreted'. As we have seen, many linguistic studies of doctor–patient interaction have variously exposed and criticised the means by which doctors exert control over patients. Yet, for a finer appreciation of the verbal conduct of the consultation, it is important to be aware of contrasting perspectives of power, including what is known as the functionalist perspective, which considers the enactment of control to be relatively unproblematic. Indeed, from a functionalist perspective the relationship between doctor and patient is essentially a reciprocal one: any occasion of conflict arising between the participants is attributable to a failure of individual competence rather than to an imbalance of power inherent in the practitioner–patient relationship itself (Bloor and Horobin, 1975: 271). Thus, according to the functionalist perspective, the consultation is not a site of struggle, a tussle where patients fight to voice their interests. Rather, medical authority is viewed as benevolent, a legitimate means of licensing doctors to perform the role of healing and thereby serve patients' best interests (Lupton, 2003: 113).

One persuasive explanation that helps to account for this status quo is that the roles of doctor and patient are socially defined and established. For instance, when people fall ill they have to fulfil certain obligations if they wish to have their illness validated and treated – if they are, to put it technically, to occupy the 'sick role' (Parsons, 1987).

According to the sick role, illness is not simply a condition but a social role which is characterised by four distinguishing elements:

Sick persons are absolved from certain social responsibilities. For example, they are exempted from being at work, attending school, etc.

The incapacity of sick persons is beyond their ability to overcome. They are not held responsible for their condition. The sick person cannot, in Parson's words, 'pull himself together' [sic] by a mere act of will' (1987: 151).

Occupying the sick role involves recognising (if it weren't already obvious) that being ill is an undesirable state, a state that should be got out of as quickly as possible.

Finally, sick persons recognise that being ill requires their seeking out appropriate help, to wit, treatment by professional physicians.

As these criteria make plain, the sick role submits ill people to rather compelling obligations; obligations, nonetheless, which are commonly taken for granted or else treated as common sense. Broadly, it is the duty of the sick to recognise that they cannot get better on their own and that they must therefore obtain professional medical care in order to recover. Naturally, this state of affairs has consequences for the maintenance of power in the doctor–patient relationship and the playing out of authority in the consultation. People experiencing illness need to acquiesce to the advice and injunctions of their doctors: a power differential between doctor and patient is thus unavoidable if doctors are to secure compliance (Lupton, 2003: 114). Indeed, licensed by the sick role, doctors apparently have little choice but to work towards maintaining 'a social difference from patients in order to meet their obligations as objective professionals' (ibid.).

There is, then, a powerful social imperative for patients to defer to the authority and technical superiority of health professionals and thereby enter into asymmetrical encounters with their doctors. Indeed, given this expectation, patients would most likely feel discomfited taking part in more symmetrical relationships (Silverman, 1987: 196). Thus it follows that if patients are tolerant of medical authority, they are also tolerant of the linguistic strategies that give rise to interactional authority in the consultation. Moreover, for patients to resist the discourse strategies of the doctors is to run the risk of their being seen to be 'symbolically challenging the status quo of medical discourse, thereby causing covert damage to their chances of recovery' (Gwyn, 2002: 74). It is in patients' interests to acquiesce.

The operation of power in the doctor–patient encounter has thus, to a not insignificant degree, become naturalised, as have the specific linguistic practices which enact power and dominance in the consultation. Naturalisation, in linguistic terms, is the process whereby discourse activities, and the ideological import of these activities, have over time, through routine and convention, become ordinary and unexceptional to the participants involved in them. As Fairclough (2001: 76) puts it, naturalisation is 'the royal road to common sense'. When an interactional routine such as the doctor–patient encounter becomes naturalised, the underlying assumptions about, and operation of, power become invisible. They are translated into neutral, conventional ways of going about things. We would dare venture that most readers, when in consultation with their doctor, are unlikely to scrutinise the turn-by-turn, moment-by-moment unfolding of interaction and remark the unwritten, yet socially sanctioned, institutional mores that give licence to this particular way of inter-acting. We might pick up on certain technical terms with which we are unfamiliar but, for the most part, we are unlikely to give much consideration to the linguistic conventions through which we communicate with our doctors.

As Fairclough (2001: 82) argues, the natural or common sense way of doing things is an effect of power, and it is only when communication breaks down during the consultation that conventional routines are rendered problematic and the workings of power exposed. What was intriguing about a number of the consultations that we considered in this chapter (the psychiatric–patient exchanges apart) was the general lack of overt challenge offered by the patients involved. The consultations appeared, at least on the surface, to be smoothly conducted (in the sense that the patients did not expressly appear to regard the doctor's style of discourse as 'oppressive or disempowering' (Gwyn, 2002: 69)). This only underscores the importance of paying micro-analytic detail to medical discourse if we are to expose tensions and problems of which the participants may well be unaware. This, in turn, raises issues about how researchers locate the operation of power in the medical interview and to what extent they consider the institutional context as contributing to the enactment of interactional authority and control.

Broadly, within the tradition of discourse-based studies of doctor–patient interaction, it is possible to identify two different approaches to power and context. Arguably, the dominant view, one espoused by proponents of critical discourse analysis, is that power in healthcare settings is a pre-existing 'structural phenomenon' (Wodak, 1997: 175). The differential rights and duties of doctors and patients are determined in advance (Treichler *et al.*, 1984: 63), and this will inevitably influence the linguistic behaviour of the participants during the consultation. Applied linguists orienting to this position take into account, or at least acknowledge, that doctor–patient talk does not occur in a vacuum, but in a specific (institutional) context, and this context will unavoidably constrain what speakers can or can't say, imposing certain interactional obligations and restrictions on them. (It would, for example, be extremely unusual for patients to interrogate their GPs about medical matters, and doctors, in response, to readily yield intimate details about their health concerns!) Situational considerations, such as the relative status of the speakers, then, are an important factor in locating power. From this perspective, particularly from a critical discourse analysis standpoint, power in medical discourse is, to put it bluntly, to do with powerful participants controlling and constraining the contributions of relatively less powerful participants (Fairclough, 2001: 38-9).

However, other analysts of doctor–patient talk adopt a more cautious approach to the influence of context upon interaction. For example, researchers from the conversation analysis tradition (see Chapter 2) reject what they refer to as the 'bucket' theory of context: treating pre-existing institutional circumstances as enclosing verbal interaction (Heritage, 2004: 224). Analysis of medical discourse, they argue, begins exclusively with the talk of the participants themselves. Talk possesses 'an internally grounded reality of its own' (Schegloff, 1997: 171). Therefore any analysis of spoken interaction must first and foremost commence with conversation, not with any consideration of situational factors.

According to this view, participants do not bring pre-existing roles (such as doctor and patient) with them to the consultation. Rather, in interaction, they orient to and talk these roles into being: they 'do' being a doctor, 'do' being a patient, and, furthermore, they 'do' doing power. All that is required to make sense of the consultation is the participants' talk itself, the spoken data alone. Indeed going beyond the data – for example, considering the institutional context in which the interaction is situated – would be an 'illegitimate move' (Cameron, 2008: 145) that would divert analytical attention away from what is relevant to the participants, to what the researcher deems to be relevant.

The key point from this perspective is that power is not a pre-determined factor liable to influence the verbal conduct of the consultation. Rather, the exercise of power must be demonstrably evident in the participants' talk. The fact that doctors and patients occupy different status positions doesn't necessarily mean that this difference should be the basis for all and every interaction between them.

Here, naturally, is not the place to attempt to resolve this ongoing theoretical debate; it is enough, at this stage of the book, for readers to be aware of it. What we would like to emphasise is that, whatever the perspective of power one adopts, any linguistic analysis of the medical interview must be based on a close examination of the interactive behaviour of the participants involved. As Treichler *et al.* (1984: 63) observe, 'power relations are negotiated within the context of face-to-face interaction'. But, of course, such a view must also take into account the institutional norms to which both doctors and patients orient themselves; norms which manifestly exist outside of the consultation and which, in Cameron's words, 'constrain participants' behaviour even if they do not fully determine it' (2008: 145).

A toolkit for interrogating power in medical interviews

Throughout our survey of the doctor–patient consultation, we have considered a range of linguistic behaviours and discourse strategies. We have argued that close scrutiny of the consultation affords penetrating insights into the linguistic behaviours of doctors and patients, as well as insights into healthcare as mode of social practice.

What we offer now is a toolkit or checklist for readers wishing to conduct their own analyses of medical interviews. The toolkit conveniently brings together many of the analytic themes and linguistic concepts that we considered throughout the chapter, serving, if nothing else, as a kind of practical summary. It is by no means exhaustive, and constitutes a tentative list of features. Nonetheless, it presents readers with a basic framework for beginning to make sense of some of the social processes that occur in the medical interview.

Exchanges

- Which speaker commences sequences of talk?
- What question types predominate: closed questions (which narrow responses) or open questions (which offer greater conversational space)?
- Do speakers interrupt each other? If so, what are the consequences of interruption (for example, how does the direction of talk alter as a result)?

Topic

- Which speaker introduces new topics?
- Are newly introduced topics accepted and sustained by speakers?
- Do doctors offer the floor to patients, allowing them to introduce and develop topics of their own accord?

Footing

- What footings predominate in the interview (do the speakers orient to the participant statuses of doctor and patient throughout or are other roles in evidence)?
- Do footings shift during the interview? If so, which speaker is responsible and how is such a change realised interactionally?
- What are the consequences of any changes in footing? Do participants, for example, realise a footing change has taken place? Do they accept it?

Medicine/Lifeworld voices

Which voice (medicine or lifeworld) dominates the consultation?
- If the patient offers lifeworld statements, does the doctor encourage them?
- What linguistic forms do the voices take? For example, are they realised in conversational forms of talk or more constraining forms of talk?

Terms of address

- How do the participants refer to one another? For example, does the patient use an honorific form such as 'Doctor' (a marker of respect that recognises the participant's status) or a more informal term of address such as a first name?
- Do terms of address change during the interview, potentially indicating a change in footing?
- What personal pronouns are used by the participants? Does, for example, the doctor use an inclusive 'we' to signal a practitioner-patient alliance: 'We should consider reducing the dosage', or an exclusive 'we' that potentially distances the participants: 'We don't prescribe that medication nowadays'?

Summary

In this chapter we have explored the doctor–patient consultation, examining its formal structure, as well as the linguistic enactment of power that commonly occurs in this routine healthcare encounter. We noted that, formally, the consultation can be resolved into six distinct phases of action, constituting what has been described as an 'Ideal Sequence'. Progress, typically, through these phases is doctor-led, but there will be occasions when patients initiate sequences. This emphasises the fact that, even if the doctor typically determines movement through the sequence, the consultation is an interactive process involving negotiation between the participants.

It was apparent that a number of the problems and tensions evident in the doctor–patient relationship were due to the different perspectives adopted by the participants, with doctors orienting to technical, biomedical matters while patients sought to make sense of their conditions by situating them in the context of their everyday lives. This gives rise to the concepts of the voices of medicine and the lifeworld. These concepts are useful for making sense of the social processes of the consultation, although we were at pains to identify some of the limitations of discretely resolving the voices into two mutually exclusive, clashing perspectives. It is better to see them as inter-penetrating rather than excluding one another.

Finally, we observed that the issue of power in the consultation is intriguingly complex and double-edged. Although many researchers have been critical of the exercise of power in medical encounters, some have described its positive effects, considering it to be an inevitable, and necessary, feature of medical interaction. However, doctors and patients have perhaps become so inured to the operation of power that it has become naturalised. The fact that power is commonly taken for granted highlights the importance of exposing its use and abuse through micro-linguistic attention.

This chapter has begun to introduce you to a number of linguistic issues surrounding the doctor–patient relationship. In the next chapter we will consider health practitioners who have been neglected in health communication research, namely, non-physician personnel, such as nurses, pharmacists and chaplains, who nonetheless substantially contribute to the litany of the clinic.

2 Spoken interaction between non-physician personnel and patients

Introduction: the bias of doctor–patient talk

The doctor is, of course, not the only practitioner in the healthcare system. Many other people play a vital part in the daily operation of the clinic, including, to name but a few, nurses, cleaners, caterers, pharmacists, physiotherapists, receptionists, porters and chaplains. Thus the talk that routinely takes place in healthcare settings is wonderfully diverse, involving a variety of personnel (both medical and non-medical) whose distinct voices unquestionably contribute to the litany of the clinic. Yet despite the ubiquity of personnel besides the doctor, the doctor is often considered to be the pivotal figure in healthcare. This assumption is borne out by the amount of discourse-based research (some of which we considered in the previous chapter) dedicated to the medical consultation. A serious consequence of researchers clustering on the doctor–patient site is that, no matter how high quality and insightful each individual study, their research findings provide a distorted account of hospital work (Hak, 1999: 441). In exploring the roles played by other staff besides doctors, this chapter aims to provide a more representative picture of the practitioner–patient exchange.

Nursing in context: some issues for applied linguistics

Despite the dominance of doctor–patient research, there has been an increase over the last fifteen years or so in discourse-based studies exploring the interactional routines of non-physician personnel. Nursing, in particular, has received not inconsiderable attention and a substantial body of literature now exists which revealingly sheds light on nursing interaction. Accordingly we devote much of this chapter to exploring the discourse of nurses, specifically how they manage the interactional demands that their workloads place upon them.

The position of nurses vis-a-vis other healthcare workers is an intriguing one. Although they are the largest body of professionals in the healthcare system, their history has been one of powerlessness and domination (Candlin, 2000: 230). Compared to physicians, nurses occupy a relatively low position in the medical hierarchy and are not uncommonly treated by doctors and patients as little more than servants (Lupton, 2003: 131). Although nurses play a central part in patient care, the social relation between nurses and patients is more complex than the doctor–patient relationship (ibid.). Nurses perform a range of tasks including routine 'dirty work', such as washing patients and changing bed pans, through to highly complex and skilled activities such as minor surgery and patient-counselling. Furthermore, nurses spend more time with patients than other health practitioners and often interpret doctors' instructions on their patients' behalf (Candlin, 2000: 231).

Unlike doctor–patient encounters, which are typically brief and predictably organised, spoken exchanges between nurses and patients are altogether more diverse and intricate. Since nursing is a continuing activity that involves many aspects of patient care, nursing interactions are likely to be conducted over longer periods of time, sometimes extending over the course of several weeks (Candlin and Candlin, 2003: 144), as well as being conducted in various locations – not just in consulting rooms or at patients' bedsides. These factors make it difficult for researchers to record nurse–patient interaction, and account for the comparative lack of research into nurses' verbal routines. It has been far easier for linguists to concentrate on collecting doctor–patient data, particularly in the primary care setting where discrete consultations are comparatively easy to access and record.

Notwithstanding the problems of data collection, the nurse–patient exchange remains a priority research site for applied linguists. The nurse–patient relationship is dependent on clear and unambiguous spoken interaction and therefore applied linguists and discourse analysts are well equipped to help identify miscommunication and interpersonal problems that may emerge during participant exchanges (Candlin and Candlin, 2003: 145). Moreover, since nursing is such a complex enterprise and therefore one which is difficult to analyse and define (Melia, 1978: 58), the linguistic interrogation of routine practitioner–patient talk offers a promising vantage point from which to understand and appreciate the work of nurses. The essence and character of nursing, we argue, is manifest, to a significant extent, in nurses' language, and in the following sections we aim to point up the role of discourse in nursing practice, particularly in light of recent changes in healthcare policy that have redefined the traditional nurse–patient relationship.

Conversation analysis approaches to nurse–patient interaction

As Salvage and Smith (2000: 1019) observe, the relationship between nurses and doctors has never been a straightforward one. Longstanding disputes over status, roles and responsibilities have undoubtedly contributed to such a state of affairs. Traditionally the dramatis personae of the healthcare system have been viewed in terms of the conventional nuclear family: the doctor-as-father, nurse-as-mother and patient-as-child (ibid.). However, recent social and political pressures have begun to undermine this old model of patriarchy. For example, patient-empowerment initiatives have led to greater involvement for patients in treatment decisions, while the reduction of junior doctors' hours has seen nurses undertaking tasks formerly performed by physicians (Doyal and Cameron, 2000:1024).

These shifts in professional boundaries have, in turn, resulted in professional groups being more regularly involved in collaborative work. Nowadays increasing numbers of doctors and nurses are organised in multi-professional teams (Doyal and Cameron, 2000:1024). Yet such collaborative working arrangements have introduced new problems for professionals to address, not least their having to reconcile differences in their unique working practices. One challenge for applied linguists, then, is to identify these differing approaches of occupational groups and how they manifest themselves during routine interactions with patients.

Recently a number of health communication researchers specialising in conversation analysis have turned their micro-analytic gaze on to the nurse–patient encounter. Conversation analysis techniques offer applied linguists a rigorous resource for analysing medical discourse, and before we examine sequences of nursing interaction in detail it is worth outlining some of the key tenets of conversation analysis and the practical utility of this method.

Conversation analysis (commonly abbreviated to CA) emerged from the writings of Harvey Sacks, Emmanuel Schegloff and Gail Jefferson in the 1970s (Sacks *et al.*, 1974). These researchers were concerned with the local mechanisms of spoken interaction and how speakers orient to and make sense of each other's turns during unfolding talk. Far from being formless and disorderly, conversation is deemed to be an intricate and cohesively patterned system of verbal exchange, possessing an 'interactional order' (Goffman, 1981). Although the mechanisms of conversation are often taken for granted, conversation analysts consider talk-in-interaction to be an interactional achievement, a collaborative activity which requires speakers to intricately co-ordinate their verbal activities. CA is therefore concerned with the minutiae of interaction and, methodologically, can be seen as a bridge between linguistic analysis and the sociological interrogation of the social world (Drew, 2001: 111).

Earlier forms of conversation analysis (what is sometimes referred to as 'pure CA') focussed purely on so-called 'ordinary' (informal, everyday, non-institutional) conversation; principally face-to-face and telephone exchanges between friends, family and acquaintances. Later analyses incorporated institutional discourse – more formal modes of interaction, including medical, legal and broadcast talk. Yet despite its widening ambit, the underlying objectives of CA broadly remain the same, namely to account for how speakers make sense of each other's talk and how they construct their utterances so as to be appropriate next actions (Drew, 2001: 112).

The 'bedrock' on which CA rests is sequencing (Heritage and Maynard, 2006: 9). A key aspect of sequencing is the organisation of adjacency pairs. Adjacency pairs are two connected utterances that perform specific verbal functions, dual utterances such as question-answer, summons-answer, greeting-greeting, and so on. Occurring one after the other in a chain-like fashion, adjacency pairs are the building blocks of conversation. Adjacency pairs, moreover, possess powerful regulatory properties. Their two constituent parts are inextricably bound together: there is a very strong expectation that the second part of an adjacency pair must appropriately follow the first part. This has two significant consequences for the conduct of interaction. For instance, when a speaker asks a question, not only is the recipient compelled to respond to this summons but they must also produce the appropriate type of response, namely, an answer.

The first part of an adjacency pair, therefore, constrains what type of turn follows it. From an analytical perspective, this powerful mechanism affords an appreciation of how speakers, regardless of their linguistic proficiency or psychological states, are often able to coordinate understanding and joint actions during interaction (Heritage and Maynard, 2006: 10). (Indeed, as we shall see shortly when considering non-native and native interaction, the sequential requirements of adjacency pairs help speakers to disambiguate problematic stretches of language and jointly recover meaning.)

As we noted in Chapter 1, CA focusses on the local context of interaction rather than the broader institutional context in which conversation takes place. Therefore attributes such as race and gender and the social and professional statuses of the participants are considered to be external to any interaction and therefore irrelevant to the analyst; such attributes are only deemed to be significant if they are made relevant in and through the actual talk of the participants themselves. Schegloff (1997) argues that talk possesses 'an internally grounded reality of its own' – and so all that one needs to conduct a conversational analysis is little more than the conversational data itself. This might seem like a rather restricting analytical point of departure, but it helps ensure a close focus on the minutiae of talk; allowing, as it were, the conversational data to speak for itself.

The analytical potential of CA has not been lost on health communication researchers. CA-based research into clinical interaction has yielded many new insights into the linguistic behaviours of medical personnel and patients. Specifically, such investigations aim to:

- identify patterns of behaviour which healthcare practitioners might more consciously take into account in their interactions with patients;
- identify interactional strategies which may facilitate patient involvement in discussions and decisions about health-care;
- explore the association between certain interactional 'styles' and certain outcomes – such as patient satisfaction, antibiotic prescription.

(Drew *et al.*, 2000: 59)

Returning to the theme of the nurse–patient exchange, one excellent illustration of a CA approach to medical interaction is provided by Collins (2005). Collins' research examines the challenges of multidisciplinary working in a diabetes clinic, particularly the consequences that collaborative working has for communication with patients. As we previously observed, inter-professional teams are becoming increasingly common in healthcare settings, requiring medical personnel to adopt new roles and working relationships (Iedema and Scheeres, 2003). By comparing the communication of nurses and doctors, Collins sheds light on their distinctive verbal strategies and how these strategies are reflective of the practitioners' respective occupational traditions.

The following two extracts feature a patient engaged in a diabetes consultation, first with a nurse, then a doctor, both of whom are part of the same inter-professional team. In these interviews the participants are discussing the results of the patient's blood test. The test, technically referred to as 'HBA1', is designed to monitor the blood glucose levels.

```
1     N:   So how have you been. this last year
2          you think.
3          (1.5)
4     P:   phhhhhh .hh I thought (I) (1.7)
5          have done alright. =
6     N:   = Right.
7          (0.7)
8     P:   Until you tell me that (0.2) my
9          H( [ )
10    N:        [HBA1 =
11    P:   = HBO1
12         (0.9)
13    N:   Was a bit high.
14         (0.3)
```

```
15   P:   (Was) hi:gh.
16        (0.3)
17   N:   Right.
18        (0.6)
19   P:   U:hm
20        (0.6)
21   N:   Well you might still have (0.6) done
22        alright! (0.5) but (0.3) the fact
23        (0.8).hh that your HBA1's high.
24        (0.4) it means- (0.3) maybe s- we
25        need to (0.6) look at (0.3) (h)ow
26        you're treated really and
27        (0.6)
28   N:   [(Maybe think about) other options. =
29   P:   [yeah yeah
30   N:   [available.
31   P:   [yeah.
32            (0.3)
33   N:   To bring it (.) more (0.6) down to an
34        acceptable level. (0.3) so that you're
35        (0.6) fine. (0.3) you can carry on
36        be[ing =
37   P:      [Yes.
38   N:   = healthy and all that.
```

(Collins, 2005: 788)

This extract opens with a question and answer adjacency pair in which the nurse enquires about the patient's well-being. A 1.5 second pause ensues before the patient, at line 4, answers the nurse's question, a response that is prefaced with a drawn out sigh ('phhhhhh .hh'). As Collins notes, this intake of breath, and the pause before it, signal a problem on the part of the patient, specifically, as it turns out, his interpretation of the test result, which he believed would reveal a lower level of glucose in the blood: 'I thought I have done alright'. The nurse's backchannelling remark, 'Right' (6), acknowledges the patient's evaluation of the test result and encourages him to continue with his turn. At line 9 the patient struggles to articulate the technical abbreviation of the test 'HBA1', but the nurse, evidently recognising his difficulty producing this clinical term, duly supplies it for him. Throughout the rest of the extract, the nurse acknowledges the patient's talk (line 17) and, significantly, picks up and recycles his words, using them in her clinical assessment of the test result (Collins, 2005: 788). For instance, at lines 21-22, she offers the explanation 'Well you might still have (0.6) done alright', an explanation which recasts part of the patient's prior evaluation: 'I thought have done alright'. Using the patient's actual words in this way, argues Collins, the nurse accommodates both patient and professional perspectives, while separating 'the patient's behaviour and responsibility from any implications the result might have for his treatment' (ibid.).

The communicative approach that the nurse takes can be contrasted with the doctor's:

```
1    D:   Okay I'm gunna set you target level
2         2 (0.6) er:: now that (0.5) that is:
3         um:: (0.5) results of some tests
4         (.)
5    P:   Yeh
6         (.)
7    D:   That we've done from the nurse.
8         an we we want ah you (.) controlled
9         to a certain level.hh (.) huh most
10        important test that we do is the
11        H B A 1 C
12   P:   ((nods)) (0.9)
13   D:   Have yuh heard of this one [before]
14   P:                              [y e s] =
15   D:   = this is the: er
16        (1.3)
17   P:   Erm
18        (2.0)
19   P:   The actual control of the: er
20   D:   Tck yeh it give [s an indication of] =
21   P:                   [uv (the) sugar]
22   D:   = how we [ll y] our diabetes is =
23   P:            [(uh yeh)]
24   D:   = con[troll]ed
25   P:        [y e s]
26        (.)
27   D:   It's actually ah measuring how
28        much glucose is combined with the
29        red blood cell pigment
30   P:   (Yes)
31   D:   And because the red blood cell
32        pigment is locked up in the red
33        cells which .hh have a half life of
34        approximately 6 to 8 weeks.
35        .hh (.) it gives us an averaging
36        out figure over that period =
37   P:   = That's right (.) yeh
38   D:   .hhh now: yours is 9 point 6
```

```
39          (0.4)
40    D:    an [d that is] hi:[gh:].
41    P:        [Yes:] [that i]s high =
42    D:    = Y[eh]
43    P:         [Ye]h
44    D:    I would like tuh see that
45          somewhere near:: (.) si-
46          between 6 and 7 percent
```

(Collins, 2005: 798)

As Collins observes, many of the doctor's turns are concerned with the technical details of the patient's blood test. The doctor, furthermore, commonly emphasises the involvement of professionals with regard to the test result: 'I'm gunna set you target level 2', 'we want you controlled to a certain level' (lines 1–3, 7–9). Little, if any, input is sought from the patient. Indeed throughout the encounter, the doctor embarks on a series of explanations of technical procedures and biomedical processes, interactionally consigning the patient to little more than acknowledging these explanations (lines 23, 25, 30, 37). On the occasion when the doctor does invite input from the patient directly – seeking his understanding of the HBA1 test (line 13) – the doctor nevertheless proceeds with his own explanation (lines 20 and 22) before the patient has yet to complete his own response. Thus the doctor subsumes the patient's understanding of the test within his own account (Collins, 2005: 789), closing down the patient's explanation.

These two extracts, then, reveal some significant differences in nurses' and doctors' approaches to communicating with patients. In the nurse–patient interview, the patient takes more of an active role in the verbal proceedings, and the nurse's contributions often issue directly and develop from the patient's observations. The emphasis is less on the technical side of clinical assessment and intervention but more on the patient's behaviour and responsibility. Conversely, the doctor's approach involves far less patient input, focussing rather on biomedical and technical concerns and professional interventions. The doctor's explanations emerge from outside the patient's talk, putting the patient in the rather passive position of merely acknowledging (instead of amending and developing) the assessment and the doctor's attendant explanations (Collins, 2005: 789).

These contrasting approaches are mirrored in the linguistic repertoires of the two professionals. Whereas the nurse's discourse is characterised by the use of lay forms of language, drawing more on everyday lexical items as well as embracing words used by the patient, the doctor's talk involves more specialised and potentially alienating forms of language. To emphasise these linguistic contrasts is not to claim that one approach is better or more effective than the other, only to draw attention to the intriguing fact that the orientations of these two professional groups are encoded in their styles of communication. To some extent, the more open structures apparent in the nurse–patient exchange reflect the emphasis in nursing on patient-centred and holistic care, an approach to medicine which recognises the importance of patients' psycho-social needs just as much as their physical needs (Candlin, 2000: 231). However, an emphasis on holistic care and the concomitant use of everyday language doesn't necessarily empower patients or assail the barriers that characteristically obtain in the doctor–patient relationship. Asymmetries in the nurse–patient relationship can also be discerned: linguistically, they are liable to manifest themselves in more subtle ways.

Task 2.1 Nursing consultation: empowering the patient   (TC)

The extract below features a 27-year-old female patient (P) in a primary care consultation with a nurse practitioner (N). The patient is presenting with a complaint of excess fatigue. This is the first time she has presented her concern at the surgery. How would you characterise the communicative approach adopted by the nurse? What discourse strategies does she use in order to engage the patient and to establish the meaning of the patient's complaint?

1	N:	I see on the little slip that Martha ((receptionist)) made out, that, uh, you're feeling tired a lot.
2	P:	Yeah, just tired.
3	N:	When did it start?
4	P:	Um, a few weeks ago. Cause I'm falling asleep early at night. Usually I can stay awake till eleven, eleven thirty and it doesn't bother me. And I've been falling asleep, like almost literally passing out, eight, eight-thirty, nine o'clock. And I'm sitting ((unintelligible)) and it's like I just run out. ((laughs))
5	N:	Um hm. Has this been true every night?
6	P:	Mnn, well, it's almost every night. Just about. I get tired, I don't know, I don't know if it's the job or what?
7	N:	Tell me, go back about your job and tell me, fill me in a little bit about what your life is like now.

(Fisher, 1991: 166)

Nursing interaction: managing the admission interview

As we have discussed, recent developments in healthcare such as multidisciplinary working practices, the increasing specialisation of practitioners and patient-empowerment initiatives have affected the professional–patient relationship and, consequently, the delivery of healthcare. Over the last 25 years, nursing, in particular, has undergone profound global changes (Jones, 2007), not least the increasing standardisation of routine nursing tasks brought about by healthcare policies that advocate the philosophy of patient-centred medicine. A consequence of these ideological changes is that nurses have to reconcile technical, clinical efficiency with holistic care. For example, as one nursing manual exhorts, nurses must always 'explore, and allow expression of, the patient's feelings' (Dougherty and Lister, 2004: 36, cited in Jones, 2007). Yet given the bureaucratic imposition of time-efficient frameworks that standardise nursing tasks, attending sufficiently to the interpersonal, psycho-social aspects of patient care is not straightforward (Koteyko and Carter, 2008), and nurses have accordingly adopted new ways to manage these conflicting demands imposed upon them.

One type of routine nursing procedure where this is apparent is the hospital admissions interview. When patients are first admitted to hospital, nurses routinely conduct an assessment of their general well-being and health requirements. This interview can be considered to be the beginning of the nurse–patient relationship (Fitzgerald, 2002) during the patient's time at hospital. As such, the interview constitutes a significant communicative event which requires sensitive and skilful handling on the part of nurses if they are to effectively assess the needs of patients, and conversation analysis research offers revealing insights into how nurses practically manage this important task. Specifically CA-based approaches have been able to identify some of the interactional strategies that nurses employ in order to conduct the assessment interview and expedite the admissions process (Jones, 2007: 212). The work of Aled Jones (2003, 2007) is particularly enlightening in this regard. The following extracts (reproduced from his 2007 study) illustrate the ways in which nurses attempt to reconcile professional directives with the actual reality of interacting with patients.

I

1	Nurse:	uhm do you live alone
2	Nurse:	(no)
3	Patient:	(no)
4	Nurse:	that's right I know they're a bit silly these questions but you have to ask them
5	Patient:	it's alright
6	Nurse:	type of accommodation
7		(1)
8	P's Wife:	house ((laughs))
9	Nurse:	semi detached
10	P's Wife:	no
11	Patient:	yeh-uh yeh yeh ((puzzled look towards the nurse))

| 12 | Nurse: | what it is you see the reason why we ask these questions because there could be some elderly people with (interesting) lives |

II

1	Nurse:	how much do you weigh
2		(1) (patient turns away to think)
3	Nurse:	any idea
4	Patient:	nine and a quarter I think
5		(2) (nurse writes in notes)
6	Nurse:	suffer with any disabilities or weaknesses
7	Patient:	no (.) no
8	Nurse:	arthritis or anything
9	Patient:	(a bit of) arthritis
10		(6) (nurse writing in notes)
11	Nurse:	does that cause you a lot of problems
12	Patient:	well yeh my leg do
13		(12) (nurse writing in notes)
14	Nurse:	speaking in uh English? =
15	Patient:	English ((laughs))
16	Nurse:	((laughs)) any Welsh
17	Patient:	no you're joking ((laughs))
18	Nurse:	are you in any pain or anything at the moment

(Jones, 2007: 219)

These two extracts occur at various stages in the admission interview. Jones notes that at no point during the encounters do the nurses officially inform the patients that the talk between them constitutes an assessment of their health needs. Instead the nurses adopt alternative types of strategies to help explicate the purpose of the interview and help preserve an interpersonal relationship. In the first extract, taken from an earlier stage in the admission interview, the nurse draws explicit attention to the act of interrogation, acknowledging what is perceived to be a personally invasive line of questioning: 'I know they're a bit silly these questions but you have to ask them'. Referring to the questions as 'silly' puts a colourfully unofficial gloss on the assessment process quite unlike that found in the professional nursing literature! Moreover, not only does the act of describing the questions in this way downplay their official status but it also distances the nurse from the discursive incumbency of having to put them to the patient in the first place. When the nurse opines 'but you have to ask them', he or she makes it clear to the patient that asking questions is not a preferred type of verbal activity but an unavoidable, predetermined one (Jones, 2007: 217).

The second extract consists of a series of questions and answers in which the nurse seeks specific details from the patient. As the interrogation unfolds, some of the questions become pared down in form, with some of their finite verb forms being elided, for example: '[Do you] suffer with any disabilities or weaknesses', '[Do you have] arthritis or anything' (lines 6, 8, 14). This rather shorthand, rapid-fire way of posing questions reveals how, in actual practice, the speech exchange of the admission interview radically differs from that of everyday conversation. As Jones (2007: 219) observes, this type of interchange creates a sequential deference structure where patients are obliged to respond to questions and have little opportunity to lead the talk. Thus it would appear that the nurses have difficulty in reconciling the patient-centred approach (an approach, recall, which advocates exploring patients' feelings and addressing their lifeworld concerns) with the exigencies of the assessment interview itself.

However, despite the rigid transactional style of turn-taking, which is purely geared towards information exchange, the participants make room for humour. At lines 15-17, for instance, they engage in mutual laughter – laughing in response to the presumably pre-formulated question 'speaking in English?'. Given that the assessment interview is taking place in a Welsh hospital, the nurse makes enquiries into the patient's linguistic background (whether they speak English and Welsh). The humour derives from the fact the patient is, quite self-evidently, conversing in English, and thus the question 'speaking in English?' is flagrantly redundant, although the nurse still has to put it to the patient as part of the official assessment procedure. But the participants' laughter here is not only a mutual reaction to bureaucratic absurdity; it also reduces the social distance between them (health professionals can laugh just like everyone else) and creates a sense of familiarity which allows the nurse to fulfil institutional goals in a way that minimises the imposition on the patient (Grainger, 2002: 14).

To sum up this section, the foregoing conversation analyses expose the reality of nursing communication in practice (Jones, 2003: 616). In the context of the diabetic consultation, for example, the focus on the interactional strategies of the nurse revealed a distinct orientation to the patient's responsibilities and behaviour. The nurse's talk was seen to develop from the patient's talk and thus the patient was actively involved in the consultation. The nurse's approach was patient-focussed, involving the patient in treatment decisions. This approach differed from the doctor's way of handling the interaction: the doctor's emphasis was on the technical aspects of assessment. Goals were set by the doctor rather than their being jointly negotiated between the two parties. Thus, in the doctor–patient exchange at least, there was little evidence of the patient empowerment philosophy which pervades contemporary healthcare (Salmon and Hall, 2004).

Contradictions were also evident in the admissions interview. Nurses adopted particular verbal strategies in order to respond to the practical necessities of performing everyday tasks. Close attention to the naturally occurring talk of nurses and patients revealed that nurses drew explicit attention to the institutional and bureaucratic routines in which they were involved with patients, in some cases even apologising for, and gently mocking, the assessment questions that they were duty bound to put to patients: 'I know they're a bit silly these questions but you have to ask them'. Herein lies the value of CA's focussing squarely on interactional data itself, its grounding insights in the actual talk of the participants. Given the complex nature of nursing, where personnel are 'faced with limited time resources and unlimited demand' (Jones, 2007: 221), it is perhaps not unreasonable to assume that there will be discrepancies between policy rhetoric and the actual working practices of nurses (2007: 213). However, the reality of such discrepancies is only evidenced and confirmed by a detailed interrogation of the actual working routines – their talk in particular – of nurses themselves. Moreover, closely examining the substance of interaction affords insight into what matters the participants deem to be relevant to themselves (rather than what the analyst from outside deems to be relevant), and how they devise strategies for managing the complex and unavoidably face-threatening encounters in which they continually find themselves.

Task 2.2 Patient empowerment or nurse control?   (TC)

Consider the two stretches of nurse–patient interaction below. Both extracts are taken from one consultation and feature the same participants, a registered nurse and a patient whom she is visiting at home after his discharge from hospital. The purpose of the nurse's visit is to dress the patient's surgical wound and to assess his health status. After studying the extracts closely, see if you can answer the following questions:

- In what ways is the patient empowered during this interview?
- Which participant dictates the encounter?
- Would you consider the way in which the patient constructs his situation to be empowering?

Extract 1

1	N:	How did you feel in yourself when
2		all this was happening
3		you know you
4	P:	Of course I couldn't believe
5		this was really happening to me you know

6		and then in the hospital em it was the first time
7		doctor was talking to me and
8		one of them asked me
9		what was my attitude towards ( ) and all this ( ) and
10		I thought oh if I die I die
11		I suppose there's nothing I could do about it but
12		I still couldn't see it happening to me
13		well nobody can can they
14		it's always someone else

Extract 2

1	N:	Yes it's not easy today with things. . .
2	P:	But it was after I was retrenched actually
3		it was five months after mum because because
4		mum because me mum passed away a week
5		or so after and then I was crook
6	N:	yeah it must have been very hard for you
7		that happening and
8		then getting sick yourself
9	P:	I suppose
10		that's the lot that's dealt out to you
11		you've got to take it haven't you

(adapted from Candlin, 2000: 233)

Nursing interaction in multilingual settings

Much discourse-based research into practitioner–patient interaction has concentrated exclusively on participants who converse with one another in their native – principally English – language. Consequently, discourse analysts such as Candlin and Candlin (2003) quite rightly argue that cross-cultural health communication should be a priority research area for applied linguists. Indeed given the increasing number of culturally diverse medical personnel (nurses in particular) working in healthcare settings (Bosher and Smalkoski, 2002), it is surprising that applied linguistic research has yet to sufficiently address this theme. Due to staff shortages, a number of European and North American hospitals have sought to recruit health professionals from overseas, employing nurses from locations such as Southeast Asia, Eastern Europe and West and South Africa (Withers and Snowball, 2003; Taylor, 2005).

Although the work of overseas nurses has been, and continues to be, invaluable to healthcare provision, the experiences of nurses working in other cultures have not always been positive (Taylor,

2005). One of the greatest difficulties that overseas nurses face is communicating with patients and colleagues (Bosher and Smalkoski, 2002). When health professionals and patients from different linguistic and cultural backgrounds interact, there is the increased possibility of miscommunication since the participants will be interacting on three levels of remove: medicine, culture and language (Cameron and Williams, 1997: 416). Cross-cultural interaction thus poses rather profound communicative challenges for both native and non-native speakers alike, and it is here that applied linguistics has much to contribute.

One of the few applied linguistic studies to explicate cross-cultural communication in clinical contexts is that conducted by Cameron and Williams (1997). Cameron and Williams' work combines insights from second language acquisition with conversation analysis and pragmatics in order to identify what constitutes communicative success (or otherwise) in exchanges between native and non-native speakers of English. Their research focusses on a series of interactions featuring a Thai nurse, her supervisor and two patients in a psychiatric clinic of a North American hospital. In some of these encounters, the nurse, Mary, converses solely with her patients, in others she interacts with both colleagues and patients. Cameron and Williams describe Mary's proficiency in English as relatively low. Nevertheless, despite her lack of competence in English as a second language, many of the interactions in which she takes part are mainly successful. This is due to a number of interpretative strategies which the participants employ, in particular their searching for relevance through the presence of contextually invoked inferences. In their joint pursuit of relevance, the participants are able to navigate communicative impasses and achieve a satisfactory level of mutual understanding (satisfactory in the sense that any momentary interactional difficulty is overcome, thereby allowing the talk to continue). We will consider the theoretical underpinnings of relevance in more detail at the end of this chapter, but for now let us consider an example of how the participants harness contextual triggers during interaction in order to resolve outbreaks of miscommunication.

1   Nurse: OK. And you know what is? ((Pointing to watch on
                  her wrist))
2   What is?
3   Patient: Huh? Quarter after ten.
4   Nurse: Oh. OK. What is?
5   Patient: It's a watch.

(Cameron and Williams, 1997: 427)

The purpose of this and other similar exchanges is to evaluate patients' speech and thereby their psychological well-being. Speech problems are potentially indicative of an underlying psychiatric disorder, and thus an accurate evaluation of a patient's linguistic behaviour plays a crucial part in reliably informing any diagnosis. As Cameron and Williams point out, 'any diagnosis of confusion or disorientation would be especially troubling if such confusion or disorientation accurately resulted from a care-provider's unintelligible speech' (1997: 419).

In the exchanges above, although the patient initially appears confused by the nurse's syntactically incomplete question ('What is?'), this confusion is quickly resolved with the patient supplying the relevant answer and thus the assessment is able to continue. Here two key factors, Cameron and Williams observe, allow the participants to overcome their difficulties. Firstly, the nurse's utterances in lines 1, 2 and 4 constitute the first part of an adjacency pair, namely, a question and answer pairing. As we noted earlier in this chapter, the first part of an adjacency pair summons another speaker to provide an appropriate response (an answer in the case of a question-answer pairing); and as can be seen in the extract above, the nurse's question duly elicits a response from the patient ('Huh? Quarter after ten'), but the summons alone is insufficient to procure the precise information she seeks. The patient only provides the right answer after he evidently realises that his first interpretation (that he is being asked to provide the time) is incorrect and so then considers the next most likely interpretation: that he is being asked what the object on her wrist is. The search for relevance is thus successfully realised by two factors: the sequential expectation of adjacency pairs and the gestural cue of the nurse's indicating her wristwatch, a gesture which, Cameron and Williams argue, closes down the available set of inferences from which the patient must choose.

Cameron and Williams identify three principle linguistic triggers which commonly give rise to miscommunication: divergent phonological features, syntactical errors, and ambiguous use of tenses (1997: 429). Yet, as we have just seen, linguistic 'deficiencies' in themselves are not an insurmountable bar to participants' understanding one another in cross-cultural interaction. For example, despite the nurse's recurring lack of tense marking, the participants are able to harness alternative lexical strategies that quickly resolve any temporal confusion. The following exchange, in which Mary questions the patient about his past relationship with his children, effectively illustrates the point:

1	Nurse:	Uh Do you uh what should I say?
2		Do you like uh give money to them or?
3	Patient:	I don't give 'em nothing.
4		They better send me some money.
5		They 27 years old. ((laughter))

6	Nurse:	Nooooo I mean in the past.
7	Patient:	Oh yeah I did.
8	Nurse:	Not now.

(Cameron and Williams, 1997: 432)

During lines 1 and 2 the nurse uses the present tense ('Do you...') to ascertain if the patient used to provide his children with financial assistance. Given the focus here on past events, the use of the present tense here appears to be inappropriate, leading to a misinterpretation on the part of the patient, whose response, which echoes the nurse's use of the present tense, describes his current state of affairs: 'I *don't* give 'em nothing' (our italicised emphasis). But Mary is alert to this misunderstanding, responding by substituting a lexical and more emphatic formulation of past time ('I mean in the past') for the prior misapplied past tense marker. This lexical substitution achieves its purpose of clarifying meaning since the patient's response (at line 7) is prefaced with an 'oh' receipt, a particle which speakers use to indicate that they have undergone a change in their knowledge state (Heritage, 1984), in this instance the patient's indicating that he has recognised the nurse's request for information about the past. After receipting the nurse's request, he duly provides the sought-after information ('yeah I did'), and, accordingly, the momentary breakdown in understanding is resolved.

Given the complex nature of medical (especially psychiatric) communication, there are occasions in cross-cultural exchanges when interactional difficulties involve more than the presence of (eminently rectifiable) linguistic shortcomings. An experienced awareness of the mores and rituals of the clinic is essential if practitioners are to achieve professional competence. For non-native practitioners acclimatising to the new culture and routines of their adopted workplaces, their fulfilling of professional goals is likely to prove especially challenging. For example, there maybe occasions when, during certain interactional routines, they are expected to present information in a particular, ritualised fashion but, due to their unfamiliarity with such routines, struggle to do so.

That said, even these more protracted difficulties between non-native and native speakers are commonly resolved, with fellow professionals providing interactional support that allows the non-native speaker to fulfil her professional goals. An example of this type of inter-professional cooperation can be seen in the following extract, in which the nurse is presenting a patient history to her supervisor (S).

| 1 | S: | mmhm OK So, we're looking at organic mood disorder with a depression, with a depressed affect that they are treating with ECT and any other drugs? |

2		Any other anti-depressant medication?
3	N:	Uh no no this time we use ECT.
4	S:	mmhm
5	N:	Before ECT we use Ritalin.
6	S:	ritalin mmhm
7		Have you noticed any changes since he came in for isolating behavior, decreased concentration?
8	N:	Uh This time we can take him to dayroom. Like
9	S:	e-He will go to the dayroom.
10	N:	Yes.
11	S:	When he is in the dayroom, what does he do?
12	N:	uh talking
13	S:	Talks to other patients?
14	N:	No.
15	S:	To who?
16	N:	Talks to me. ((laughs))
17	S:	Talks to you.
18		Does he initiate that conversation?
19		Does he start the talking or do you have to -
20	N:	No no
21	S:	to start?
22	N:	I have to start.

(Cameron and Williams, 1997: 434-435)

Presenting the patient history involves detailing not only the biomedical aspects of patients' conditions but also their personal, social histories. Cameron and Williams note that the communicative breakdown in the sequence above is brought about by the nurse's failure to provide sufficient information regarding the patient's social behaviour. She produces only short, stunted utterances – contributions that are evidently inadequate for the purpose of providing a fulsome history, since the supervisor has to continually probe her for further information (at lines 9, 11, 13, 15, 17-19, for example). Here the supervisor's questions perform the pedagogic function of scaffolding (Bruner, 1990). Scaffolding, a form of collaborative interaction often used in second language classrooms, aims to pre-empt and address communicative breakdowns, with one speaker, typically a teacher, providing close interactional support for another (Walsh, 2011). In the extract above, the supervisor constructs a chain of questions which elicit specific details from the nurse – questions composed of pieces of information already provided by the nurse in her previous turns (Cameron and Williams, 1997: 434). In this way, the participants, in systematic, step-by-step fashion, build up a more informed picture of the patient's social life than would be provided by the nurse alone and thereby work towards constructing a successful case history.

Although this scaffolding procedure might appear to be a one-sided interactional process, in the sense that the supervisor continually has to prompt and direct the nurse, it is very much a collaborative enterprise. The nurse herself introduces new, if small, pieces of information into the talk and the supervisor, in turn, develops these incipient themes. Despite the extra responsibility placed on the supervisor, scaffolding, as this example illustrates, serves as an effective means of conducting collegial interaction, assisting non-native personnel to express themselves (Walsh, 2011: 119). Yet, interestingly, the use of scaffolding in the foregoing example raises the complex question of precisely where second language proficiency (that is, being able to provide appropriate description in the target language) ends and professional competence (knowing what sort of information to provide) starts (Cameron and Williams, 1997: 434). For health communication researchers, resolving this conundrum continues to be an ongoing endeavour.

Other voices: pharmacists, physiotherapists and chaplains

So far in this chapter we have examined how nurses, during certain of their everyday activities, interact with patients and colleagues. We have also considered how nurses perform these tasks against a backdrop of an ever-changing healthcare system that continues to place increasing emphasis on patient-empowerment and multidisciplinary working. Yet nurses are not the only set of health workers to be affected by these developments. Professional groups including pharmacists, physiotherapists and occupational therapists have also experienced changes in their working practices, changes which reflect not only these aforementioned shifts in healthcare ideology, but also other professional concerns.

Pharmacy, for example, is a profession that has changed rapidly in recent years (Pilnick, 2001). Technological advances – the availability of ready prepared drugs and increased computerisation – mean that there is now less need for traditional medicine formulation skills, resulting in a situation where more routine dispensing work is being performed by less qualified personnel (2001: 1928). Yet if the role of the pharmacist has declined in certain areas, it has extended in others. Patient counselling now plays a prominent part in pharmacy practice. Pharmacists are increasingly taking on more of an 'advisory role', a broad, if indeed somewhat boundless duty, which requires them to offer advice on myriad matters ranging from staple concerns about drug dosage through to more protracted advice touching on lifestyle choices and health promotion (Pilnick, 2003: 835). Intriguingly, this advisory role is, Pilnick observes, not clearly defined by the bodies that govern pharmacy, such as the Pharmaceutical Society of Great Britain (RPSGB). It assumed that advice-giving (a linguistic activity which we explore in detail in chapters 7 and 8) is a skill that pharmacists already possess, a skill that can be called upon at will when the situation demands (Pilnick, 2001: 1929). In their daily practice pharmacists have the difficult job of managing the delicate task of informing and directing patients; patients who may already have considerable experience of pharmaceutical services and the particular conditions for which they are seeking treatment.

(TC)

Task 2.3 Patient-empowerment in physiotherapy: the problem of goal-setting

As with pharmacists, the working practices of physiotherapists have also been subject to change and increasing professional regulation. For instance, professional standards documents encourage physio-therapists to actively involve patients in goal-setting (Parry, 2004: 669). However, during actual physiotherapy sessions, involving patients in goal-setting is no straightforward interactional task: powerful social constraints render goal-setting problematic. (We discuss the nature of these constraints in the commentary to this exercise).

The extract below features a physiotherapist (T) and a patient who has recently suffered a stroke. The purpose of the encounter is to set goals for the patient in order to promote his rehabilitation. Study the extract then answer the following questions:

- How does the physiotherapist involve the patient in goal-setting?
- To what extent are the goals proposed by the physiotherapist taken up by the patient?

1	T:	just to get a good picture of what you're able to do so that
2		we can work out where there's problems and what we
		can do
3		about them is that OK
4		(1.5)
5	T:	what would you say your biggest problems are
6		(2.0)
7	T:	whilst you're here in hospital
8		(2.0)
9	P:	my left and right arm
10	T:	your left and right arm ((questioning tone))
11		(2.0)
12	P:	when fell (h)it both the elbows here
13	T:	ri[ght]
14	P:	[(they're)] (very) painful
15	T:	so the pain in your left and right arm is your biggest
		problem
16		(0.5)
17	P:	yeah
18	T:	OK: Ohh do you (.) is there anything that you can't do at
		the

19		mome:nt (.) um that you'd like to be able to do by the time
20		that you go out of hospital
21	P:	put me socks on
22	T:	put yer socks on OK so what limits you putting yer socks on

*Lines omitted in which these limitations are discussed.
The therapist asks the patient to demonstrate the
difficulties by reaching downwards. The transcript
recommences as he ascends back towards upright sitting*

45	T:	and back up again hh so (.) we could probably: (e) set a goal
46		then for you like a g- like a joint goal that we'll- I'll (.) look at
47		achieving with the occupational therapists hh that you can
48		reach and put yer socks on maybe we should <u>sav</u> within (.)
49		two weeks that you can do that d'you think that's fair enough
50	P:	I (.) put them on now by laying on the bed
51	T:	ri:ght so you've found one method of doing it
52		but would you nor:mally when you're at home do it in sitting
53		(0.5)
54	P:	normally

(adapted from Parry, 2004: 673)

The case of the healthcare chaplain

Non-physician personnel such as nurses, pharmacists and physiotherapists indubitably constitute professional groups, each having charters and sets of official regulatory guidelines. However, the professional position of the hospital chaplain is, according to Woodard, 'not a neat one' (Woodward, 2001: 92). As Woodward explains, despite there being a move towards the professionalisation of spiritual and pastoral carers, hospital chaplains have not been regarded as healthcare professionals alongside other (medical) professionals (2001: 90). Although valued by other health professionals and patients, the work of the hospital chaplain and other non-medical personnel has featured far less prominently in health communication research, which, as we have noted, has focussed more on the discourse of clinicians.

The primary function of the hospital chaplain is to provide spiritual and pastoral care to the healthcare community, a community which comprises not only patients but also visitors and healthcare workers. Chaplaincy is a verbal practice, enacted through face-to-face communication with patients at their bedsides. Chaplains help patients to express their anxieties and fears, to share feelings with someone who is not directly involved in their medical treatment. The discourse of chaplains therefore is characteristically exploratory and non-programmatic. Patients are accorded a great deal of interactional space and freedom to discuss not only spiritual and religious issues and matters concerning medical treatment, but also social and emotional concerns, talk germane to their own world of experience (Ribeiro, 1996). As Cobb (2001) observes, the role of chaplains exists in relationships with patients, relationships which are established in and through supportive talk and sympathetic listening.

The following extract provides an illustration of how a hospital chaplain interactionally manages the activity of eliciting personal information from patients (necessarily a face-threatening task) while, at the same time, developing and maintaining a relaxed, supportive and intimate conversational atmosphere. The sequence features a Catholic priest (C) conversing with a middle-aged man who has recently suffered a stroke. The extract represents just one of the many routine conversations conducted by the chaplain during the course of his regular spiritual and pastoral duties at a British hospital.

1	C:	You were saying that you were er feeling a bit bored today
2	P:	(That's right yeah)
3	C:	Uh uh
4	P:	Because it's pretty boring in the hospi=
5	C:	Yeah (just lying in in in the)
6	P:	Bed fed up
7	C:	Uh hu yeah
8		(5)
9	C:	You finding it a bit frustrating to be
10	P:	Yeah because I had a stroke
11	C:	Yes
12	C:	That makes it a lot worse
13	C:	Yes uh uh
14	C:	Would you be able to tell me a little bit about how that
15		affects you? How having this
16	P:	((unclear))
17	C:	having had this stroke affects you?
18	P:	It affects in just about everything honest
19	C:	Yeah
20	P:	I can't talk properly ((unclear)) speech
21		got brain damage so I can't explain just like that
22	C:	Yes uh uh I understand but it has always seemed
23		to me that you you you explain things very well
24	P:	Oh if you say so ((laughs))

25   C: Uh hu. Yeah
26   P: I try to
27   C: Yes
28   P: explain as best I can
29   C: Uh hu

A characteristic property of the chaplain's talk is his use of vague language. Common in informal conversation (Carter and McCarthy, 2006), vague language performs an important interpersonal function, as is apparent in the sequence above. The interchange commences with the chaplain sensitively encouraging the patient to discuss his feelings in relation to the effects of the stroke and his recent time in hospital. A recurring strategy employed by the chaplain to elicit this personal information is his use of the vague quantifier 'a bit' (lines 1, 9, 14). Although only a relatively small and seemingly inconsequential phrase, its cumulative use helps not only to establish and maintain an informal tone of interaction but also facilitates the discussion of extremely sensitive topics.

For example, although the vague statement 'You finding it a bit frustrating...' (line 9) could easily be interpreted as an understated assessment of the effects of the patient's stroke, the chaplain's referring to frustration in this vaguely mitigated way nevertheless appears to help the patient to talk about his difficulties. The use of the vague quantifier also functions as a deference strategy, a marker potentially indicating that the chaplain does not wish to make bold assumptions and assertions about the patient's feelings or intrude too much into his private affairs. Similarly, at line 14, as part of the process of eliciting further personal and potentially painful disclosures from the patient, the vague formulation 'a little bit' in the chaplain's utterance serves to mitigate the force of his request. The demand on the addressee to provide information is softened, affording the patient the option to supply only as much information as he feels able to disclose.

Structurally, the exchanges between the participants appear to resemble those of casual conversation more than the tightly controlled exchanges common in other forms of professional–patient interaction (such as doctor–patient communication). Although the interaction possesses a discernible pattern and structure, there doesn't appear to be any obvious pre-allocated system of turn distribution or adherence to a specific topical agenda. Moreover, unlike the clinical detachment which is a common characteristic of doctor–patient talk (Treichler et al., 1984: 69), some of the chaplain's responses constitute more than neutral acknowledgements of the patient's problems. (Consider, for example, the utterance: 'it has always seemed to me that you explain things very well', in which the chaplain offers a personal evaluation of the patient's linguistic abilities.)

However, despite its relation to ordinary conversation, chaplain–patient interaction nonetheless remains a form of institutional discourse, organised as it is towards specific transactional ends. For example, the chaplain is evidently in an institutionally licensed position from which he is able to ask questions of the patient and to pursue particular topics regarding the patient's presence in hospital. In turn, the patient provides the information requested of him. The exchange of information is mainly one way: although there is nothing stopping him from doing so, the patient does not ask questions of the chaplain. Finally, both participants orient to specific institutional roles, and this orientation inevitably confines the contours of their interaction.

Cooperation, implicature and relevance: pragmatics theories and health communication

Earlier in this chapter we considered how native and non-native speakers engaged in healthcare exchanges are able to resolve breakdowns in interaction. In these instances what enabled the participants to make sense of one another was an awareness of the structural imperative of adjacency pairings (that one utterance compels another) and the availability of contextual triggers that prompt speakers to infer certain meanings over others. The latter sense-making activity involved the participants searching for relevance, the pursuit of which allowed the various troubled interactions to recover and resume successfully (Cameron and Williams, 1997: 415). For the remainder of this chapter, we shall consider the notion of relevance in the broader context of pragmatics, a branch of linguistic study concerned with 'the meaning of utterances in specific contexts of use' (Jaworski and Coupland, 1999: 14).

Pragmatics is an extremely broad field of enquiry and so our focus here will be confined to a few key theoretical concerns (readers interested in pursuing this fascinating subject might wish to consult the Further Reading section for recommended texts). Very broadly speaking, pragmatic theories of language examine speaker (and writer) meaning. Pragmatics accounts for how people are able to interpret certain instances of language which on the surface are different from the meaning intended by the speaker. Consider the example of the nurse who, after an exhausting, frantically non-stop twelve-hour nightshift, returns to her car only to find a parking ticket affixed to its windscreen. 'Fantastic,' she says to herself, 'just what I needed.' Given the context of the situation (our understanding that receiving a parking ticket is not a pleasant experience – the authors, at least, know of no-one ever having rejoiced at the prospect of paying a parking fine – coupled with the fact the nurse is likely to be tired after a long, taxing stint at work), we can confidently interpret her remark as one of sarcasm. What she really means (implies) is quite the opposite from the literal meaning, the surface form, of the words she utters to herself. In saying something different from what she means, the nurse generates an implicature, an additional unstated meaning. She conveys more than what she says.

One influential pragmatic theory of language that accounts for how speakers convey more than they actually say (and how listeners are able to apprehend unstated information) is provided by Grice (1975). Grice advanced the notion of the Cooperative Principle. According to Grice, when people interact with one another, their talk does not characteristically consist of a series of disconnected remarks. Rather their utterances are cooperative efforts: 'each participant recognises in them, to some extent, a common purpose or set of purposes, or at least a mutually accepted direction' (Grice, 1999: 78). Grice sought to account for this purposeful linguistic behaviour, formulating his Cooperative Principle (CP) in the following famous terms:

> Make your conversational contribution such as is required, at the stage at which it occurs, by the accepted purpose or direction of the talk exchange in which you are engaged.
>
> (Grice, 1999: 78)

Although well known among coteries of applied linguists and discourse analysts, Grice's phrasing here is open to interpretation. Although the CP is expressed as a set of imperatives ('make your conversational contribution...'), Grice not so much proposes a set of rules as assumes that people generally observe these conversational criteria when engaged in interaction. The CP, in other words, is not a prescription for effective communication. Furthermore, the notion of cooperation that Grice posits is quite different from the conventional sense of 'cooperation'. Cooperation in the Gricean sense doesn't necessarily involve speakers harmoniously working together in order to achieve some mutual goal outside of understanding one another. Rather it entails speakers operating with a shared set of assumptions about communication and their mutually adhering to certain linguistic norms (Thomas, 2001: 122). People can argue and disagree with one another, even subject others to the most devastating invective. Yet for all their abuse and discord, if they intend their utterances to be meaningful, they will still be adhering to the Cooperative Principle. The point is that people generally try to make themselves understandable to one another, and they do this by being as truthful, informative, relevant and clear as they can. They observe a set of conversational maxims or categories, which Grice described thus:

Quantity:	Make your contribution as informative as is required (for the current purposes of the exchange).
	Do not make your contribution more informative than is required.
Quality:	Do not say what you believe to be false.
	Do not say that for which you lack adequate evidence.
Relation:	Be relevant.
Manner:	Avoid obscurity of expression.
	Avoid ambiguity.
	Be brief (avoid unnecessary prolixity).
	Be orderly.

(Grice, 1991: 78-79)

When speakers observe all the above four maxims, they typically produce meaning in a clear, unambiguous fashion. But language in use is, blessedly, ever colourful and dynamic and replete with hidden depths. People often fail to observe the maxims. Doing so can be intentional or otherwise. However, failing to observe a maxim doesn't necessarily mean failing to be linguistically cooperative. People often deliberately fail to observe maxims (a process that Grice called 'flouting') in order to produce a level of meaning in addition to what they literally mean (Thomas, 2001: 122). When people flout a maxim they are still adhering to the Cooperation Principle: they have no intention of misleading others. Rather their intention is to prompt others to recover a hidden or implied meaning. In the example above, the nurse who literally rejoices in her receiving a parking ticket flouts the maxim of quality. Constituting an outburst of agonised sarcasm, her remark is patently untrue. Nevertheless, we can still easily infer her implied meaning, the meaning she intended to communicate: her annoyance at receiving a parking fine.

As this parking ticket vignette demonstrates, flouting maxims, the maxim of quality in particular, often involves the use of figures of speech – sarcasm, irony, hyperbole, understatement, and so on. Speakers sometimes flout maxims to make their utterances more playful and rhetorically appealing. Flouting maxims can also produce humorous and interpersonal effects. It is not surprising, therefore, that in certain sensitive healthcare encounters practitioners and patients may resort to verbal play in order to alleviate any potential tension and conflict. The following nurse–patient exchange illustrates the point. In this extract the nurse is assisting an elderly patient to bathe herself – naturally a delicate, sensitive nursing procedure.

1   N: oh! I've heard of bubble bath but this is ridiculous (.) I
            think there's more bubbles than water in there

2   P: ((laughs))
3   N: ((in mock baby talk)) you can play games with all the
           bubbles
4   P: lovely
5   N: ((baby talk)) yeah.
6   P: you help me
7   N: right ((laughs)) we'll sit here and play games with all the bu-
           we'll sit here and flick them at everybody who walks in
8   P: that'd be an idea love (.) I've been dying to that for years
9   N: what flick bubbles?
10   P: yeh
11   N: right then (.) you stand up then my love ((nurse helps
           patient to sit on the bath hoist)) (and pull these) you sit
           yourself back down there nice and gently

                                                (Grainger, 2002: 7-8)

This short exchange is characterised by humour and verbal play. There is laughter throughout (lines 2 and 7) and sustained reference to gameplaying (lines 3-10). The nurse speaks in a babyish voice and, at line 1, produces a hyperbolic remark which clearly flouts the maxim of quality: 'I think there's more bubbles than water in there', an exaggeration to which the patient responds with laughter, thus evidently treating it as a humorous remark. In their laughing at the prospect of playing with bubbles, the nurse and the patient jointly assert their solidarity in the bathing task (Grainger, 2002: 8). Moreover, since there is no pre-existing closeness between the participants, the verbal play (the exaggeration and the implicit mocking of the bathing procedure) which they engage in helps to promote a sense of familiarity between them, a familiarity which, according to Grainger, is 'motivated by the need to legitimise the intimate help by a non-intimate other, to which the elderly adult is obliged to subject herself' (ibid.).

Relevance: strong and weak communication

Although speakers (and writers) are liable to flout all four maxims (and sometimes more than one simultaneously), the maxim of relation is arguably the most commonly exploited (Short, 1996: 244). Relevance is central to inferential communication. Indeed Sperber and Wilson's Relevance Theory (1986) proposes that the basis of all communication is relevance-based, to the extent that the maxim of relevance subsumes all the other conversational maxims. According to Sperber and Wilson, relevance determines the usefulness or otherwise of human communication. Consequently an essential feature of human cognition is the search for relevance, a process which language users undertake whenever they are confronted by and wish to make sense of a stretch of discourse. Sperber and Wilson propose two general principles with regard to their theory of relevance:

> [1] The *cognitive* principle that human cognition tends to be geared to the maximisation of relevance; and [2] the *communicative* principle that every act of inferential communication communicates a presumption of its own optimal relevance.
>
> (Wilson, 1999: 719)

To put it another way, language users are implicitly aware that they are motivated by relevance, and that when they produce an utterance they intend listeners to assume that it is relevant enough to be worth attending to (Lycan, 2008: 166). Thus all utterances possess a presumption of their own relevance. But, of course, language processing, searching for relevance in a particular act of communication, involves mental effort. The greater the effort needed to process (or make sense of) a communicative act (such as a spoken utterance, written sentence or non-verbal gesture), the less relevant that act will be. Conversely the smaller the mental effort needed to make sense of a communicative act, the more relevant it will be. Thus relevance can be situated along a continuum, with some instances of language use being more relevant and readily comprehendible than others. Reflecting this scalar phenomenon, Sperber and Wilson posit the idea of weak and strong communication, each occupying opposite ends of the relevance continuum. Strong communication, at one of the scale, involves language and/or gesture that 'enables hearers to pin down the speakers' intentions about the explicit content of an utterance' (1986: 60), whereas weak communication, at the other end, is comparatively vague and more open to interpretation, requiring greater processing effort on the part of the listener. In other words, strong communication is speaker-dominated in that it constrains the range of relevant meanings that a hearer can infer, while weak communication is hearer dominated since a wider range of inferences are made available to the listener (Cameron and Williams, 1997: 418).

Having provided an (admittedly brief) overview of Relevance Theory, let us conclude by practically demonstrating, as it were, the relevance of relevance in a specific health communication context. Cameron and Williams (1997) usefully extend the notion of weak and strong communication to examining interaction between native and non-native speakers. Earlier in this chapter we considered the authors' analysis of a set of exchanges that featured a Thai nurse, Mary, interacting with patients and her supervisor. Cameron and Williams argue that Relevance Theory offers an effective means of accounting for how the participants overcome communicative difficulties that arise due to the nurse's lack of English proficiency. In the following extract, the various instances of miscommunication might appear to render the talk between Mary and her supervisor problematic or halting at the very least. However, recourse to the concepts of relevance and strong and weak communication provide a more optimistic linguistic assessment.

1	Nurse:	mmmhm Mr Tuh PTSD patient
2		He comes here because uh
3		(daily flashback of an accident that occur at the Operation Desert Storm)
4		uhhuh he uh he is unable to concentrate or function at work
5		and uh get along with others
6		He has low appetite
7		And he has difficulty to sleep
8		No suicidal ideation for this case mmhhmm
9		The history, I mean
10		uh recent history he started on amitriptyline HS two (tams) {times or terms}
11		And then he has uh short (tam) {time or term} therapy
12		one (tam) {time or term} before he came here
13	Supervisor:	What-what do you mean by short-term therapy?
14	Nurse:	He uh short [tam] {time or term} therapy
15	Supervisor:	At uh ou-out-patient clinic?
16	Nurse:	Yea
17	Supervisor:	Yea like how many weeks or days?
18	Nurse:	Just one [tam] {time or term}
19	Supervisor:	o-oh one time
20	Nurse:	One (tam) {time or term} by Dr D
21	Supervisor:	mmhhmm So he saw him once
22	Nurse:	mmhm
23	Supervisor:	And he was put on amitriptyline
24	Nurse:	amitriptyline
25	Supervisor:	For two days, before he came?
26	Nurse:	umm
27	Supervisor:	You said twice
28	Nurse:	Yes, twice
29	Supervisor:	I didn't know what that meant. So he had that for two, just two days of that

(Cameron and Williams, 1997: 426)

The instances of miscommunication that recur throughout this sequence, part of a case history summary, occur as a result of the nurse's divergent pronunciation, specifically her phonetic rendering of the word 'tam' (lines 10, 11, 12, 14, 18, 20). It is not clear whether she means 'time' or 'term', and her ambiguous expression prompts the supervisor to seek clarification: 'What-what do you mean by short-term therapy?'. The nurse's pronunciation renders the two words 'time' and 'term' as potential homophones – the vowel sound in 'tam' not being clear enough to distinguish the one possibility from the other. As Cameron and Williams (1997: 426-7) observe, this mispronunciation potentially has significant consequences for the construction of the case history. Is the nurse reporting that the patient has had two courses ('terms') or two doses ('times') of the drug amitriptyline? Both are perfectly valid interpretations. Yet there are insufficient contextual assumptions surrounding the nurse's utterance that prompt the supervisor to make the correct interpretation. The utterance constitutes an instance of weak communication, placing the burden of interpretation on the supervisor, who has a variety of interpretations to choose from. Given the open-endedness of the nurse's expression, the most straightforward way for the supervisor to establish its relevance is through interaction. Accordingly, at lines 13, 17, 25 and 27 the supervisor resorts to questioning the nurse and seeking clarification from her until she is able to establish the relevance of the nurse's utterance. Through the use of the supervisor's probes, it is a fairly straightforward matter of arriving at the correct interpretation, and thus the sequence concludes successfully.

The foregoing illustrates how participants in medical interaction search for relevance in one another's utterances. The pursuit of relevance becomes more acute in cross-cultural healthcare encounters where imbalances in the participants' language proficiency may give rise to instances of weak communication. Nevertheless, when confronted by weak communication, speakers are often able to compensate for such a shortcoming, drawing on communicative strategies in order to resolve episodes of miscommunication.

Summary

In this chapter we have examined the interactional routines of non-physician personnel – professionals whose roles in the healthcare system tend to be overshadowed by the work of doctors. We have sought to provide readers with an insight into the communicative routines of nurses, pharmacists, physiotherapists and chaplains, and how these professionals conduct interactional affairs with patients and other professionals. Although it has been impossible to do justice to the rich variety of communicative activities in which these non-physician personnel routinely take part, this chapter illustrates a number of the interactional and institutional pressures that confront professionals and how they skilfully manage them during exchanges with patients.

We have sought to situate these various professional–patient encounters in the context of an ever-changing healthcare system which places increasing emphasis on the notions of patient-centred care and patient empowerment. Although a patient-focussed ideology pervades much contemporary healthcare, it is not necessarily the case that such idealism always faithfully translates into the practical delivery of healthcare. For instance, a number of the professional–patient interactions that we explored reveal practitioners negotiating the expectations of professional standards documents with the practical necessity of actually conversing with patients in situations not easily conducive to patient choice and involvement.

In order to make sense of the range of non-physician interactions that we covered in this chapter, we explored the utility of a number of discourse-based frameworks and theories drawn upon by applied linguists. We reviewed the theoretical underpinnings of conversational analysis (CA) and the role this approach can play in explicating nurse–patient interaction. Although, unlike Critical Discourse Analysis approaches, it has not traditionally been in the purview of CA to criticise interactional practices, the use of CA in interrogating nurse–patient discourse powerfully exposes some of the realities of healthcare interaction in practice, and how these realities might be at odds with theoretical assumptions about patient engagement.

Finally we considered how pragmatic theories of language are able to enrich our understanding of health communication. Focussing specifically on Grice's notion of implicature and Sperber and Wilson's Relevance Theory, we looked at how speakers in healthcare interaction work together in recovering implied meanings, and how, through a search for relevance, participants in cross-cultural exchanges resolve episodes of miscommunication.

The emphasis in these first two chapters has been on the language of health professionals. In the next chapter, we offer a complementary perspective, devoting our attention to the language of patients, specifically their experiences of health and illness rendered through the sense-making resource of narrative.

3 Patients' narratives of health and illness

Introduction: the need for narrative

Storytelling is common: everyone can recall the experience of listening to and telling stories. Yet this mundane phenomenon is also the oldest form of history and entertainment, and a powerful tool that, driven by our imagination, can transport us to different places or offer a window into someone else's world. Stories are therefore valuable: for storytellers they are important because they can help instil meaning and structure into an otherwise incoherent cascade of events and experiences; whereas listeners may appreciate how stories can take them away from the pressures of everyday lives. This relation of storytelling to our understandings of the world, others and ourselves has led to a growing research interest in narratives, their various uses, functions, and benefits. The notion of narrative is therefore central to an array of approaches within a number of disciplines, including anthropology, linguistics, psychology and psychiatry. We will examine some of these studies further in this chapter, as we focus on the role and significance of narrative in relation to patients' understandings and experiences of their illness.

For now, however, let us further consider the importance of narrative by examining how telling a story can help the narrator reflect on and reconstruct the past. Here personal interest can influence how storytellers go about connecting events and making them meaningful for their audience. In this way, the choice of what to tell, and how to tell a story, is often strategic. Hyden (1992), for example, has shown how narratives are used to interpret the past in cases of domestic violence. In this study, male perpetrators were found to prefer words and narrative devices that emphasised purpose (why they acted as they did), whereas their victims foregrounded how they were abused and the physical and emotional consequences of their ordeal. In a similar vein, in his narrative investigation of tales of the unexpected, Wooffitt (1992) observes how speakers retailing stories of purported supernatural happenings are prone to harness a range of discursive strategies in order to make their accounts both believable and dramatic – their being worthy of telling and listening to. Consider the following extract, reproduced in Cameron (2001: 152):

ah came home from work at lunchtime (1)
an I walked into the sitting room door (.)
in through the sitting room door (1.5)
an:: right in front of me (.)
was a sort of alcove (.)
and a chimney breast (.)
like this (0.7) ((pointing to the wall))
and a photograph of our wedding (1)
came off the top shelf (0.2)
floated down to the ground
hh completely came apart
but didn't break

The first thing that you might notice about this extract is its textual realisation, the way in which it has been rendered, from speech to writing. The transcript of the original spoken narrative is larded with orthographical features, such as dots, colons and pairings of letters (hh). As with the practitioner–patient exchanges we examined in the previous chapters, these symbols (see Appendix for details of the transcription code) aim to accurately account for some of the spoken characteristics of the original oral narrative. However, we mustn't lose sight of the fact that the transcription of spoken language into written/ graphic form is very much an interpretative act, a type of reading which will almost certainly vary according to who is undertaking the transcription. The analyst who wishes to transcribe spoken material has to decide exactly how to render it into a form that meets the aims and objectives of their research. This might seem like a rather obvious point, or one we might easily take for granted, but we need to be alert to the fact that spoken discourse can be set down in many different ways, hence giving rise to an infinite variety of textual realisations which will vary in faithfulness with regard to the original spoken text. The striving for accuracy when transcribing talk is a perennial issue for linguists working with spoken discourse, whether they are concerned with oral narratives or any other spoken activity.

Now let us return to our discussion of the speaker's use of linguistic strategies to construct both a vivid and plausible narrative event. As Cameron (2001: 152) comments in her analysis of this narrative sequence, a striking feature is the number of pauses which appear in the speaker's recounting of the supernatural event (or if not supernatural then at least very unusual event). Pauses are not, of course, uncommon in speech (they allow, for instance, narrators to consider what they are going to say next, and the manner in which they are going to say it). But here the pauses appear to be of special significance: not only are there a large number of them, but also they are of extensive duration (a silence of a second or more is potentially a long time in talk). As

Cameron suggests, the narrator is here using the prolonged sequence of pauses for dramatic effect, 'artfully building up suspense' (ibid.), keeping the audience on tenterhooks and so compellingly maintaining listeners' interest.

Apart from their dramatic impact, the pauses also serve to punctuate the introduction of what are rather trite and everyday details: the coming home at lunchtime, the walking into the sitting room, the encountering of the chimney breast. This build-up of commonplace details situates the tale in the familiar and mundane, making the extraordinary event that follows (the picture that weirdly floats down to, and comes apart on, the ground) all the more unexpected but, nonetheless, plausible. The narrative, therefore, is just as much about the personality, the credibility, of the speaker, as it is the drama, the supernatural nature of the tale.

When telling stories which describe unbelievable occurrences, speakers have to anticipate and negotiate the audience response that they are cranks, are deluded or otherwise unreliable and, therefore, not to be taken seriously. Through the use of commonplace detail, narrators construct themselves as ordinary people, involved in ordinary activities and are thus able to ward off the imputation of their being unable to distinguish between fantasy and fiction. As Cameron (2001: 151) puts it, in locating his or her tale in the 'flow of very routine events, the narrator claims credibility as a normal, even dull person whose account of a non-normal occurrence should therefore be taken seriously'.

Overall, narratives are useful in research and practice precisely because narrators interpret the past, rather than reproduce it as it was; they take into account their audience; and they try to make sense of their experience. Consequently, the importance of narrative accounts lies not in their truthful representations of a past event or phenomenon, but in the connections they engender among past, present, and future and the purposes these connections may be intended to serve. We hope that our exploration into the role of narratives in the rest of this chapter may be of use not only to health professionals (as suggested by Greenhalgh and Hurwitz's (1999) plea for narrative-based medicine), but will also have a wider relevance and resonance in the broad field of health communication. We will highlight four areas in particular which, according to Greenhalgh and Hurwitz's summary, can derive most benefit from narratives: the therapeutic process, the diagnostic encounter, education of patients and professionals, and research.

Narratives and empathy

Moore and Hallenbeck (2010) believe that attention to patients' accounts of illness, self-reflection and 'deeper listening to the other'

(474) can enable participants to move towards better and, more importantly, mutually constructed stories during diagnostic encounters. This, in turn, will result, they argue, in improved decision making and healthcare outcomes. They see such an approach as based on 'narrative empathy'. The view is based on the premise that along with scientific expertise, health professionals need to acquire an ability to listen to the narrative of the patient (what the authors call 'narrative competence'). In the words of Greenhalgh and Hurwitz (1999) this perspective treats narratives as 'the phenomenal form in which patients experience ill health' (48). Furthermore, narratives are seen as constituting an important resource for promoting understanding between clinicians and patients, as well as allowing for 'the construction of meaning' (ibid.).

Careful attention to narratives of illness, then, will ensure that the needs and goals of patients are communicated, and would ideally allow health professionals to respond appropriately. Crucially, the notion of narrative empathy also targets culture as the primary frame of reference, and includes an objective on behalf of the clinician to listen to and empathetically respond to culturally specific narratives. This is an important but also an extremely complex task which, in our view, merits further elaboration.

Over the last two decades the role of health beliefs in doctor–patient encounters (seen as static, culturally specific beliefs separate from language) have received increased attention (Gumperz, 1999). However, as Roberts *et al.* (2005) point out, rather than fixed health beliefs, it is the language and cultural issues concerned with relating to and representing illness to the clinician that tend to cause misunderstandings. It is not difficult to imagine how this may lead to misperceptions about whether empathy exists in doctor–patient encounters. From this perspective, a focus on the language/culture axis will help us recognise that cultural groups will vary in the types of stories they most value, how they tell them, and also how they expect to be responded to. As more recent research into intercultural healthcare exchanges (Candlin and Candlin, 2003) demonstrates, misunderstandings and miscommunication occur when native and non-native English speakers talk 'past' each other by using culturally different styles of communicating.

For example, Roberts *et al.* (2005) examined 232 video-recorded consultations that took place in Lambeth, South London (an ethnically and linguistically diverse area of the United Kingdom). These encounters regularly featured patients who were non-native English speakers and whose English-speaking ability was of variable quality. Of the 232 consultations, 48 involved either minor or more involved episodes of misunderstanding or moments of apparent discursive unease (trouble, confusion or disruption in interaction). The following sequence, which features a Nigerian patient presenting with a dog bite, reveals some of the linguistic processing difficulties experienced by the doctor:

```
1    D:    what kind of dog was that (.) it was somebody's (.)
2          [dog
3    P:    [yes somebody's
4    D:    it was a stray dog
5    P:    no no it was somebody's dog
6    D:    right
7    P:    yes I:: made an enquiry they said that – they
8          they told me
9          the dog go to the vet regular
10   D:    right okay
11   P:    but that's what they said
12   D:    right (.) right right so did you know the
13         owner or [did
14   P:    [I know the owner=
15   D:    =oh fair enough (.) so
16   P:    erm:: ((laughs)) (but)
17   D:    did you see any doctor then
18   P:    no
```

(Roberts et al., 2005: 414)

As Roberts *et al.* (2005: 414) comments, the doctor and patient clearly possess the same lexical and grammatical system (their lexical choices and grammatical structures do not result in any evident confusion). What causes the misunderstanding in this sequence is the participants' differing use of stress and intonation. At the start of the extract, the doctor, in seeking to ascertain whether the dog is a stray or not, probes the issue of the patient's requiring a rabies vaccination. Given the subsequent responses from the patient, who confirms that he knows the owner of the dog and that the animal, according to the owner, receives regular veterinary care, the doctor appears satisfied – 'oh fair enough' – with the patient's confirmation. As a result of the patient's account the doctor decides to forego the vaccination.

Yet the patient's turns (at lines 7–9, 11) communicate a degree of scepticism with regard to the owner's prior mentioned assurance. This incredulity is expressed by the patient's particular use of stress and intonation: 'they said that – they they told me the dog go to the vet regular', 'but that's what they said'. The tonal stress on the underscored words 'they' and 'what' is characteristic of the patient's intonation system which places emphasis on the agent ('they', the dog owner) and the content of the agent's report ('what'). This pattern is at odds with the doctor's British English use of stress and intonation who, as a result of this difference, fails to apprehend the patient's suspicion.

Narratives and identity

Traditionally, identity has been viewed as something that is fixed and immutable. It was believed (and some theoretical accounts still espouse the belief) that one's identity was given, was something 'essential' and hence something that couldn't be changed. In other words, you are who you are. However, research, particularly in the social sciences, has recently come to challenge such an essentialist view of identity construction, where one's identity is conceived in terms of being stable and unitary. Identity has come to be seen as 'something shifting and multiple, something people are continuously constructing and reconstructing in their encounters with each other and the world' (Cameron, 2001: 170). According to this 'constructionist' view, identity is not given and fixed: identities are something upon which we work, which we can modify, as we interact with other people.

As it will by now be apparent, spoken narrative is an important aspect of social life which, through the processes of recalling, recounting and reflecting on their lives (Benwell and Stokoe, 2006: 130), affords people a powerful resource for shaping their personal identities. The particular strength of the narrative approach is that it enables us to situate analyses in how human beings typically understand and represent their lives. One of the most profound life events that can undermine our sense of self is our experience of illness, particularly serious illness. When individuals experience sickness, narratives commonly involve a search for meaning, a searching for patterns and regularities or ways of managing the condition. In a sense, narratives represent the sufferer looking for alternative ways of being ill, or even alternative ways of being well.

In order to illustrate how, in the face of serious illness, narrative is utilised to construct particular identities, let us consider the story of 'Burt', the subject of Riessman's (1990) research into the strategic presentation of self and illness. Burt, a middle-aged man with advanced multiple sclerosis, was interviewed in relation to his recent divorce (he had been married for 25 years). Although the interview schedule focusses on his divorce, Burt, Riessman observes, redirects the interaction at every opportunity towards the issue seemingly important to him: that of refashioning a positive identity against a background of chronic illness and dependency on state support. Through his manipulation of narrative, Burt seeks to guide the impression others form of him, constituting a positive masculinity in the roles of husband, father and worker despite his recent separation and loss of physical function.

Burt, according to Riessman, moves quickly to influence the interviewer's impression of him. At the start of the interview he produces a preface, elaborating his definition of events – that, as the good husband, he is not to blame for the divorce.

> Well. I can go back to 1975 when I first found out I had MS. And when she was told by the doctor that it eventually would cripple me, put me in a wheelchair. Seems like back in 1975 that she seemed to drift apart from me, that she didn't accept the disease.
>
> (Riessman, 1990: 1196)

Although, as Riessman notes, the two events of Burt's diagnosis and divorce are unrelated temporally (the diagnosis occurred 9 years before his separation), he effectively joins them together in a cause-and-effect relation. He implies that his MS is responsible for the divorce, not he himself, an intimation that is further elaborated in his ensuing narrative. As follows:

[p= pause of 3 seconds or longer]

1   OK, when she left me in February
2   we tried to get back together in May…[tells of going to see her in a motel and asking her to 'come home' and she said 'I'm not coming home.']…
3   That night about (p) about twelve o'clock
4   there was a call (p) and it was her
5   and Susan [daughter] picked the phone up
6   and she had been drinking
7   and she said she wanted to come home
8   so Susan went down to the motel and picked her up…
10   brought her down here
11   she slept here that night
12   she came into my room
13   gave me a big hug and a big kiss
14   said 'I'm glad to be back'
15   I said 'I'm glad you're back'
16   I says 'We have all missed you.'
17   The following day
18   she seemed like she had a split personality
19   seemed like she changed into a different person.
20   She got up in the morning
21   I came out and sat in the chair here an'
22   she went back to the same routine that she had done before she (p) decided to move out.
23   She's telling me that I'm gonna be put in a nursing home
24   …she's going sell the house.
25   And I said 'hey, look, no, nothin' is gonna change
26   it's not gonna be any different than before we were married.
27   Now if you want to stay here you can, you know,

28   you gonna be – act the same way you were before you left.'
29   So she just packed up and left.

(Riessman, 1990: 1197)

Throughout his account Burt presents himself as the devoted husband and as willing to forgive, thus laying full responsibility for the divorce on his wife (1990: 1197). Burt's supportive story maintains a positive identity for himself in the face of physical disability and loss. Further, his story also enables him to reassert his vital position as a man, a husband and father firmly situated in the family hierarchy. As Riessman (1990: 1197) comments, 'Despite his confinement to a wheelchair, the point of the story is that he stood up to his wife, refusing to allow himself to be defined as incompetent'.

Task 3.1 Identity construction in narratives of illness   (TC)

During subsequent phases of the interview, Burt produces a further account of his illness in order to construct a specific version of events relating to the onset and diagnosis of his illness. Against a backdrop of his loss of physical function, what identity does he create for himself? How does he position himself in relation to his disability? How is this achieved in the text?

1   Well in '75 I was diagnosed
2   you know, at that time I was still able to walk but I had to
3   drag my right leg
4   and as the years went on
5   the leg got worse
6   my right arm started to get weak
7   I'd start losing my balance
8   my coordination was going
9   and un then I – naturally I had to start using a walker
10   and I don't think she liked the idea of
11   having to help me all the time in the morning
12   help me get dressed
13   lift me out of bed in the morning
14   help me sometimes with my bowel movement and things
15   like that
16   you know, she couldn't take it anymore
17   so she started drinking (p) very heavily.

Approaches to the study of illness narratives

In this section, we examine various narrative models which might be applied to accounts of health and illness, and narratives of depression in particular. Despite their differences, the approaches to narratives that we study below can all be profitably applied to illuminate different facets of interview-based narratives. We will pay particular attention to how interview narratives can give voice to depressed people themselves, privileging an alternative standpoint from which it is possible, among other things, to 'hear what depression feels like, what it means to receive an 'official' diagnosis, what depressed individuals think of therapeutic experts', along with what meanings 'patients attach to taking psychotropic medications' (Karp, 1996: 11).

Labov's model of narrative

One of the most well-known approaches to the analysis of narrative structure is that proposed by William Labov. Originally designed to explain narratives in a particular speech community, Labov's model has been applied to a range of communicative contexts, as well as to both spoken and written narratives.

Labov emphasises the sequential nature of narrative. Narratives occur in and through time, involving at least two pieces of information presented in a certain sequence. If the order of the sequence were to change, then so would the meaning of the narrative – it would be a different story altogether. Consider the following illustration provided by Toolan (2001: 145).

1 John fell in the river, got very cold, and had two large whiskies.
2 John had two large whiskies, fell in the river, and got very cold.

Although these two small narratives contain exactly the same formal features, the different ordering of the clauses (or events) produces two distinct stories, with separate cause-and-effect relations between the events. As Toolan observes, any audience listening to these narratives is bound to evaluate them differently: in the first narrative, John's ordeal might be viewed sympathetically, while in the second, the audience might respond to his alcohol-spurred accident with comments such as 'serves him right'.

The element of sequence, then, distinguishes narrative from other forms of information production and reception. Narrative can therefore be seen as:

depending upon a specific construction of temporality, in which events occur within and across time. Narrative is the form of human representation concerned with expressing coherence through time: it helps to provide human lives with a sense of order and meaning. By imposing an orderly sequence of events upon an inchoate mass of experience, expanses of time can be retrospectively structured and, in the process, made meaningful.

(Gwyn, 2002: 140).

Labov (1972) proposed that narratives can be broken down into six potential components, these being:

Abstract: What, in a nutshell, is this story about?
Orientation: Who, when, where?
Complicating Action: What happened and then what happened?
Evaluation: So What? How or why is it interesting?
Result or Resolution: What finally happened?
Coda: That's it, I've finished and am 'bridging' back to our present situation.

(Toolan, 2001: 148)

The abstract outlines the narrative to the listener; it appears outside the story proper and is no way intrinsic to the telling of the narrative. As Toolan (2001: 150) explains, 'a typical abstract outlines or advertises the story...but is never a proper telling of it'. Orientation involves the narrator setting the scene of the story; it is likely to appear at the beginning of the narrative but its position is flexible. Orientation, moreover, may recur throughout the telling of the story as new background information and detail are introduced prior to another complicating action.

The orientation is followed by one or more complicating actions which unfold through time. Complicating actions appear in sequential order and promote the tellability or significance of the narrative. As Gwyn (2002: 145) puts it, 'Events in the complicating action "take us through" the narrative'.

The evaluation is where the point of the story becomes evident to listeners. During the articulation of the story, the narrator will invariably harness various linguistic and paralinguistic features to embellish the narrative, features including: intensifiers, gestures, repetitions, tense changes, and so forth. In addition, the narrator may momentarily interrupt the telling of the story in order to provide an assessment of the narrated events so far or offer an aside which has some bearing on the story.

The resolution describes the end result of the event, or events, of the complicating action, while, lastly, the coda indicates the sealing off of the narrative, relocating the discourse back to the present time and situation of the telling.

Of course, not all narratives are so neatly shaped, nor fall crisply into the above categories. The abstract and coda, for example, may not be present in a narrative since they stand outside the events of the story itself: in telling a story, speakers might begin *in medias res*, that is, directly commencing the narrative with the complicating action (with minimal orientation). Indeed only the complicating action is vital to the production of a narrative. For example, the following very short narrative contains only two complicating actions, but, for all that, remains a complete narrative:

> Another boy threw a bottle at him right in the head
> and he got seven stitches
>
> (Labov, 1972: 361)

Thus it is the 'what is done', the complicating action, that constitutes the foundation of a narrative. The other elements in the narrative schema serve to embellish stories – to promote tellability and hence to hold the listeners' attention. Perhaps the worst outcome for story tellers after completing their stories is to be confronted with the response (or a response similar to): 'So what? Can't see why you bothered to tell me that.'

Despite the centrality of the complicating action, it is important not to overlook the significance of the evaluation element in Labov's narrative schema: the 'what is said' about the narrated events, the reason for telling the story. The evaluation informs the audience of why the story is worth telling in the mind of the teller (Gwyn, 2002: 146). In relation to personal narratives of health and illness, evaluation episodes have particular significance for understanding how people experience and deal with illness. In their study of women's illness narratives that were published in a lifestyle magazine, McKay and Bonner (2002) describe how many of the stories contained each of Labov's six narrative phases. Yet it was principally during the evaluation phase of these narratives when the tellers constructed their personal and social meanings as sufferers, or when family members attempted to explain the significance of their illness experiences in relation to their lives. The evaluation typically occurred in the penultimate paragraph of the story, at a point in the narrative when the plotline was momentarily suspended and the narrator–patient sought to make meaning of her experience.

Labov's classificatory model can be applied to a range of narratives, not just to the type of narrative for which the model was originally intended. However, its dependence on the discrete structural elements of a story means that as an analytical tool for interrogating narrative it lacks flexibility. Many narratives, particularly spoken narratives, are fractured and disparate or otherwise interrupted and so cannot be readily resolved into Labov's six-part schema. Narratives are more than a sequenced order of clauses encoding temporal events. Moreover, Labov's model of narrative does not tell us anything about the story that is being recounted or, in the context of a conversation, the interaction within which it takes place (Gwyn, 2002: 150). Making sense of a story involves more than simply carving it up into a series of structural chunks, and only a particular type of narrative – to wit, a temporally predictable narrative – can be resolved into formal categories.

Labov's version of narrative, then, is dependent on formal aspects of language. Yet speakers and writers make use of a range of culturally available narratives that do not readily yield to this formal arrangement. As Kemp observes 'narratives do not always recapitulate discrete events in a temporal sequence or in the past tense and narrativised discourse is often hypothetical, counterfactual or habitual' (2003: 191). Consequently, Kemp (2003) and other scholars advocate 'a more flexible notion of narrative', one which is better able 'to facilitate the interpretation of personal stories of illness where such experiences are often disrupted or disordered and where events are overlapping, undefined and recurrent, thus deviating from the formal linguistic [Labovian] definition' (ibid).

Prince's approach to narratives: degrees of narrativity

According to Kemp, a more flexible approach to narrative is that proposed by Prince (1982). Prince's view of narrative construes discourse as having more or less narrativity. 'Narrativity', in this sense, is the property that all stories possess, although some narratives (prototypical or core narratives) will exhibit greater levels of narrativity than others. The properties of narrativity include:

- a beginning, middle and end format;
- presentation of discrete and positive events;
- temporality through a sequence of narrative clauses;
- the presence of a conflict situation;
- recognition by listeners that what is being told is a narrative.

As Kemp points out, some of these elements are present in Labov's model of narrative. Thus prototypical narratives, which possess most of the above (specifically the beginning-middle-end and temporalisation properties), may overlap to some extent with Labovian narratives. However, even if a given stretch of language is low in narrativity (possessing only a few of the above criteria), it is still for all intents and purposes a narrative and can be analysed and interpreted as such. This model of narrative or 'narrativity' makes it possible to interrogate stretches of discourse that traditionally (in the Labovian sense) wouldn't be considered pure narrative but which still possess narrative elements.

In order to illustrate the narrativity approach to health discourse, let us examine an extract taken from a series of interviews which Kemp (2003) conducted with women who spoke of their personal experiences of emotional distress. The extract that follows is taken from an interview with Sue, an educated middle-class English woman in her mid-thirties, and details her account of struggling against depression. For the sake of analytical convenience, the text is divided into three sections: lines 1-28, 29-43, 44-8, 49-50.

Part I

1   I tend to get really anxious,
2   before I get depression:
3   I'm really struggling not to get like that,
4   but it's almost
5   I'm like erm like a swan y'know under the water
6   with the legs going
7   trying not to sort of slide into this depression.
8   And I'll do everything
9   I can to try and make:
10   you know,
11   'cos the minute I sort of go on this slidey slope down to a deep
12   depression I can't seem to get back up again,
13   it's like another year or so.
14   So there's real, you know, panic.
15   But erm: then I take,
16   I take:
17   everything goes out,
18   completely out of co:
19   completely out of of:
20   what's the word I'm looking for – out of:
21   I dunno.
22   Everything small seems large.
23   It's like,
24   you know,
25   I get really worried –
26   I get really worried
27   that I can't, say, pay bills
28   or do normal things.

Part II

29   Then I started having these, these stupid routines like
30   writing it down in my book
31   to forget
32   to remember that normal things
33   that I would do in my stride:
34   and I would be writing them down in a book, say,
35   and trying,

36   you know,
37   trying to keep tabs on:
38   'cos everything just seemed out of control
39   and it was:
40   it was just awful.
41   And I just:
42   it was like leading up to the depression,
43   everything's just like going out of control.

Part III

44   And then, one day, it's like:
45   I can't cope.
46   And it's, you know,
47   And I just slide
48   And that's it.

Part IV

49   Then I just don't do anything.
50   And I just sit there like a vegetable.

(Kemp, 2003: 195)

This account of emotional distress does not slot very easily into Labov's narrative schema. For instance, apart from lines 29 and 44, there is very little else in the way of narrative clauses or anything that could be interpreted as a complicating action. Kemp notes that rather than order her experiences through a series of chronological clauses, presenting her troubles over and through time, Sue describes her lead up to depression by way of a recurring, continuous and hence predictable state of affairs. Her account exhibits a low degree of narrativity. It possesses little event structure and reports generalised experiences in which events are repeated that have no clear boundaries. The present tense ('I tend to get') and continuous aspect ('I would be writing them down') emphasise this repeated and habitual nature of her depressive experiences (Kemp, 2003: 194). Thus Sue recounts her experiences in 'habitual narrative' (Riessman, 1990) which reports 'a general course of events, rather than what happened at a specific point in the past'.

However, despite this lack of temporality, Sue's account of depression nevertheless does contain a discernible outline of plot. Although no beginning, middle and end are apparent in the ordering of her experiences, Sue's story, as Kemp observes, is centred around a loose plot line which follows an irresistible plummet into depression that involves her struggling against this fall, a struggle to cope and assert some control over her life. The turning point at line 44 marks a significant departure in plot development where Sue's personal agency appears to crumble entirely: 'And then, one day, it's like: I can't cope. And it's, you know, and I just slide and that's it'.

Kemp relates the fissured structure of the events that Sue describes (i.e. the frequent lack of clear boundaries between the events that befall her) to the fact that her experiences resist temporal or traditional narrative ordering. Therefore the low level of narrativity which characterises her account can, in part, be seen as a 'function of the disrupted nature of what is being recounted' (2003: 195). Kemp elaborates, 'If narrative depicts agency, then narrative incoherence and low levels of narrativity are available to speakers for depicting experiences in which agency has broken down'. Kemp, therefore, suggests a link between personal agency and the temporal re-ordering of experience: 'a speaker's agency drives the discursive processes of narrativisation' (ibid.). Thus the collapse of Sue's agency, her inability to resist depressive states and regain personal control, is reflected in her story where events are presented haphazardly and unclearly, as though the events which she seeks to make sense of resist temporal and logical reconstruction. The only sense of narrative order that emerges is brought about, Kemp argues, by a plot line featuring an extended metaphor which describes her inexorable descent towards a 'negatively valued end state', during which she passes through the process of losing control, right through to being completely out of control, before finally realising a position of utter lifelessness: 'And I just sit there like a vegetable'.

A theory of narrative that strictly depends on temporal sequence, then, is liable to be inappropriate for understanding events that, as with Sue's generalised experience of psychological distress, are habitual and repetitive. Not all narrative analysis depends on the strict temporal and sequential ordering of events that take place in a specific point in time. This is particularly so for narrative analysis concerned with experiences of illness. Illness, specifically chronic and serious illness, is persistent, and its effects are liable to be suffered on a routine, day-by-day basis. Consequently, people's rendering of their experiences will reflect the habitual and recurring nature of their conditions. Yet, for all that, as Sue's story demonstrates, such narratives are no less compelling or important: they are still able to dramatise and animate significant events, while drawing the audience deeply into the narrator's private experience.

Karp's approach: four stages of mental illness narratives

Despite the powerful analyses of social scientists (e.g. Goffman, 1961) and the anti-psychiatry of thinkers such as Szasz (1970) in the 1960s and 1970s, there has been a revolution in psychiatry that has resulted in 'the hegemony of biological explanations for affective disorders and a nearly universal consensus among psychiatrists that such disorders are most effectively treated with drugs' (Karp, 1993: 358). Thus a substantial part of the medical literature is taken up by studies that adopt a biomedical perspective, particularly research that describes the use of different drugs for treating mental illness (Karp, 1996: 11). Such studies are predominantly logical-scientific, relying on quantitative assessment, and privilege the perspectives of health professionals over the voices of people actually experiencing emotional distress.

This neglect of personal experiences of mental illness has given rise to research that aims to describe the unfolding of depression as opposed to its cause (Smith, 1999). For instance, David Karp's seminal work has sought to document people's subjective experience of depression. One theme that consistently runs through Karp's research, which we will now explore in some detail, concerns the meanings that depressive patients attach to their taking of antidepressant medication (e.g. Karp, 1993, 1996). His in-depth interviews with people experiencing depression have elicited a series of rich narratives in which sufferers describe the course of their depressive careers and their responses to psychiatric treatment.

Among the various stories, Karp identifies an underlying trend in the way that respondents evaluate the course of their drug regimen. This involves four stages: resistance, trial commitment, conversion, and disenchantment; all of which we shall illustrate with narrative examples.

Passing through each of the above stages constitutes a process of socialisation, a process which, according to Karp, is akin to a religious conversion (and, in some instances, de-conversion) where 'one's willingness to begin, sustain, and sometimes stop a doctor-prescribed regimen of anti-depressant medications must be understood in the broader context of adopting a new, identity-altering view of reality; namely that one suffers from a biochemically based emotional illness' (Karp, 1993: 355). At first, during the *resistance* phase of the socialization process, respondents speak of a reluctance to embark on a course of psychiatric medicine, since taking anti-depressants would only affirm that they are people with a stigmatised emotional disorder, as the following excerpt reveals:

> I didn't want to be told that I had something that was going to affect the rest of my life, and that could only be solved by taking pills. It was sort of definitive. I had a label and it was a label that I thought was pejorative. I didn't want to be this quietly depressed person, that there was something wrong with me.
>
> (Karp, 1993: 344)

As their turmoil increases, the narrators abide by the recommendations of doctors and enter the phase of *trial commitment*. However, as Karp notes, this acceptance of a medical version of reality is by no means unequivocal: this decision to undertake a course of medication is negotiated, with the respondents still not fully accepting the doctors' assessment of their having a biologically based disorder:

> And the only reason I would take it [Prozac] is that he promised I would be on it for three months. I ended up being on it for nine months, probably longer, nine or ten months. If I had known that, I don't think I'd ever have gone on it.
>
> (Karp,1993: 347)

After the patients have 'accepted and internalised a rhetoric of biochemical causation' (1993: 349), they have, according to Karp, reached the *conversion* phase of their depression narrative, during which they are committed to obtaining the most suitable pharmaceutical treatment. Yet the pursuit of the right medication is often fraught with difficulties, with the respondents entering into drawn out phases of profitless experimentation with assorted medications. Karp describes these various experiences as little less than 'horror stories', with a number of patients retailing accounts of intolerable therapy regimens, such as the following vignette narrated by a hospitalised woman whose treatment combined physical exercise with stupefying antidepressants:

> I'll never forget – tennis…I was so drugged up I could barely see my fingers and this therapist took us out to the tennis courts. He was hitting balls and I couldn't even see the ball. This asshole, I couldn't even see and he's worried about my backhand. It's stupibid [sic]. You know, at the time I don't think I thought it was too funny. I thought, 'What's wrong with me.' So things went from bad to worse.
>
> (1993: 349)

However, a few of the respondents were able to find a drug that positively influenced things for the better. Such a discovery was narrated in terms of what Karp (1993: 350) refers to as a 'spiritual awakening'.

> All I can tell you is, 'Oh my God, you know when you're on the right medication.' It was the most incredible thing. And I would say that I had a spiritual experience.
>
> (1993: 350)

The final stage of the respondents' journey involved experiences of *disenchantment* which were characterised by feelings of despondency and, at the very least, ambivalence towards the role of anti-depressant medication. Yet even when medications failed to have any effect on their depressive symptoms, the respondents still narrated a psychological dependence on them. Having commenced a course of anti-depressants, and thus accepted the biochemical underpinning of depression, they felt unsure about abandoning their medication regimens, a predicament succinctly narrated in the following account:

> I mean, it's almost to the point now where I take it sometimes but like I really don't feel like I have the need for it. But I'm sort of afraid not to take it...I'm on such a low dosage [now]. He's (doctor) got me on one pill a night. And it's taken, you know, ten years [to get to that point].
>
> (ibid.)

The narratives presented here offer a counterweight to the perspectives of mental health experts (particularly psychiatrists) that dominate research into mental illness. The stories which we have considered above powerfully illustrate how individuals do not instinctively cleave to clinical versions of reality. Although a number of the respondents eventually came round to this version, accepting the biochemical nature of their condition, their conversion is, in the end, incomplete since faith is lost in the effectiveness of drug treatments to the extent that, in some instances, medication is abandoned altogether.

Narrative theory in health and illness research: harnessing analytic opportunities

In this last section we discuss in more detail the uses and, according to some scholars, abuses of narratives in health communication research. Following the by now familiar work of Greenhalgh and Hurwitz (1999), we focus on how narratives may help to set a patient-centred agenda, challenge received wisdom, and/or generate new hypotheses. At the same time, however, we note that the increasing enthusiasm for using narratives as research tools that followed the narrative turn in humanities and social sciences (Atkinson, 1997) does not always engender systematic analysis. According to Atkinson and Delamont (2006), some scholars tend to collect and study narratives in an uncritical fashion, for example, when researchers refer to their informants' voices as 'speaking for themselves', or assert that biographical materials provide a direct access to participants' personal experiences or an 'authentic' self. (As we noted earlier, it is questionable whether there is such a thing as an essential self since we constantly present different versions of ourselves when we interact with other people.)

This is why throughout this chapter and further on in this book we emphasise the point that the collection and analysis of stories, whether interview accounts, biographies, patients' narratives during diagnostic encounters or online accounts of illness, should start from a detailed study of the social and cultural contexts in which these accounts are produced (see Chapter 4 in particular). Furthermore, this focus on context should not be sidelined when analysis is in full swing and should aim to highlight the often forgotten fact that narrative conventions differ from culture to culture, from one context to another. As Atkinson and Delamont observe, 'traditional' societies have various 'forms of narrative and oral performance, but the significance of narratives is by no means confined to face-to-face cultures' (2006: 165). Modern societies are characterised by complex institutional cultures that display a wide variety of narrative forms, whether written, spoken or digital. In addition, the advent of the Internet has led to a creation of new conventions and norms of narrative and narration (Orgad, 2005), which we explore in more detail later in the third part of this book.

To begin with, and following Atkinson and Delamont's critical essay, we hope that our study of mental illness narratives in the preceding sections demonstrates the importance of treating narratives as 'accounts' as well as 'performances'. The analysis of personal narratives as accounts stems from Scott and Lyman's (1968) work that highlights how narratives share many characteristics with speech acts, or may incorporate speech acts. In other words, as Atkinson and Delamont (2006) maintain, narratives must be first and foremost analysed 'in terms of their rhetorical, persuasive properties, and their functions in constructing particular versions of events, justifications of actions, evaluations of others, and so on' (167).

The work of Jonathan Potter, Derek Edwards, Margaret Wetherell and their colleagues exemplifies the 'performative' and 'rhetorical' view of narratives espoused by Atkinson and Delamont. These scholars developed a framework known as discursive psychology that aims to counteract assumptions regarding essentialist identity outlined at the beginning of this chapter. Potter (2000: 31) describes discursive psychology as focussing on 'the production of versions of reality and cognition as parts of practices in natural settings.' From this perspective, the process of identity construction is fluid and not always conflict free. In their talk, people can strategically deploy a set of discursive resources or 'interpretative repertoires' (Potter and Wetherell, 1987) in order to suit the rhetorical demands of the interactional context. This means that during interviews, for example, participants can use different terms or accounting devices, and switch between them, in order to implicitly reconcile contradictory aspects of their identities. This is why Atkinson and Delamont (2006) argue that narratives elicited through research interviews should be examined as performative acts, through which identities are enacted, and actions and behaviours are justified and accounted for.

The approach of discursive psychology is particularly suitable for the analysis of not only what people make relevant in their personal narratives, but also how they accomplish this in linguistic terms (and, consequently, how they manage their identities in the process of sharing their views with others). Equipped with discursive psychology and conversation analysis (see Chapter 2) as analytic tools, Monzoni and Reuber (2009), for example, examined narratives of people with epilepsy in order to learn more about their coping behaviour. The authors found that on the level of thematic analysis participants in their study were keen to communicate that they were in control of their illness. Eight out of nine patients did not explicitly describe epilepsy as causing any major problems in their everyday lives (2009: 656). This was particularly evident in those participants who started talking about their seizure symptoms without specific prompting in the opening phase of the interview. However, once the authors examined the narratives more closely through the lens of the discursive psychology framework, they arrived at a different conclusion.

Specifically, the analysis of linguistic and interactional features showed that despite their unsolicited 'normalization' attempts, it emerged that epilepsy actually was quite problematic for the majority of narrators. Features such as formulation effort associated with the description of seizures or reluctance to describe seizure symptoms, or a complete avoidance of any references to seizures, indicated a degree of anxiety about seizures and their consequences. Consider an example of David's talk (D) provided by the authors to illustrate this finding:

```
1    I:    i wonder whether you could (0.2) tell me what
2          your expecTAtions were from (0.25) coming here
3          this week;
4          (0.75)
5    I:    what you were hoping to get out of it?
6          (0.5)
7    D:    .h expectations? (0.75) erm (1.3) find out (0.25) why
8          (1.5) i get these (0.25) reactions;
9    I:    mh,
10   D:    ((smacks lips)) (0.25) and (0.50) i've had encephalitis
11         eighteen months ago, (0.50) and ever since (0.2) then
12         (0.50) i've BEEN havin (0.25) a reaction (1.3) we
13         (0.50) cos its with my chin they thought was
14         EPIlepsy; (0.75) er: (1.2) some of 'em MUST be,
15         (0.6) i think are (0.50) some of 'em (-) i don't
16         think ARE cause i can stop 'em meSELF;
```
(Monzoni and Reuber, 2009: 656)

As Monzoni and Reuber comment, the participant responds almost immediately to the opening question (lines 7, 8). He then proceeds to give background information (lines 10, 11) and uses self-coined terminology (line 12, 'a reaction') to refer to seizures. Although most participants showed a readiness to describe subjective seizure experiences in great detail, David avoids focussing on potentially frightening seizure symptoms through the use of medical jargon (for example, 'tonic–clonic seizures'). He displays a subtle form of distancing from seizure experiences by resisting the use of explicit labels such as 'seizure,' 'fit,' or 'attack' and instead uses the term 'reactions'. He then describes his seizures (line 13) and differentiates between different types of seizures (lines 14–16).

Other participants in Monzoni and Reuber's study paused immediately before saying 'seizure' or employed discourse markers such as 'you know' through which they explicitly avoided naming the problem (2009: 656). In this way, the authors demonstrate that a detailed linguistic inspection of narratives produced by patients in conversations with clinicians can enhance our understanding of patients' thoughts and feelings about illness. It can also provide an explanation as to why problems coping and associated with emotional disorders (such as anxiety and depression) tend to be overlooked in epilepsy clinics that often rely on conventional assessment tools such as questionnaires.

The discursive psychology approach also highlights the importance of the wider socio-cultural context in the analysis of how people choose different linguistic resources to produce their accounts. In this regard, Koteyko (2010), for example, draws on this approach to explore the variation in articulations concerning eating preferences and alerts us to the subtle ways in which the practices of purchasing novel food are discursively bound up in descriptions of appropriate or inappropriate behaviour. The study demonstrates that participants' accounts of eating and buying yoghurts containing probiotics (or 'good bacteria') are understood both in the context of health and well-being and in the broader context of social norms and moralities of eating. Consequently, in describing their reasons for purchasing or not purchasing probiotics, the participants related their talk to wider cultural assumptions and existing moral presuppositions on how individuals should behave (i.e. discourses around 'good' and 'bad' food). The moral context of purchasing what was perceived to be 'healthy food' was visible through different constructions of the probiotics benefits. Thus, whereas food with perceived health benefits was often bought for oneself as part of rational self-improvement behaviour, the purchase of the same food for others reflected the moral values residing in performing the right role, conforming to the socially approved role of caring partner, father or mother (2010: 598–599).

In a similar vein, if we now recall the dominant theme of individual control over epilepsy identified by Monzoni and Reuber, we can also see a moral streak in patients' accounts of epilepsy. In this regard, Bury (2001) talks about a moral facet of illness narrative in that it involves an evaluative dimension concerning the relationship between the individual and their social world, how it might have been changed by illness, and how the individual is expected to behave as a result of this change. This echoes earlier work by Frank (1997) who suggests that through such narratives people may be trying to be 'successfully ill' (Frank 1997: 117). He then proceeds to suggest that illness and suffering present people with a 'moral opening for witness and change' (141) and the associated opportunity to change one's identity.

Overall, then, when using narratives as data one must ensure that participants' stories are not treated 'at face value', as if they display a coherent representation of a reality that is independent of the accounts themselves (Atkinson and Delamont, 2006). Rather, we, as researchers, have to bear in mind that 'narratives, and the accounting devices they enshrine, create the realities they purport to describe' (2006: 170).

Summary

In this chapter we have begun to examine the importance of narrative. In particular, emphasis was placed on describing the powerful role that narratives can play in creating and giving meaning to social reality. Narrative is not simply a form of representation (as it was to early generations of researchers), but conveys something of the self-image of the narrator (Hyden, 1997: 50). As we have seen in our accounts of illness (as well as the other types of stories examined), narratives supply context and perspective for the teller's predicament, offering a possibility of understanding which could not be arrived at by other means (Greenhalgh and Hurwitz, 1999). Stories offer their narrators a way of re-imagining their lives and (re)creating identities. They can therefore be harnessed as powerful sources informing health professionals about patients' feelings, and also as the means of fostering understanding and catalysing empathy in doctor–patient encounters. The narrative approach to textual analysis, then, is an essential resource for making sense of experience and how people fashion identities for themselves, particularly in light of experiences which are chaotic and meaningless (such as illness).

We have also considered definitions of narrative, exploring various narrative models which might be applied to accounts of health and illness. Narrative has been formulated in various ways, particularly in relation to time: from strict notions of temporality and consequentiality (as in the Labovian sense) through to habitual narratives which emphasise a general course of events rather than a specific blow-by-blow temporal unfolding (for example, the low 'narrativity' accounts that featured in Kemp's narrative analysis of emotional distress). Although most researchers define narrative on the basis of its having a beginning, middle and end, narratives of health and illness are typically too complex to be reduced into the tidy structural schema of abstract, orientation, complicating action, evaluation, resolution, coda. Consequently, while not denying the temporal and sequential significance of narrative, many studies of illness and narrative are likely to privilege the content and themes of illness accounts (i.e. the story itself) and how they are formulated, rather than their structural arrangement alone.

Through our examination of different approaches to mental illness narratives, we aimed to demonstrate how personal accounts can offer a counterbalance to the perspectives of mental health experts, as they give voice to depressed people themselves and can highlight alternative standpoints. For example, some of the stories that we have explored above illustrate how individuals do not automatically adopt medical versions of reality.

In the final section, we explored some of the recent work on narratives and associated theoretical standpoints. Given the current proliferation of illness accounts in the general context of the 'interview society', we argue that there is a need for a critical evaluation of existing studies in order to avoid misconceptions about the aims and applications of narrative research.

Part II

Written health communication

4 The patient record

Introduction: written language and the patient case record

A significant part of the first section of this book was devoted to exploring the (often unequal) relationships between health practitioners and patients and how these relationships were determined and constrained through spoken exchanges, principally during consultations of some kind. By examining specific aspects of spoken interaction, such as question and answer formats, turn-design and topic control, it is possible for the analyst to identify and describe sequences where practitioners enact interactional control at the expense of the patient's perspective. Conversely, it is possible to account for linguistic cooperation between the participants, such as acts of shared decision making.

Spoken language is dynamic, often conducted in real-time, unfolding moment-by-moment, with speakers' alignments and footings potentially changing many times within the duration of a single turn. Spoken language possesses prosodic and paralinguistic features that allow speakers to communicate subtle meanings and imbue portions of speech with certain emphases. Additionally, during real-time interaction, speakers can query and interrupt one another in order to seek confirmation and check their understanding, as well as providing supportive feedback. Given its comparatively static, linear formation, written language would appear, at first sight, to constitute less of an interactive resource for dynamic interchange.

However, as Stubbs (1983: 211) points out, many features of discourse (such as lexical cohesion, propositional development, implicatures and speech acts, and so forth) operate equally in both spoken and written communication. Although taking place in a context which the writer and reader are unlikely to share temporally and spatially, written communication similarly constructs and constrains relationships between participants, and mediates personal experiences. In the context of healthcare, writing doesn't simply reconstruct events that have taken place; it is not ancillary to speech, merely a means of providing 'post-hoc representations of past decisions and investigations' (Berg, 1996: 500). Writing is constitutive. The process of translating or coding patient talk into professional language, for instance, determines outcomes and pathways for future action (Prior, 2003: 54). Whereas spoken language is ephemeral (disappearing as soon as it is uttered), writing is permanent, or at least possesses some degree of permanence, and is therefore associated with authority and credibility. If an utterance can be written down, we are, in the (written) words of Halliday (1985: vii) 'much more likely to believe it'.

The aforementioned properties of written language need to be taken into account when examining the medical case history or patient record. The patient record is brought into being through the process of writing, the active business of selecting, ordering and ultimately reformulating persons and events (Berg, 1996). The fact that the record is a written, permanent document allows it to accompany the patient on his or her passage through the healthcare system; it can be consulted at various times during the journey and referred to long after the patient has been discharged. As Kleinman (1988: 131) observes, the patient record is a multi-authored, inter-group document that will be read by a variety of people (doctors, nurses, medical students, medical ethics committees and, in special cases, lawyers, judges and juries); it is also a legal document that is used to assess the quality of care in malpractice claims (Iyer, Levin and Shea, 2004); it is a document consisting of standardised language forms that requires its authors to adhere to certain (stylistic and bureaucratic) conventions and protocols such that completing the record incorrectly may constitute a dismissible offence (Brown *et al.*, 2006: 110).

The patient record, then, is an intriguing topic for linguistic investigation, figuring, as it does, as a key and constitutive aspect of medical practice (Berg, 1996). Moreover, given its transformational power – its ability to translate the flesh and blood patient into a written, fictional case (a theme we pursue in more detail shortly) – the patient record affords applied linguists a rich seam of linguistic data for exploring the rhetorical processes through which patients are represented.

From talk to text: the practice of record writing

The patient record is a key aspect of the medical case history. As a communicative process, the medical case history is compact of a number of activities, including: case presentations, medical interviews and published case reports; activities, broadly speaking, whereby practitioners impart 'information about patients to peers, superiors and consultants' (Anspach, 1988: 357). Yet as an official account of clinical care, it is the patient record that shapes the various activities that constitute the medical case history, as well as determining what practitioners 'take seriously' in these antecedent activities (Donnelly,

1997: 1045). The patient record serves a number functions, including: recording information provided by the patient (such as symptom presentation and biographical details), describing the results of laboratory tests and physical examinations, detailing the author's diagnostic impressions, and justifying the therapeutic plan proposed by him or her (Charon, 1992: 120).

But there is more to writing the patient record than these routine practices betray. Its construction is 'a profound, ritual act' of written transformation (Kleinman, 1988: 130), whereby 'illness is made over into disease, person becomes patient, and professional values are transferred from the practitioner to the "case"' (130-1). Illness is the personal, lived experience of sickness – symptoms and suffering which are 'innately human' (Lupton, 2003: 93), whereas 'disease' refers to the biomedical perspective of the clinician, a categorical formulation that construes pathology as a discrete entity existing within the patient's body. The biomedical model is the 'conventional, chronological account of the onset and course of symptoms of disease' (Donnelly, 1997: 1047), and differs profoundly from the patient's view of their condition, which is likely to include concerns about the impact of disease on their life, work and relationships, the experience of pain and anxiety, and uncertainty about the future. Illness is often chaotic, confusing, and rarely easy to render into words. Disease is quantifiable and diagnosable. Disease, moreover, is not confined to humans: plants and animals too have disease. But they do not have illness.

Whereas the patient's language, in relaying his or her illness experience prior to or during the construction of the case history, is liable to be open, unconstrained and 'unbounded by biological plausibilities' (Charon, 1992:117), the doctor's language is constrained by 'physiological categories, which are themselves determined by conceptual categories' (ibid.). In constructing the medical record, health professionals transform 'the sick person as subject into an object first of professional inquiry and eventually of manipulation' (Kleinman, 1988: 131). Accordingly, the language of the patient record is predictable, pared down – almost 'aphoristic' (Hobbs, 2003: 454). In the words of Hunter (1991: 90), it is 'cool and objective'. It is the standard clinical shorthand that helps to shape how practitioners 'learn to organize their thinking' (Warshaw, 1989: 52).

Our discussion so far has been rather abstract. In order to illustrate the practice of constructing the medical case (and therewith a number of the issues outlined above), let us consider the following practitioner–patient exchange, along with the doctor's subsequent write up of the interview in the patient record. The data is taken from Kleinman's (1988) classic study of illness narratives and features the protagonists Dr Staunton Richards (DR) and Melissa Flowers (MF) in consultation.

Kleinman describes Melissa Flowers as a thirty nine-year old black mother of five children. She has hypertension and resides with her mother, four of her children and two grandchildren. She is the single head of the household (both of her previous husbands having deserted her) and currently works in a restaurant to support her family. Her 59-year-old mother is partly paralysed due to a stroke that resulted from long term and poorly treated hypertension. Matty, Melissa's oldest daughter, is pregnant and has had a drug problem. Her other daughter, Marcia, who is fifteen, is also pregnant. Her 18-year-old son, JD, is currently serving a prison sentence, and her youngest son, Teddy, who is 12, is truanting from school and has other behaviour-related problems. A year ago, Melissa's long-term partner, Eddie Johnson, was killed in a fight in a public bar, and, recently, Melissa has been increasingly distressed by memories of Eddie. She is also upset by the predicaments of her children, particularly the impact of prison on JD, and worries about Teddy falling into drug use like his older brother and sister. The following sequence commences just after the greeting phase of the interview.

1	DR	You been taking your medicines as you ought to?
2	MF	Sometimes I do. But sometimes when I don't have no pressure I don't take it.
3	DR	Gee whiz, Mrs. Flowers, I told you if you don't take it regularly you could get real sick like your Mom… You been eating salt again?
4	MF	It's hard to cook for the family without salt. I don't have time to cook just for me [...]
5	DR	a low-salt diet is essential for your problem.
6	MF	I know, I know. I mean I do all these things, but I just plain forget sometimes. I got so much else goin' on and it all seems to affect the pressure. I got two pregnant daughters at home and my mother is doin' much worse. I think she may be senile. And then I worries about J.D., and here comes Teddy with the same problems startin' up. [...]
7	DR	You said you had headaches?
8	MR	Sometimes I think my life is one big headache. These here ain't too bad. I've had 'em for a long time, years. But in recent weeks they been badder than before. You see, a year ago last Sunday, Eddie Johnson, my friend, you know. Uh huh, well, he died. And –
9	DR	Are the headaches in the same place as before?

10   MF   Yeah, same place, same feelin, on'y more often.
            But, you see, Eddie Johnson had always told me not to
            bother about –
11   DR   Have you had any difficulty with your vision?
12   MF   No.
13   DR   Any nausea?
14   MF   No. Well when I drank the pickle juice there was some.
15   DR   Pickle juice? You've been drinking pickle juice? That's got
            a great deal of salt. It's a real danger for you, for your
            hypertension.
16   MF   But I have felt pressure this week and my mother told me
            maybe I need it because I got high blood and –
17   DR   Oh, no. Not pickle juice. Mrs. Flowers, you can't drink
            that for any reason. It just isn't good. Don't you
            understand?

Based on the above interview, and subsequent physical examination of
Mrs. Flowers, the doctor writes up the medical record as follows:

April 14, 1980

39 year old Black female with hypertension on hydrochlorothiazide
100 mgs. daily and aldomet 2 grams daily. Blood pressure now
160/105, has been 170-80/110-120 for several months, alternating
with 150/95 when taking meds regularly. Has evidence of mild
congestive heart failure. No other problems.

Impression:
1 Hypertension, poorly controlled
2 Noncompliance contributing to (1)
3 Congestive heart failure – mild

Plan:
1 Change aldomet to apresoline.
2 Send to dietician to enforce low salt diet.
3 Social work consult because of financial questions.
4 See in 3 days, regularly until blood pressure has come down and
  stabilized.

Signed: Dr. Staunton Richards
(adapted from Kleinman, 1988: 132-3)

What vividly stands out when comparing the transcript of the medical
interview with the written patient case record is how the latter
completely fails to represent many of the personal and social concerns
that the patient seeks to introduce during the consultation. During the

interview, Dr. Richards interrupts Melissa on at least four occasions when she seeks to elaborate her lifeworld concerns (note, for instance, her worries about her family, her exhausting work at the restaurant, her relationship with her deceased partner Eddie Johnson, and her viewing her physical afflictions through the prism of folk medicine (turns 9, 11, and 17 respectively)).

The patient record suppresses the patient's perspective even further (nowhere can her voice be discerned in the written report). As Kleinman (1988: 134-5) notes in his commentary on the document, the person of Melissa Flowers is reduced to, and considered purely in, medical and physical terms: her high blood pressure, her failure to adhere to her treatment regimen, her early signs of heart disease, and her medicine for hypertension. The written case history records no details of the personal, domestic travails, the severe social pressures that confront her and undoubtedly exacerbate her condition. The doctor's strategy of regarding Melissa as little more than a receptacle for disease reduces her to a case such that her 'problem is transformed into a manageable one' (Hewett *et al.*, 2009: 122).

(TC)

Task 4.1 Narrating the case report

The extract below (from Hunter, 1991: 99) is taken from a hospital case report. This case report is a written record of an oral presentation in which clinicians were discussing a patient's medical history. Despite the heavy use of medical and technical terms throughout the extract, it is still possible to produce a meaningful reading or at least a stylistic impression of the report. Study the text carefully and then consider the following questions:

- How would you describe the way in which the case report is narrated?
- What linguistic elements are absent from this account?

CASE REPORT

A 51-year-old white man had a heart murmur which was first discovered during routine examination at age 18. He was asymptomatic until aged 30, in 1958, when he had two episodes of syncope while running. Over the next six years, light-headedness, dyspnea on exertion and fatigue, orthopnea, paroxysmal nocturnal dyspnea, angina, hemoptysis and episodic acute edema developed. He was therefore sent in 1964 to Strong Memorial Hospital, where the diagnosis of hypertrophic cardiomyopathy was established...Because of the severity of his symptoms, he was referred to the National Institutes of Health where a successful myotomy and myectomy were performed in October 1964.

Linguistic interventions: frameworks for interrogating clinical texts

As an example of the practice of constructing the patient record, Kleinman's illustration above is illuminating. But for all its insightfulness, it reveals little about the rhetorical structure of the document. Accordingly, we now consider approaches to evaluating the linguistic character of the patient record, closely examining the precise textual means by which medical authority is written into it and the way in which the patient is translated into a clinical case.

As we have noted, the patient record is a written document whose creation involves a set of routine procedures; it makes use of conventionalised linguistic rituals, and deploys a stylised vocabulary and telegraphic syntax (Hobbs, 2007: 283) that reveal 'tacit and subtle assumptions, beliefs, and values concerning patients, medical knowledge, and medical practice' (Anspach, 1988: 359). The language used in the patient record is commonly taken for granted and, consequently, the meanings it generates may not be readily apparent to the practitioners who use it (ibid.). Accordingly, institutional personnel are liable to take medical records to be an 'unproblematic' account of their routine activities (Cook-Gumperz and Messerman, 1999: 146).

In order to better appreciate the textual organisation and the communicative import of the patient record, it is important to be aware of the institutional conventions that determine the form and content of the document. When writing the medical case history practitioners commonly follow the stages encoded in the acronym SOAP, which stands for: Subjective, Objective, Assessment, Plan (Hobbs, 2003: 454). The concept of SOAP constrains the writing of the record and ensures that practitioners, using this problem-oriented formula, obtain and record appropriate data with which diagnostic and treatment decisions can reliably be made.

The first component of SOAP, the 'subjective' element, involves the documenting of the patient's history or complaint; it is encoded through the use of reporting verbs such as 'states', 'claims', 'reports' and so forth, verb forms or 'account markers' (Anspach, 1998: 363) which designate the patient's testimony as 'subjective rather than fact' (Donnelly, 1997: 1045). The 'objective' component of the record relates to the practitioner's initial, physical investigation of the patient's complaint, a medical examination that is conducted in a strict order, beginning with the patient's head and systematically moving down the body to the limbs (Hobbs, 2003: 455). The 'assessment' and 'plan' elements of SOAP relate respectively to the practitioner's evaluation of the problem and the course of treatment to be followed. These elements take on specific linguistic forms: assessments are typically expressed as direct factual assertions (for example: 'Status post late-term cesarean section delivery, day three'), while plans are couched in the form of unmitigated directives: 'Discharge home per Dr. Garner on oral ampicillin' (Hobbs, 2003: 456). The SOAP formula thus gives rise to a unique discourse structure, a rigid, strictly-to-be-followed format which marks off patients' accounts, relegating them to 'the domain of the subjective – a negatively valued category in the world of science' (Fleischman, 2001: 477).

Although the SOAP concept determines the format of the patient record, it is the document's aggregate linguistic features that contribute to the derogation of the patient and his or her experience of illness. Research into the patient record has described a range of problematic linguistic usages. For example, Donnelly (1997), himself a clinician, identifies what he labels as the seven 'language maladies', a number of which overlap one another, while, in her US-based study of the case history, Anspach emphasises four key linguistic and rhetorical elements which determine the way information about the patient is represented. The elements described by Anspach (1988: 363-9) are listed below and taken together provide a useful framework for interrogating the patient record. We will consider each feature in turn.

1 Depersonalisation
2 Passive voice and agent omission
3 Treating medical technology as the agent
4 Account markers

Depersonalisation

The process of depersonalisation involves the lexical stripping away of patients' personalities, representing them, through the deployment of an impersonal, technical register, as general objectified types or parts of a class. In the medical record, individuals are not named but referred to as 'the patient'. A 'baby', in the context of obstetrical and gynecological care, is lexicalised as a 'product' – a 'product' of a 'gestation' (Anspach, 1988: 366). The use of such an impersonal, technical lexis reflects a subtle set of assumptions that emphasise biological processes over human agency. In other words, biological processes are divorced from human individuals. Further examples provided by Anspach help to illustrate the point:

the *pregnancy* was complicated by...
SROM (spontaneous rupture of membranes) occurred
the *bruit* (murmur) has decreased significantly
the vagina and the cervix were noted to be clear

(Anspach, 1988:366)

According to Anspach, these occurrences invite the question 'To which person?' or 'Whose organ?'. Attention is drawn to a body part or disease and, as a result, the whole person is effaced.

Passive voice and agent deletion

Besides the phenomenon of depersonalisation, another common rhetorical element in the medical record is the passive voice (and the concomitant omission of the agent). According to Porter (2005: 10), the choice of whether to employ the active or passive voice is one of the most significant choices that a writer can make when representing reality. Research into the language of the patient record indicates that the passive voice occurs more frequently in the document than the active voice (Hobbs, 2003). The two voices place different emphasis on the events and participants they are representing. The passive voice can be contrasted with the active voice thus:

Active   The doctor took her blood pressure.
Passive Her blood pressure was taken by the doctor.

In both the active and passive clauses, the doctor is the agent, the 'doer' of the action described by the verb (the process) 'took'. The passive voice, however, unlike its active counterpart, allows for a further option that can significantly affect the representation and perception of events, namely, the removing of the agent. Thus:

The blood pressure was taken.

Removing the agent is commonly referred to as, not unsurprisingly, 'agent-deletion'. It is an important linguistic resource, the use of which helps to explain the recurring presence of the passive voice in contexts where the emphasis is on describing a process rather than the individual performing it. By contrast, to use the active voice is to draw attention to the performer, the agent at the heart of an event. Thus, the impersonal, agentless nature of the passive voice makes it suitable for use in the case history, in which biological processes overshadow personal agency.

In the medical case history, the agentless passive, notes Anspach, is often introduced using an existential 'there'. For example, 'There was no mention of bleeding pattern...' (1988: 366), a representation of a verbal process that begs the question: 'no mention of bleeding' by whom? Some further examples illustrate the removal of medical personnel from the actions and verbal processes they produce:

The infant was transferred
The baby was noted to have congestive heart failure

She was treated with high FiO2's (respirator settings)
The patient was admitted to the hospital

(Anspach, 1988: 366)

All these examples (whether the writers are aware of the effects of their language choices or otherwise) draw attention to what was done, the clinical processes, rather than who actually performed particular actions. Mention of how and why a decision was taken to conduct a specific course of action is also removed. Using the passive voice, moreover, constitutes another rhetorical strategy: it confers the patient record with a veneer of epistemological authority, that is, it records events from the perspective of 'an omniscient, anonymous narrator' (Donnelly, 1997: 1045). Since deleting the agent removes personal involvement and responsibility from the processes described in the record, it obfuscates the practitioner's role in collecting, processing and structuring the information used to create the medical history (ibid.). Omitting the person responsible for an action (an action, for example, such as observing a patient or recording test results) potentially obscures the possibility of misinterpretation of information (or other malpractice) on the part of the agent (for human agents are, of course, always fallible!) in the activities so documented. Consequently the patient record is imbued with the status of categorical truth, veiling the fact that all medical knowledge, 'from the initial history to autopsy result – is uncertain, tentative, incomplete and subject to change' (ibid.).

The pervasive application of the passive voice and agent deletion in the patient record has consequences beyond the construction of clinical omniscience and unquestionable authority. The effect of 'Olympian detachment' (Wilkinson, 1992: 322) produced by use of the agentless passive is also liable to obscure the source of patients' complaints that arise as a result of domestic and social problems. For instance, sociological and applied linguistic research by Warshaw (1989), which investigated the medical records of women receiving treatment as a result of physical abuse, describes the way in which the agentless passive (and other features of standard medical shorthand) serve to obfuscate the most significant problem, the abuse itself, experienced by the women concerned. The medical record below exemplifies the linguistic behaviours identified by Warshaw:

NURSE TRIAGE NOTE: was hit on upper lip. teeth lose and c dislocation. Happened last night.
MD RECORD: Patient 25y/o BF c/o [complained of] swelling and Pain on the mouth after was hit by a fist about 5 hours ago. No LOC [lack of consciousness], no visual symptoms, no vomiting, no nausea.

PHYSICAL EXAM EXAM: Afebrile, hydrated, conscious, oriented x3 [time, place, person]. HEENT [head, eyes, ears, nose, throat]: has swelling in the upper lip and loose teeth. No evidence of Fx[fracture]
XRAY: No Fracture
DISCHARGE DIAGNOSIS: Blunt Trauma Face
DISPOSITION: Ice Packs, Oral Surgery Clinic appt, Motrin
(Warshaw, 1989: 512)

Through the use of disembodied language, the record presents the 'mechanism of injury' (Warshaw, 1989: 512), specifically how the physical violence affects the body but not the person herself. What, of course, is grossly absent from this account are details of the individual responsible for the assault, along with the circumstances surrounding the violence. Not only does the agentless passive – 'Was hit on the upper lip' – omit the attribution of responsibility for the physical action to a specific person (the assailant), the passive construction here also deletes the grammatical subject of the clause (the woman), removing her entirely from the clinical picture. The entire event of physical abuse is thus reduced to and represented by body parts – an exchange between fist and eye, with the latter removed from the individual attached to it (1989: 512-13). As Warshaw observes, 'the passive voice slides over the real action' and, as a consequence, 'obscures both the etiology and meaning of the women's symptoms' (1989: 513).

Treating medical technology as the agent

Although the passive voice occurs frequently in the patient record, the active voice also plays a significant part in the construction of the document. The active voice is commonly associated with Anspach's third linguistic feature of the case history: treating medical technology as the agent. Here the active voice is used by practitioners to report medical processes, but rather than clinical personnel occupying the agentive role (the performers of a particular test, procedure or operation), technology and equipment take on the agentive role. For instance:

Ausculation of the head revealed a very large bruit, and *angiography* showed a very large arterio-venous malformation in the head...

Follow-up CT scans have showed the amount of blood flow to be very minimal...

The path reported revealed endometrial curettings...

In these examples the use of technology as agent, Anspach notes, extends the process of objectification even further than the passive voice. This is because not only do the writers fail to mention the personnel who performed a given diagnostic process, they also exclude mention of 'the frequently complex processes' by which such technical procedures are interpreted (1988: 368). Representing medical technology in this way (as though it were the agent of the various processes documented in the record) upholds a view of knowledge where instruments, rather than human beings, create and read data. The (unavoidably) equivocal process involved in interpreting the results obtained by, say, x-ray or biopsy is suppressed. The effect of this is that test data is made to appear as though it were emanating from nothing less than 'scientific revelation' (ibid.).

Account markers

The fourth and final linguistic feature of the case history is the use of account markers. As we observed when discussing the SOAP formula earlier, these linguistic markers take the form of verbs such as 'note', 'report', 'claim' – verbs which express some commitment to a claim in knowledge. The use of account markers varies for professionals and patients. Whereas practitioners typically 'observe', 'note', 'find'; patients 'claim', 'report', 'state', deny' – account markers which are selected by medical case writers to emphasise the subjective nature of patients' accounts (Anspach, 1988: 368). Where practitioners imbue the physical examination and diagnostic machinery with unfailing objectivity ('CT scans have *showed* the amount of blood flow to be very minimal'), they treat patients' reports with skepticism: as subjective accounts with only tenuous connections to reality. Practitioners' use of the account marker 'deny', for example – 'Pt denied fever' (Hobbs, 2003: 465) – indicates a negative response to a query, one that hints at a degree of untruthfulness (Donnelly, 1997: 1045).

Although the range of rhetorical features we have examined above certainly contributes to reductive written practices such as objectification and depersonalisation, they cannot simply be treated as careless and unreflective linguistic practices on the part of health practitioners. The acquisition and use of technical language is seen among clinicians as a significant step on the way to becoming a fully socialised professional (Crawford *et al.*, 1995: 1141). Adopting such a register facilitates professionalism and prevents descriptive diversity which could potentially result in ambiguity that leads to inaccurate assessment and inappropriate care (Crawford *et al.*, 1998). Moreover, not only does the use of medical discourse contribute to professional socialisation, confirming one's insider status, the process of objectification, of reducing patients to their malfunctioning organs or diseases, also serves as a protection strategy, a means of shielding healthcare providers from the 'human tragedy of illness' (Charon, 1986: 61). As Charon puts it, 'A malignant hepatoma seems easier to face than a twenty-six-year-old man who will die soon from a rare and fatal liver problem' (ibid.). However, although such formulations have the effect of distancing professionals from the human suffering they often encounter, adopting such linguistic strategies (and the biomedical perspective they encode) risks transforming the practitioner into 'an anatomist': he or she becomes a 'curator of specimens' (ibid.) rather than a carer of human beings.

Collaborative construction: patient records as multi-authored texts

The linguistic approaches we have just considered reveal much about the textual intricacies of the patient record and, significantly, the social consequences of its construction. Although health professionals are unlikely to disclose their beliefs and assumptions about patients when interacting with them directly (Anspach, 1988: 358), it is possible, by interrogating the written discourse of the patient record, to identify some of the assumptions and values that professionals display when communicating with one another (358). The construction of the patient record is indisputably a collaborative endeavour, one that not only helps to determine the patient's trajectory (Berg, 1996), but one that also communicates inter-collegial relations between medical personnel, as the various participants encode their particular medical allegiances or 'speciality memberships' (Hewett et al., 2009: 134). The medical case record thus bears witness to inter-professional negotiation and decision-making and, with these activities, the 'projection of professional identities' (Hobbs, 2007: 283).

In order to pursue the issue of professional collaboration further, we shall now, in the final part of this section, turn our attention to exploring how the patient record is jointly constructed by different medical personnel, and the consequences that joint discursive action has not only for inter-group allegiances, but also for the representation of the patient. Since the focus on the patient record so far has been in the context of general medicine rather than specialist medical domains, we shall consider one such specialist context: that of psychiatric care.

As we noted in Chapter 1, relatively little is known about the everyday language practices that take place in psychiatric settings (Buus, 2008). One important body of work in this area, which is worth considering in detail, is Robert Barrett's (1996, 1999) discourse analytic and ethnographic research into the care and treatment of patients passing through psychiatric institutions. Barrett's research investigates how practitioners in a multidisciplinary team – including psychiatric nurses, psychologists, social workers, and psychiatrists – communicate with one another and how their verbal exchanges are transformed in the process of writing up their communications in the patient record. Barrett, a psychiatrist by profession, was able to immerse himself in the clinical settings he was studying. Doing so enabled him to elucidate the 'cycle of interpretation that alternates between talking and writing' (Barrett, 1999: 244) as hospital staff participate in a range of day-to-day communicative activities, such as reading case records, interviewing patients, discussing patients with colleagues and entering their observations and opinions in patients' records.

For the analyst concerned with medical documentation, it is important to examine both these frontstage and backstage communicative events since, as Prior reminds us, the patient record is 'tied into and anchored within other aspects of organizational life such as conversations at the nursing station' (2003: 56). In adopting an ethnographic approach that examines these various formal and informal interpenetrating communicative events, the researcher is able to render them unfamiliar, thereby exposing aspects of clinical practice which are typically unremarkable to participants and which therefore might go unnoticed in the daily run of events (Hak, 1999: 434).

A key insight of Barrett's applied linguistic intervention reveals how, in the context of the medical case history, speech and writing are observed to penetrate each other: 'written language is dictated by oral discourse and infused with figures of speech, and conversely [...] speech itself is captive to the writing process, and shot through with written idioms' (1999: 245-6). This interpenetration of speech and writing has implications for the representation of patients. Barrett identifies three key linguistic mechanisms through which psychiatric team members express moral judgements about their patients, as well as displaying the professional values and beliefs unique to their specific disciplines, to wit: 'pseudo-technical idioms', 'pseudo-lay language' and 'epigrammatic appraisals', each of which we will examine in turn. Focussing on the use of these central features affords a survey of both the frontstage and backstage settings of the clinic since all three are ubiquitous linguistic practices, occurring in both formal and informal spoken events (such as formal case presentations and informal collegial chat) as well as, crucially, in the written medical record itself.

Pseudo-technical idioms

In the official patient case conferences that Barrett observed, the multidisciplinary team's talk was strewn with pseudo-technical idioms. Taken from the written discourse of the patient record itself, these linguistic forms, according to Barrett, enable team members to make value judgements about patients. For instance, the following technical idiom describes a patient experiencing severe psychological distress: 'He's thought disordered plus plus plus' (Barrett, 1999: 260). What is immediately evident about this formulation, Barrett notes, is that it appears as though the speaker is reading directly from the case record (though in fact they aren't). The standardised written format, the medical shorthand of clinical documentation, appears to have infiltrated the verbal discourse of the clinicians (the 'plus plus plus' in the spoken utterance relates to the typographical '+++' notation, symbols which denote 'a lot', 'a great deal'). Other pseudo-technical idioms which featured commonly in the speech of professionals, and which similarly attribute value judgements to patients, include lexis from the Diagnostic and Statistical Manual (DSM), a document used universally by clinicians. As a system of psychiatric classification, the DSM is the most authoritative text of its kind for defining and identifying mental disorders, a technical document that translates 'particular observed behaviours into symptoms' for diagnosis (Crowe, 2000: 69).

The use of technical jargon is of course common in clinical settings. However, in the context of the psychiatric care (not to mention other workplace settings, medical or otherwise) jargon is likely to be taken for granted (Kohr, 1999: 1055). Rather than being deployed carefully as part of the operation of defined diagnostic criteria, Barrett observed that technical terms imported from the DSM were liable to be used loosely, extravagantly, and instinctively with a deliberate pejorative inflection, metonymically reducing patients to symptoms or categories. The following formulations illustrate the trend:

She's an out and out borderline.
He's obsessional to the nth degree.
Passive-aggressive plus plus plus.
She's a grand hysteric.
He's a real thorough-going little sociopath.

(Barrett, 1999: 260)

Pseudo-lay language

As with technical idioms, pseudo-lay language is a key aspect of the verbal repertoires of mental health workers and possesses a similar evaluative function. According to Barrett, the most 'quintessential' examples of pseudo-lay language are found not in formal discussions, such as official case conferences, but, intriguingly, in more informal, backstage settings and activities, such as during tea breaks (where personnel are more likely to interact with one another unguardedly and the talk so produced, unlike the discourse of official verbal routines, lacks accountability). For example, in these backstage settings practitioners variously described their patients as 'not with it', 'away with the fairies', 'off in her own little world', 'off the air', 'off', 'mad', 'crazy', or 'mad as a cut snake' (1999: 261). Examining these formulations in this domain of so-called unprofessional talk is revealing indeed since the practitioners' use of these constructions reveals the mobilisation of moral positions and attitudes towards patients – beliefs that, as Barrett discovered, were later recycled during the conference forum and subsequently appeared in the case record itself. In other words, 'What began off the record was ultimately translated back into the record' (ibid.).

Epigrammatic appraisals

The final linguistic concept on which Barrett draws to make sense of psychiatric communication is that of the 'epigrammatic appraisal'. Epigrammatic appraisals take on a number of forms of varying sizes, from larger vignettes down to sentences and phrases, each of them, however, possessing vivid rhetorical force. Given their compact size, epigrammatic appraisals are liable to occur in the swift course of conversation and, as Barrett observes, convey a detailed knowledge of the case. They are used to morally evaluate the patient as an active subject, specifically, the extent to which patients are in control of their situation.

The power of the epigrammatic appraisal can be demonstrated by summoning a specific case. Barrett describes the history of Ms Treloar, a 59-year-old spinster, who had been admitted to the psychiatric clinic with a diagnosis of paranoid schizophrenia. In the first conference, a formal and detailed presentation concerning Ms Treloar took place, followed, a week later, by presentations from each member of the team reporting on their additional investigations into her condition. From here on a more informal discussion ensued in which the consensus was that Ms Treloar, despite her schizophrenia, was ultimately an 'incorrigible old eccentric', her illness only being a problem in so far as it was a nuisance to people around her. The mood of the mental health team was one of wry acceptance: whatever treatment the patient received, she would still continue to do what she wanted. The following epigrammatic appraisals reflect this shared belief:

Trainee psychiatrist:	*She functions reasonably well, it's just that she terrorizes the next door neighbours.*
Social worker:	*She can cope with her illness, she can get on top of it, but she gets on top of everyone else as well.*
Psychiatric nurse:	*She gets enjoyment out of annoying people.*

(Barrett, 1999: 263)

These appraisals reveal not only the 'pseudo-lay quality' of their linguistic make up, but also their ability to capture a version of Ms Treloar's character in a 'persuasive, pithy utterance' (Barrett, 1999: 263). The language of these appraisals is typified by so-called common sense diction, language that is lay-like, jargon-free. Their demotic nature, Barrett claims, functions as a bridge between team members whose different specialist backgrounds may lead to conflicting points of view. Yet this 'egalitarian style of talk' (ibid.) further functions to mark off and point to the speakers' various occupational specialities, with the expert concision of the appraisals disclosing the precise and detailed command of the patient's case each team member possesses.

Epigrammatic formulations such as these demonstrate the power of mental health workers to 'summarize and encompass all that was known about a case, without having to say anything complicated at all' (Barrett, 1999: 263). Thus epigrammatic appraisals allow professionals of different stripes to achieve consensus while, in spite of the negative and reductive evaluation of the patient, preserving a degree of professional autonomy.

Overall, then, what Barrett's linguistic and ethnographic analysis provides is a thorough survey of the communicative routines of the various clinical staff in a modern day psychiatric hospital, a survey which reveals much about the life and culture of the clinic itself. Combining the linguistic analysis of spoken and written texts with ethnographic techniques (such as participant observation) yields acute insights into the shared decision-making processes among clinical practitioners and their moral assessment of patients. Although most professionals consider the moral evaluation of patients to be 'antithetical to humane care and effective treatment' (1999: 259), for the practitioners whom Barrett observed, moral evaluation was vital to the treatment process; the key objective of medical intervention being to transform the patient from a case with schizophrenia into a person who is responsible for their own actions. This process involved subjecting patients and their behaviours to moral scrutiny, a process which, in turn, produces the detrimental notion of the good and the bad patient.

Barrett's integrated approach to psychiatric discourse raises questions about whether the study of the language of clinical communication alone (be it written documents or verbal interaction) is sufficient to produce meaningful insights that make sufficient sense of the workaday practices that take place in healthcare settings. This is a moot theoretical point we follow up in the next section.

Theorising the patient record: perspectives on language and researcher involvement

Our review of the patient record has sought to demonstrate, among other considerations, how this essential clinical document is no mere repository of information, but constitutes a vital, transformational text that helps to determine patients' trajectories (Berg, 1996: 520), a text that encodes practitioners' evaluations of patients and inscribes professional identities and allegiances. In this final, theoretical section we will examine some of the assumptions that underpin the discourse of the patient record (and medical discourse more broadly), drawing further on the seminal work of Anspach (1988) as a means of accounting for some of the linguistic consequences of the case history. We will also explore some of the further implications of the discourse of patient record, seeking to answer the question: What does the language of the document reveal about assumptions underpinning the medical ideologies that shape contemporary patient care? Finally, we will consider recent ideas in applied linguistic thinking concerning the role of analysts involved in health language research and the extent to which they need immerse themselves in the clinical site if they are to produce robust and convincing analyses of medical documentation.

When analysing written discourse (whether medical or otherwise), it is important to realise that linguistic data can yield many readings. No reading of a text is ever truly exhaustive or utterly beyond doubt. This equally applies to the language of clinical documentation. Various interpretations concerning the communicative import of the patient record can be made, not just the linguistically inspired readings we have examined throughout this chapter. With regard to the patient record, linguistic findings consistently reveal problematic discourse practices or what Donnelly (1997: 1045) more vividly refers to as 'language maladies'. Although these findings and interventions are (and continue to remain) persuasive (derived as they are from close empirical scrutiny of real-life texts), a key issue is whether the language of clinical texts has the same kind of significance for practitioners themselves, the individuals who produce and interpret clinical documents on a daily basis. For instance, just because, say, patients are often written in the record as 'biological specimens' (Donnelly, 1997: 1045), described in terms of body parts and organs rather than as people, doesn't mean that practitioners automatically construe such instances of language as acts of de-personalisation, attributing the same 'deeper meanings' (Anspach, 1988: 370) to language forms that discourse-fixated researchers do. The language of the patient record constitutes an 'occupational register', and it can be argued that such a register merely has the function of transferring information among professionals (Fleischman, 1999: 99). Occupational registers are not uncommon, existing widely outside the sphere of healthcare: the domains of law, science and advertising, for instance, all employ various specialist 'economy registers' (Bruthiaux, 1996), many of which similarly use reductive and depersonalising devices (such as the agentless passive) not unlike those found in the patient record.

Medical writing not only describes the patient, but also constitutes his or her treatment (Prior, 2003: 57). The language of the patient record, therefore, reveals some deep-seated medical assumptions about disease and the treatment of disease, assumptions that have consequences for clinical practice. For example, the recurring use of the various discursive practices that we examined above gives rise to what Anspach refers to as the 'mitigation of responsibility' and 'the surrender of subjectivity' in professional medicine (1988: 370). Devices such as the passive voice and agent deletion play down, we noted, the involvement of human actors, deflecting attention away from clinicians and the decisions they make. Couple this with the active, agentive role accorded to diagnostic technology and it is possible to apprehend a distinct 'epistemological hierarchy' at work, with technological information being valued over practitioners' observations which, in turn, are considered superior to patients' own accounts of their histories (Anspach, 1998: 370).

Such a state of affairs arises, according to Anspach, as the result of the 'structural imperative in the medical profession to shield itself from scrutiny' (1998: 370). Legal accountability, the ever-present threat of malpractice claims, for instance, plays a significant part in how health providers document procedures and present information about patients in medical records. As we noted at the beginning of this chapter, the patient record is a multi-authored legal document that is read by a diverse audience (not just health providers), and clinicians are acutely aware that the document constitutes a legal artefact that can be used in a court of law (Annandale, 2004: 191). The account markers which professionals use to code information for reliability (Hobbs, 2003) reflect a preoccupation with accuracy; and this striving for precision can be seen as a 'defence mechanism' (Annandale, 2004: 190), a means of 'covering oneself' against potential malpractice claims.

Making sense of the patient record: are linguistic approaches alone sufficient?

Another key theoretical concern that applied linguists need to consider when investigating the patient record (or indeed any text or instance of discourse within medical settings) is just how robust and convincing are linguistic interpretations alone? Do other forms of communication have to be interrogated alongside the record if we are to make sense of clinical documentation and apprehend both its intended and unintended meanings and consequences? Is it essential that researchers possess intimate knowledge of the clinical setting (and its procedures) in which these medical texts are written, read and acted on? To what extent, if at all, should analysts immerse themselves in settings to make sense of the communicative phenomena they are investigating?

The question of whether outsiders (researchers who are not themselves practitioners) can read the contents of medical records appropriately – that is, whether they can appreciate what such documents are talking about (Garfinkel and Bittner, 1967) – raises a number of important theoretical and methodological concerns. In an early and often-cited study of clinical records, Garfinkel and Bittner (1967) draw attention to the composition of the patient case folder.

> In their occasionality, folder documents are very much like utterances in a conversation with an unknown audience which, because it already knows what might be talked about, is capable of reading hints. As expressions, the remarks that make up these documents have overwhelmingly the characteristic that their sense cannot be decided by a reader without his [sic] necessarily knowing or assuming something about a typical biography and typical purposes of the user of the expressions, about typical circumstances under which such remarks are written, about a typical previous course of transactions between the writers and the patient, or about a typical relationship of actual or potential interaction between *the writers and the reader.*
>
> (1967: 201-2, emphasis in the original)

Although the documents, the 'folders', to which Garfinkel and Bittner here refer are psychiatric outpatient records and intake application forms, the comments the authors make equally apply to the peculiar texture and situated construction of the patient record. A key point that Garfinkel and Bittner articulate relates to the interpersonal dynamics of speech and writing. The written entries in the patient record can be seen as being similar to spoken utterances in that they are contextually dependent: one turn at talk – like one written entry – depends on another for it to make sense, to be interpreted correctly, and to cue subsequent turns or entries. Although the participants who produce and read one another's written entries in the patient record are unlikely to share the same temporal and spatial context, they are still able – like interlocutors co-present in unfolding speech – to 'read hints', to complete ellipses, to fill in missing details. However, analysts who approach the patient record from outside and who conduct purely an interrogatory reading (one, of course, very much different from the purpose than that for which the document was originally intended) will find themselves, in Coulter's words, 'cut adrift from [the] immediate and situated conditions and constraints' that pertain to the interactive production of the record (1994: 690). In other words, without the appropriate background information, the outside analyst will be unable to fill in the missing details and therefore fail to make sense of the document (at least in terms of the purpose of its original production).

Although Garfinkel and Bittner are here describing the plight of sociologists whose prime concern is not necessarily linguistic, their remarks apply to researchers of all stripes approaching clinical documents from the outside (including linguists who may be concerned solely with the textual make up of written texts rather than the social organisation and workflow of the medical setting more broadly). As Hak (1992: 142) puts it, since researchers do not possess the relevant knowledge regarding the patients to whom the record relates, nor the individuals who produced the written entries, nor the organisational principles that determine the clinic's day-to-day operation, they will be unable to read such texts correctly. Hence problems of interpretation may well arise.

In the context of applied linguistic research, this theoretical predicament can be demonstrated through a specific example: the use of the passive voice. Recall that previously we identified the agentless passive as a significant component of the patient record, a rhetorical device which imbues the statements of medical personnel with a degree of objectivity and authority, as well as obscuring the involvement of actors in reported clinical procedures. The agentless passive is one of the key sources of textual evidence on which researchers who critically interrogate the patient record base their claims concerning reductive effects, such as depersonalisation. This is not surprising since using the passive voice can produce (whether deliberately or otherwise) opaque and dispassionate forms of discourse. Yet, despite the imprecations of generations of self-styled English language advisors (e.g. Gowers, 1954; Strunk and White, 2009; Heffer, 2010), avoiding the passive voice does not necessarily lead to a 'good strong style' (Phythian, 1979: 3) or a more transparent form of representation. Its presence in many forms of writing, including the patient record, is not remarkable and nor does its use in a clause make a sentence necessarily impenetrable.

In many circumstances, the use of the passive is natural, innocuous – indeed even essential. However, to appreciate this (in the clinical context at least), one has to have a close situational understanding of its use. Porter (2005: 8-9), in an enlightening study of nurses' use of the passive voice, provides the following illustration. The two patient record entries below describe the removal of an intravenous line (IV):

1 Disconnected IV.
2 IV Disconnected.

For the researcher unfamiliar with the day-to-day practice of nursing, the significance of these two formulations is unlikely to be registered.
   The first description, which is in the active voice, can be restated as:

'I disconnected the IV' or
'Patient disconnected the IV'.

The second example, the passive counterpart, can be interpreted as:

'The IV was disconnected by me' or
'The IV was disconnected by patient'

Porter makes the point that only with specialist insider knowledge can the reader of the above common formulations appreciate that the active statement 'Disconnected IV' describes, in actuality, the patient's disconnection of the IV, while 'IV Disconnected' relates to the practitioner's removal of the device, specifically the person who wrote that particular entry. Without being privy to such insider knowledge, the analyst who interrogates these statements might well believe that agency, whether consciously or unconsciously, is being obscured as a result of the use of these linguistic choices. Yet such a reading would be inaccurate since, for the practitioners engaged in writing and reading the record, responsibility for the actions and procedures documented is clear. Agency, in these instances at least, is neither obscured nor concealed by the writers. Responsibility for an action will only appear absent or obscure in the eyes of those unfamiliar with the mores of clinical document construction. Thus written entries such as the above take on particular meanings within communities of healthcare practitioners (Porter, 2005), meanings that will not necessarily be apprehended by linguists unless they have familiarised themselves sufficiently with the routine and culture of the clinic whose written practices they are investigating.
   The foregoing concerns with interpretation alert us to the problem of researchers relying solely on textual data (be it the patient record or any other aspect of medical discourse) and failing to get to grips

sufficiently with contextual data. As Candlin and Sarangi argue, applied linguists need to 'acknowledge that despite their adherence to language, linguistic means are only one of a range of semiotic modalities through which significant action may be coded' (Candlin and Sarangi, 2004: 4). Accordingly, examining the language of written documents or transcripts of spoken interaction at the expense of other communicative behaviours will only provide a partial description of the culture and practice of healthcare settings. Numerous discursive activities take place within the clinic, many of them behind researchers' backs – backstage activities that are never captured in official documenting procedures or are beyond the reach of recording equipment. These discreet activities are equally important sources of data to consider if analysts are to make greater sense of the clinical routine, or to corroborate the themes or issues that they have identified during their linguistic analyses. Relying on text-based discourse analytic approaches alone is liable to provide a distorted picture of healthcare settings and the work that takes place inside them (Hak, 1999: 430).

Therefore, analysts concerned with interrogating clinical discourse need to consider immersing themselves in workplace contexts if they are to understand and explain why the communicative practices within them 'are the way they are' (Sarangi and Roberts, 1999: 2). For researchers investigating the discourse of the clinic, securing access to workplace sites involves considerable negotiation with health providers (not to mention satisfying the requirements of research and development and ethics committees). Nonetheless, if analysts are committed to conducting research that not only enhances theoretical knowledge (thereby addressing fellow linguists' concerns and interests) but is also to be of practical relevance to professionals and patients, then linguists need to 'engage with the "real world" of the institution of medicine' (Roberts and Sarangi, 2003: 341).

The applied linguistic approaches to the patient record that we have considered throughout this book all, to varying extents, cleave to this principle. The research of Anspach (1988); Donnelly (1997); Barrett (1999) and Hobbs (2003, 2007), for example, is not confined to the analysis of clinical documents outside the context of their production, but is supplemented by other modes of investigation. For instance, Anspach's and Hobbs's linguistic enquiries are complemented by ethnographic insights (such as observations of procedures and interviews with clinical staff), while Donnelly's and Barrett's research is informed by their professional experience as clinicians.

Of particular note is Hobbs' research (Hobbs, 2003, 2007). In order to understand the 'daunting complexities of clinical practice' (Hobbs, 2007: 274) through the linguistic analysis of patient records, Hobbs, a former lawyer without medical experience or training, immersed herself in the professional milieu of medicine, spending weeks meeting with doctors, discussing and reviewing cases – partaking in such activities in what she describes as a '"doctor-like" fashion' (Hobbs, 2003: 453). As a consequence of her total immersion in the work of the clinic she acquired a comprehensive understanding of the construction and interpretation of the patient record (Hobbs, 2007: 275) indeed perhaps more so than other applied linguist hailing from a non-medical background. Now this exemplar is not to suggest that applied linguists wishing to pursue health communication research need take up medical training or completely immerse themselves in the ways of the clinic to the same ineffable extent that Hobbs did. It is rather to highlight the importance of their being prepared (to an extent) to socialise themselves into the discourse of medicine if they wish to comprehend and explicate 'the linguistic and non-linguistic aspects of communicative events' (Circourel, 1992: 294).

Task 4.2 Remedying the record

In his article, 'The Language of Medical Histories', William Donnelly (1997: 1047-48) proposes seven modest remedies to mollify the depersonalising and objectifying effects of the patient record. In producing these salutary recommendations, Donnelly's research is not only concept driven – that is, aiming to enhance linguistic theory – but is also outcome orientated, aiming to contribute to change (no matter how small) in the world of medicine.

Contemporary thinking in applied linguistics underscores the importance of the practical relevance of discourse-based research. Although the term 'applied' in applied linguistics is commonly used to refer to real-world communicative settings and the practices that constitute them (Roberts and Sarangi, 2003: 340), the notion of 'applied' also entails providing solutions to real-world problems. If, as Candlin and Candlin argue, applied linguistics is to be 'truly problem driven, then it needs to be equally outcome focused' (2003: 146). In the sense that his research seeks to contribute to social change, Donnelly's work embraces a version of applied linguistics that construes 'research and application as a joint enterprise' (Sarangi and Roberts, 1999: 40).

Consider Donnelly's seven language remedies below then answer the following questions:

- How effective are these linguistic recommendations?
- Would the implementation of these changes result in a more holistic representation of the patient and their clinical care? Would any information be lost as a result?
- Do these changes respond to all the linguistic problems of the patient record that we have examined in the preceding sections of this book?

1. Introduce the patient as a person: for instance, 'Mr Kevin Harvey, a 39-year-old sociolinguistics lecturer, who lives with his family in South Nottinghamshire'. Throughout the rest of the record, aim to refer to the patient by name as often as possible.
2. Record the patient's complaint in his or her words. In addition, use the term 'chief concern' rather than 'complaint' in the record since it 'is less likely to be translated into biomedical language' (Donnelly, 1997: 1047).
3. Avoid linguistic descriptors that promote the credibility of medical data and undermine what the patient reports.
4. Construct a two-perspective history of the patient's condition: one account that records illness (the personal, social reality of the patient's sickness – how the patient understands their condition and its impact on his or her life, work, family, relationships, etc.), and a second account that describes disease (the biomedical formulation of sickness, such as the chronology and onset of symptoms and details of any previous diagnosis).
5. With regard to the SOAP (subjective, objective, assessment and plan) formula for constructing the patient record, replace the term 'subjective' with the more inclusive 'history'. Also substitute the more precise word 'observations' for 'objective'. This lexical reshuffling gives rise to the new abbreviation HOAP, a formula which strikes a more upbeat note than its antiseptic, though equally memorable, counterpart.
6. Consider that a patient's sadness (and his or her understanding of their condition) may simply relate to a human situation that is more appropriately described in lay language than in technical, pathological terms such as 'denial' or 'depression'.
7. Use the term 'history' or 'patient perspective' to signal patients' updated, changing points of view concerning their condition. Record in the record what the patient understands rather than simply what he or she has been informed about.

Summary

We began this chapter by describing some of the (technical, stylistic, legal) aspects of the patient case record and illustrating how talk between doctors and patients (and talk between medics themselves) is radically transformed when written up as a record, obscuring the original verbal content. Much of the personal and social context of the patient's illness is effaced, leaving behind only accounts of biomedical details and technical processes. The patient, as a person, is, as it were, effectively written out of the record.

The depersonalising, objectifying effects of the patient record are brought about by a number of linguistic practices and can be summarised as follows:

- use of the passive voice which downplays the role of human agents;
- the recurring presence of technical terminology which substitutes general objectified types for people;
- treating technology as the agent, a practice which objectifies the patient, obscuring the involvement of human agents;
- the use of account markers, that is, verbs such as 'note', 'report', 'observe', 'claim'.

Although interrogating these features offers a promising approach to making sense of the patient record, we also emphasised the importance of examining the context in which the document is produced. Patient records are not produced in a vacuum and therefore any reading of them will be incomplete, not to mention potentially misinformed, if researchers are not familiar with the conventions attending their construction. Researchers should not depend on language as their sole means of analysis since observations based on linguistic behaviour alone provide only a partial account of the culture and practice of the healthcare environment.

As we noted throughout this chapter, a significant amount of extant research into the patient record is supplemented by ethnographic approaches, such as observations of routine procedures and interviews with clinical staff. Although language plays a central part in the enactment of healthcare, health communication is encoded in a range of ways, and researchers should aim to ensure that they explore as wide a variety of communicative behaviours as possible and, ideally, familiarise themselves closely with the routines of the clinic.

5 Print media representations of health and illness

Public health communication: exploring print media representations

In this chapter we look at public health messages and documents produced for distribution via channels of mass communication, paying particular attention to print media representations of infectious disease outbreaks. We will also discuss the importance of metaphors in public debates and outline the implications of their use for risk communication.

Public health communication is concerned with creating, tailoring and disseminating health promotion and disease prevention messages to the population as a whole. Communicators are typically issued with guidelines that stress the importance of knowing the audience, avoiding jargon and, as far as media professionals are concerned, delivering 'accurate' information. Although such guidelines appear to be straightforward and applicable to a range of communicative situations, it is increasingly evident that there is more to public health communication than the simple transmission of information. As the SARS and recent swine flu outbreaks have demonstrated, crisis communication is far from a straightforward act of raising public awareness and transmitting information in an objective manner, not least because health professionals and journalists may differentially understand and communicate about health risks and their prevention. Rather, it is a complex and inherently political process that requires taking decisions that prioritise certain solutions, courses of action, and groups of people over others. In other words, it is a process immersed in a specific cultural, political and historical context where the senders, messages, and receivers do not remain static.

The recognition of communication as a process highlights the social dynamics involved in defining, negotiating and understanding health and illness and, subsequently, the crucial role of language in public health discourse. Here pragmatic functions of language, aspects of text production and reception, as well as resources and channels of communication come to the fore as we focus not on the dissemination of information as such, but on the human processes of communication in which such information is embedded (Carey, 2009). As a result, the traditional information dissemination model largely concerned with the one-way transmission of particular messages is being increasingly replaced by models incorporating a number of variables that can affect health behaviour and practice. One example of such a context-based approach is the UNAIDS new communication framework for HIV/ AIDS (Airhihenbuwa *et al.*, 2000) that recognises five levels of context: government policy, socio-economic status, gender relations, spirituality, as well as culture and language.

One of the most apparent examples of communication to benefit from such a context-sensitive model is crisis communication during an infectious disease outbreak. Decisions regarding human and animal travel and transportation, trade restrictions, distribution of antivirals, quarantines and immunisation procedures are all dependent on communication and are inherently political acts that need to be carefully balanced to ensure that different parties benefit from such provisions. During such turbulent times, it is not uncommon for opposing political groups to voice their criticism of public health decisions in the media and in this way shift the public attention from the disease threat to matters of accountability and blame (Wallis *et al.*, 2005). If we want our communication to be effective in such circumstances, and not drowned out in the rhetoric of blame that often dominates in such situations, we need to understand both the linguistic means with which certain messages will be created and the broader political, social and cultural environment in which the communication will take place. For this purpose, a study of how medically significant scientific claims have already been linguistically rendered in the public domain via the channels of mass communication is crucial (Rundblad *et al.*, 2006).

Personal reflection

It is interesting to consider whether – and, if so, how far – keywords for emerging diseases function differently in different contexts. Compare the use of different phrases and terms in media reports and scientific articles referring to the 2009 swine flu pandemic (for example, 'swine flu' and 'H1N1'). Does the use of these seemingly equivalent words trigger the same associations? What about 'pandemic flu' or 'Mexican flu'? Note down phrases or sentences that demonstrate any relevant differences you find.

From the perspective of health communication research, the media represent a vital link between health professionals, scientists and the larger public by enabling mass communication about matters of health and illness. In this highly complex process of knowledge popularisation, originally specialised claims by medical scientists are diffused into the public domain via print media articles. If we now come back to the multi-level model of communication outlined above, it becomes clear that this involves not only a mere *reformulation* of scientific claims, but in particular also a *recontextualisation* through adaption to different socio-cultural constraints, including the constraints of the media, e.g. those of the broadsheet or tabloid press in which they appear (Calsamiglia and Van Dijk, 2004).

The media's role as a source of up-to-date information about an often remote event is particularly important due to the potential to influence public perception of the severity of the risk. Earlier risk communication research was predominantly based on the psychometric paradigm of risk pioneered by Paul Slovic and his colleagues in the late 1970s (Slovic *et al.*, 1979). In contrast to the individual perceptions of risk, which were the focus of this psychometric paradigm, more recent approaches have started to explore the social and cultural environment in which risk perceptions are formed. That is, rather than attempting to calculate the likelihood of an adverse event, present studies are also exploring how risks are explained and communicated in particular ways, as well as how they become interpreted and integrated into the public mind. In this field, scholars have reflected upon the ways in which social and individual processes work to amplify or attenuate the sense of risk. Here the Social Amplification of Risk Framework is drawn upon as a model that addresses both the perception and communication of risk and accounts for the role of channels, risk signals and the culture of social institutions (Kasperson *et al.*, 2003:13).

Several studies have already explored a number of ways in which journalists can position their texts in order to conceptualise the possibility of certain risks, for example, a construction of a link between MMR vaccines, inflammatory bowel disorder, and autism (Rundblad *et al.*, 2006). In another applied linguistic study of risk, Wallis *et al.* (2005) examined the framing of severe acute respiratory syndrome (SARS) as a 'killer', and Washer and Joffe (2006) describe how social representations of methicillin-resistant Staphylococcus aureus (MRSA) in newspapers link it to issues of the management of hospitals and the erosion of authority and morality. In a similar vein, earlier studies into AIDS have shown that communication about disease and action are closely linked via metaphors, images and narratives.

The above studies draw attention to the fact that the different ways in which society defines and categorises disease, as well as the ways and mechanisms of attributing different causes to ill health, can influence societal responses to risk and health problems. According to this view of risk as an inherently social and communicative phenomenon, 'non-compliant' individuals may be subject to stigma

(Brown *et al.*, 2009), and certain actions and processes may be viewed as preferable because they are in line with dominant cultural models. Research by Nathanson (1999) on the anti-tobacco movement, for example, identifies the following key dimensions of framing public health risks that have the potential to influence policy responses: whether the health risk is presented as 'acquired deliberately or involuntarily (and the victim correspondingly as culpable or innocent)'; whether it is portrayed as 'universal (putting us all at risk) or as particular (only putting *them* at risk)'; and whether the risk is constructed as 'arising from within the individual or from the environment' (1999: 430-441).

Metaphors and framing

As the issues around risk and uncertainty are particularly problematic notions to convey, lexical devices used in print media articles to formulate risks as well as define and describe diseases demand a careful study by linguists and sociologists. One of the main semantic means of establishing links between two domains of experience and in this way providing explanation is metaphor, and it is therefore not surprising that it plays a central role as a recontextualisation device. The research interest in metaphor illustrates the broader impact of the 'linguistic turn' (which we discussed in Chapter 1) and the emergence of 'cognitive linguistics' (Lakoff and Johnson, 1980) outside the health communication field. Metaphor is defined as 'understanding and experiencing one kind of thing in terms of another' (Lakoff and Johnson, 1980: 5). As a cognitive phenomenon realised in language through metaphoric expressions, metaphor involves a *mapping* of semantic features from a source to a target domain. For example, all of the following individual linguistic expressions – *our relationship has hit a dead-end street, we are at a cross-roads* and *we may have to go our separate ways* – are based on the conceptual mapping LOVE IS A JOURNEY where the love relationship is regarded as travelling through space (Lakoff, 1993). In this way, the source domain, a journey, is *mapped* on to the target domain, the love affair. It is a convention of cognitive linguistics to use small capital letters for the statement of conceptual metaphor and italics for metaphorical linguistic expressions.

As metaphors always highlight certain aspects of a phenomenon while other aspects remain obscured, metaphor analysis aims to explore the reasons behind the choice of certain metaphors and seeks to clarify our shared assumptions. Consider some of the metaphors traditionally used in medicine – seeing the body as a machine, for example. Some assumptions stemming from this popular view have played an important role in the practice and public understanding of medicine – such as seeing the heart as a pump. The danger of this widespread mechanistic approach, however, is that by using machine metaphors medical professionals can imbue the body, and with it the patients, with other machine-like qualities and attributes. This in turn renders patients passive, inanimate and de-individualised, and above all 'fixable', and can therefore lead to an automatic preference for engineered solutions to ill health (Hodgkin, 1985). Furthermore, as health policy analysts Evans and Stoddart (1990) warn, such a mechanical view of medicine results in an equally mechanical notion of healthcare policy that prioritises observable and measurable interventions (such as new drugs) instead of attending to 'a wider range of relationships among determinants of health' (1990: 1349) such as class, and levels of education and income.

Military metaphors are another prominent example of how metaphoric expressions can play a ubiquitous, but often unrecognised role in popular and policy discourses. The metaphor 'MEDICINE IS WAR' where doctors 'fight the battle' with diseases may lead to assumptions that taking action is a justification in itself. Doctors and diseases become the main protagonists in this metaphorical scenario, where technologies are weapons and medical authority cannot be questioned. In the realm of public policy, such military thinking places the emphasis 'on the physical, sees control as central, and encourages the expenditure of massive resources to achieve dominance' (Annas, 1995: 746).

Such studies highlight the fact that metaphors can be not just representational, but performative (Nerlich and Halliday, 2007), that is leading to a certain course of action (Searle, 1969). This is in line with a well quoted statement from the media theorist Robert Entman, who suggests that frames (realised through the use of metaphorical expressions) can simultaneously define a problem, diagnose causes, make moral judgements, as well as invite a certain course of action by providing implicit or explicit solutions (Entman, 1993). In their role as 'framing devices', metaphors can therefore be used rhetorically by different social actors to shape visions of the past and/or the future and in this way affect our socio-political actions in the present (Wallis et al., 2005).

This was the case with the foot and mouth outbreak in the UK in 2001, when the use of militaristic and plague metaphors dominated media coverage. Consider the following examples of media reporting on the outbreak in Cumbria:

THERE was less sign of smoking pyres in Cumbria yesterday as the battle against foot-and-mouth continues. [...] Nick Utting, the area group secretary with the NFU, was at yesterday's daily briefing in Carlisle. He said: "It's war, and that's precisely what we have with the military out there fighting to try to get on top of this disease.

They are having to use military tactics. All round them they have farmers who have lost their stock and others who are trying to survive this terrible plague." (The Scotsman, April 13, 2001)

The killing continues as the UK total of confirmed cases of foot-and-mouth disease steadily climbs towards four figures. However, at yesterday's regular briefing held by the National Farmers' Union of Scotland at Ingliston, the union's president, Jim Walker, once again expressed some highly cautious hopes that in Dumfries and Galloway the plague is close to coming under control. (The Herald (Glasgow), April 3, 2001)

"Look, Britain is being badly damaged by this foot-and-mouth disease. The Americans think we are a plague ship and tourism is being crucified. Holding a general election will demonstrate to the world than Britain is open for business." That argument still carries weight. (The Sunday Herald, April 1, 2001)

Here the use of war (for example, 'the battle against foot-and-mouth', 'it's war') and plague ('survive this terrible plague', 'a plague ship') metaphors framed the issue in such a way as to make the slaughter policy seem inevitable and entirely justifiable. As a result, the millions of animals that were killed in this metaphorical battle against an invisible enemy were not really seen as victims but as a necessary sacrifice. Moreover, it became possible to overlook the fact that only a small fraction of them were actually infected with this animal disease virus that poses no risks to human health (DEFRA, 2011). As Nerlich *et al* (2002) observe:

In the UK, by framing the handling of FMD as a battle against an evil virus, as a struggle against a deadly plague, and as combat against dark and evil forces, the media found occasion to write stories that people wanted to read and provided the government with a framework that allowed them to ask the nation to pull together to fight a common enemy. The metaphors, images and associations spun by the media in its reporting on FMD thus tapped into a wider network of social and cultural representations and of collective myths and beliefs that eventually buttressed the government's policy decisions.

(Nerlich *et al.,* 2002)

In this instance, as the authors point out, scientists, policy makers and journalists all resorted to culturally available and widely used metaphors to conceptualise policy responses to this crisis, without initially reflecting on the wider implications their lexical choices might have – that is, what came to be seen by many as a needless slaughter of millions of animals.

Another way of exploring how risk is communicated in the media is to study how the experts such as scientists and public health authority figures, rather than diseases, are represented and quoted. Whereas scientific publications rarely use verbatim quotations, media texts often provide quotes from various experts, and use a number of strategies to do so. One of the main aims of such frequent referencing can be interpreted as the intention to signal authority (Rundblad *et al.*, 2006). Source quotes may suggest to the readers that the reporter has access to important information and that the information presented is believable (and the reporter in turn is trustworthy). Furthermore, direct verbatim quotations may be perceived as more authentic than paraphrasing or indirect quoting (ibid.). Previous studies have shown that scientists can be quoted in a way which induces moderation rather than fear (Lewison, 2008), whereas in other cases, as we will explore in the next section, scientists' warnings about health risks can be intentionally or unintentionally amplified through frequent citation in the media. Nerlich and Halliday (2007) therefore call for linguistic analyses of how metaphors and other rhetorical devices are used not only by the journalists but also by the experts when conveying health risks to the public in crisis situations. Such studies may be aimed at identifying which rhetorical devices are employed to create early warnings and how their repeated use might have unintentional consequences such as cynicism and dismissal of the necessity of preventative measures.

In this section, we have discussed that metaphors as framing devices can have a considerable discursive power. Hence we must be aware of the importance of framing in public debates. As Nerlich *et al.* (2002) maintain, 'the more successful the metaphor, the more peoples' thinking becomes entrenched, and the harder it becomes to change direction. There is no good way out of this – except by careful choice of the first metaphor to be used.' In the next section, we will study in more detail how the use of both metaphors and 'risk signals' (Kasperson *et al.*, 2003), which include what linguists call 'pragmatic markers', can have direct implications for public action and the allocation of resources during infectious disease outbreaks. This problem is particularly acute in the case of outbreaks of novel or emerging infectious diseases where the strategic deployment of framing devices may serve to create what Nerlich and Halliday (2007) describe as a 'rhetoric of fear'. Although such rhetoric may have benign intentions behind it, such as to emphasise the need for a timely and appropriate course of action, the ambiguity inherent in metaphorical framing can contribute to the sense of uncertainty and confusion – which in turn are major obstacles for effective public health communication.

Task 5.1 Metaphors in avian flu reporting

The statements quoted below appeared in UK print media articles during the outbreak of avian flu in 2005. Try to identify the metaphoric expressions realised linguistically in these texts and then establish the conceptual mapping on which they are based. You may want to start by identifying the contextual meanings of words and then check whether these can be contrasted with a more basic sense of that same word. If the contrast can be resolved by comparison, the word is used metaphorically (see Pragglejaz, 2007 for detailed instructions on metaphor identification). Can you tell if the statement belongs to a public health expert, scientist or journalist? (The answer is provided later in this chapter.) Discuss the potential of these metaphorical framings to shape perceptions as well as the implications they may have for outbreak management.

> This virus is likely to be far more lethal. At least half those infected could die. It could strike anytime but I think it is probable it will come here sooner rather than later. All it needs is one carrier getting off a jumbo jet and then it is away in the general population. (*The Express*, 4 March 2005)

> I have put avian flu at the top of my list of world threats – this is the biggest threat to the human race. It far outweighs bio-terrorism, this is natural bio-terrorism. It won't spare anybody. (*The Express*, 4 March 2005)

> Forget al-Qaeda, the biggest terrorist threat we face today is Mother Nature ... (*The Guardian*, 20 March 2005)

> The virus, when it breaks into the human community, will go on and on until it finds the last person not infected. (The Express, 27 October, 2005)

Linguistic tools for interrogating print media reporting on health and illness

This section introduces the linguistic analysis of framing devices that can be drawn upon in the study of health and illness reporting. We will examine how analysis of metaphors and pragmatic markers can be used to expose definitions of problems and solutions (as well as assumptions) that underlie their use in print media reporting on infectious disease outbreaks.

In what follows we

- introduce the concepts of 'discourse metaphor' and 'pragmatic marker' drawn from the applied linguistic research as ways of studying framing devices;

- look at how different framing devices are exploited in media articles reporting the bird flu outbreak in 2005;
- discuss the perfomative role of expressions and consider the implications for risk communication.

Applied linguists are well equipped to make a valuable contribution to studies of disease and representation that involve analysis of media texts. As the sociologist Clive Seale notes in his review of media articles on health and illness, such textual analyses may 'investigate the formal properties of media messages as linguistic, narrative or semiotic systems' (2003: 515). As part of an overall discourse analytic framework, linguistic methods can also be called upon to uncover ideological biases, or establish how particular themes and constructions have come to dominate the coverage, as well as reveal how certain messages and metaphors can promote or impede communicative efforts to enhance health or prevent ill health. In this section we will explore in more detail the last point, namely the application of linguistic techniques to provide an in-depth analysis of how particular lexical choices may influence health communication efforts by prompting readers to conceptualise the possibility of a certain risk.

While discourse analysts explore social interactions and representations through the analysis of language in its widest sense, including non-verbal symbols and images, here we narrow our attention to words and word combinations that, depending on the context, can prompt certain attitudes and courses of action[1]. This is in line with the well-known postulate of Critical Discourse Analysis scholars that our words are never neutral (see discussion later in this chapter). The words we use in our everyday interactions convey how we see ourselves and others, our professional standing, values and beliefs. Consequently, choice of language and context of communi-cation can be said to contribute to the way people think about issues. This has important consequences from the perspective of public health communication, as even one word can convey a strong meaning through its connotations and underlying assumptions, and in this way can potentially influence public reactions to the risk message.

The variability in our interpretation of words is due to the fact that meanings are often assigned on the basis of the cultural knowledge of the participants rather than coming from the standardised definitions registered in the dictionaries (these dictionary-recorded meanings are variously referred to as denotational, literal, basic or 'context-free,

---

1   Whether the use of such words then directly leads to the social amplification or attenuation of risk as studied by social psychologists is another matter which we cannot address in such linguistic analysis.

semantic meaning' (Gibbs, 2002: 475) in the linguistic literature). Connotations associated with one word, or meanings arising from word combinations, metaphors and other figures of speech, can signal the genre where the word is used, as well as its evaluative polarity. As an example, consider the different associations stemming from the use of the terms 'H5N1' and 'bird flu' to refer to the same virus. Although they can be used synonymously in certain contexts, the terms also signal different registers (scientific versus popular/journalistic) to the reader. Furthermore, a personification of this virus with the help of the metaphoric expression 'killer flu' in tabloids, for example, presents us with an altogether different version of a story, where flu is represented as an active and malevolent agent that preys on its 'victims' (Larson *et al.*, 2005).

Earlier in this chapter we briefly explored how, through underlying values and assumptions, the metaphoric use may serve to emphasise certain policy positions. In doing this, we reasoned, metaphoric expressions can 'frame' a narrative. From this perspective, framing refers to the way a story is told – its selective use of particular symbols and metaphors, for example – and to the way these cues, in turn, trigger the shared cultural schemas that people use to make sense of their world (Goffman, 1959). The identification and analysis of frames, however, is a difficult issue that has attracted a lot of discussion in media studies (Van Gorp, 2007). Here we will not get involved in this debate and instead consider how applied linguists can contribute to the identification and analysis of framing devices on the level of lexis, such as words used figuratively and pragmatic markers. Such an analysis can be used to explore how discourses are realised linguistically in the text, and in this way contribute to a sociological enquiry by delineating different discourses and lines of argument. (As mentioned earlier, however, in discourse and sociological analysis the study of framing devices is not limited to the domain of lexis and can include visuals, or sound tracks that have the potential to trigger an existing idea.)

Metaphors are among the most frequently used framing devices that offer opportunities for an in-depth study of texts dealing with issues of health and illness. A body of work is focussed upon *discourse metaphors* – defined as 'relatively stable metaphorical mappings that function as a key framing device within a particular discourse over a certain period of time' (Zinken *et al.*, 2008). Nerlich and Halliday's (2007) work on avian flu, for example, examines how the discourse metaphors from the domains of *war, journey,* and *house* were used as major framing devices in media articles covering the outbreak in 2005. Their analysis shows how the metaphorical mapping DISEASE IS A WAR/INVASION and TRYING TO CONTROL DISEASE IS WAR worked to construct disease as an attack by foreign bodies that have to be destroyed, as well as how such discourse metaphors as THE SPREAD OF

A VIRUS IS A JOURNEY and THE APPEARANCE OF A VIRUS IS AN INVASION became activated in the context of viral spread and viral infection.

Before we proceed to analysing the framing role of metaphors in sample texts, however, it is necessary to consider non-metaphorical lexis that co-occurs with metaphors in media reports. Such lexical devices are often used with the intention of keeping the readers' interest alive by dramatising events. Here it is useful to pay attention to the pragmatic rather than semantic aspect of meaning, as the field of pragmatics deals with the meaning or force of utterances used in situation. From a pragmatic point of view, utterances can be analysed on three levels (Austin 1962): locutionary act (what utterances say, their ostensible meaning), illocutionary act (what utterances do – perform), and perlocutionary act (what utterances achieve, such as persuading, convincing, or scaring; in other words, getting someone to do or realise something, whether intended or not). As Nerlich and Halliday (2007: 49) explain, the sentence 'This dog is dangerous', gives us the information that this dog is dangerous, but at the same time it can 'have the illocutionary force of warning someone about this particular dog' (as can be put more explicitly in the expression 'I hereby warn you that this dog is dangerous'). Consequently, this utterance also can have the perlocutionary effect of frightening or alarming the person to whom it is addressed.

On the pragmatic level, single words and phrases used alongside metaphors can intensify a rhetorical effect, and therefore can be seen as part of what some social amplification of risk theorists, such as Kasperson *et al.* (2003), might call 'risk signals'. Specifically, as we will explore below, such pragmatic markers can intensify the 'rhetoric of fear' when the media frames a novel danger with the help of traditional militaristic metaphors. The use of the illocutionary force markers, as in 'scientists *warn* that…', or such verbs as 'alarm' and 'frighten' can also help us analyse how different (and often negative) expectations are created in the process of the recontextualisation of scientific knowledge by the media. For example, scientists can issue direct and/or indirect warnings through the media early in the outbreak expecting their audience to take appropriate action – in this case, to intensify national or international outbreak preparedness efforts. From this perspective, an infectious disease outbreak involves not only a communication about a threat but also an opportunity for the authorities to mobilise resources for a co-ordinated response (Nerlich and Halliday, 2007).

Let us now apply the analyses of lexis discussed above to three excerpts from UK media articles in order explore further how the use of metaphors and pragmatic markers can weave the journalists' and experts' voices together, draw attention to certain actions over others, and potentially contribute to the social amplification of risk. The article excerpts come from *The Independent* and *Daily Star* and were published in the second half of 2005 – a period of great speculation in the newspapers about the consequences of the bird flu outbreaks in Hong Kong and later in Eastern Europe. The common name 'bird flu' refers to an emerging and highly pathogenic influenza H5N1 virus that has a potential to cause a pandemic.

Although avian flu is one of a series of infectious diseases such as AIDS, BSE, FMD and SARS, back in 2005 it was still a relatively unknown and remote illness about which the UK media could not easily write human-interest stories. Following the research agenda outlined by Nerlich and Halliday (2007), we want to explore the following questions as part of this linguistic contribution to the sociological study of media reporting: Which rhetorical devices were used and by whom – biomedical experts or journalists? What they were used for – to inform/explain, to warn, to blame etc., and, in this process, to mobilise what kind of action?

1. BIRD FLU: IS IT THE NEW BSE? Last week we broke the news that bird flu could soon arrive in Britain. (*The Independent on Sunday*, 28 August 2005)

> [...] Back in January, Professor John Oxford, one of the world's leading authorities on flu, likened it to 'a tsunami rushing towards us'. Another, Professor Michael Osterholm of the University of Minnesota, a key US government bioterrorism adviser, added: 'I cannot think of any other risk, terrorism or Mother Nature included, that could potentially pose any greater risk to society than this.' [...] One of the country's top experts, Professor Hugh Pennington, president of the Society for General Microbiology, is even more pessimistic: he told The Independent on Sunday in March that up to two million Britons could perish. Small wonder that Lee Jong-wook, the director-general of the World Health Organisation, has called this 'the most serious health threat facing the world'. His top experts have warned that 'we are closer to the next flu pandemic than we ever were', and that it is now 'knocking at our door'. [...] Smaller, much less serious, pandemics struck in 1957 and 1968.
> (Full text can be accessed via *The Independent* newspaper website: http://www.independent.co.uk/news/science/focus-bird-flu-is-it-the-new-bse-504547.html)

2. JABS FOR ALL IN BIRD FLU PANIC; EXPERTS WARN OF EPIDEMIC AS DISEASE HITS EUROPE (*Daily Star*, 14 October 2005)

> Every EU citizen should be given a jab to prevent an epidemic of deadly bird flu, health chiefs warned last night. EU Health

Commissioner Markos Kyprianou's call came after the disease reached Europe from Asia. Kyprianou, 45, said all 458 million people should be considered for jabs as scientists confirmed the deadly H5N1 strain of the virus had been found in Turkey. The H5N1 has already killed 60 people in Asia and experts fear it could mutate into a virus which spreads easily among humans, possibly killing millions. Experts warn as many as 500,000 Brits could be wiped out. They say it is inevitable bird flu will arrive in Britain "within weeks" through migrating geese.

(Full text is available via the Daily star archive
http://www.ukpressonline.co.uk)

3. BIRD FLU TREATMENT STOCKPILED BY GOVERNMENT MAY BE INEFFECTIVE (*The Independent*, 22 December 2005)

[...] The New England Journal of Medicine, which publishes the findings today, describes them as frightening. Governments around the world, including the UK, are stockpiling Tamiflu to be used as the first line of defence against a flu pandemic. [...] Yesterday, Sir John Skehel, director of the National Institute for Medical Research in London, and one of the world's leading virologists, said: 'The fear is that all the virus that comes here might be resistant.'

(Full text can be accessed via *The Independent* newspaper website:
http://www.independent.co.uk)

The above texts contain a number of direct and indirect quotes of scientists and public health authorities. Whereas direct quotes provide a high degree of explicitness and similarity to the source, in the case of indirect reported speech a receiver has no guarantee that the writer is using the actual wording of the reported text (Rundblad *et al.*, 2006). In the examples below, we can see several framing devices used by the journalists to introduce both the direct and indirect quotes.

Small wonder that Lee Jong-wook, the director-general of the World Health Organisation, has called this 'the most serious health threat facing the world'. His top experts have **warned** that 'we are closer to the next flu pandemic than we ever were', and that it is now 'knocking at our door'.

[...] and experts **fear** it could mutate into a virus which spreads easily among humans, possibly killing millions. Experts **warn** as many as 500,000 Brits could be wiped out.

Instead of using the verbs such as 'say' or 'state' for example, the writers opted for the pragmatic markers 'warn' and 'fear'. Together with such verbs as 'threaten', 'alarm' and 'frighten' further down in the excerpts such phrasings are used to signal concern and in this way to introduce a sense of urgency.

The direct quotations also allow us to see that pragmatic markers are used not only by the journalists but also by the experts themselves. The last excerpt, for example, cites 'one of the world's leading virologists' as saying 'The **fear** is that all the virus that comes here might be resistant.' In text 3 another pragmatic marker is used in a less direct attribution: 'The New England Journal of Medicine, which publishes the findings today, describes them as **frightening**'. Moreover, the experts do not shy away from what Nerlich and Halliday (2007) call 'scare statistics', that is using numerical statements to refer to mortality rates from previous flu outbreaks, for example, or to predict a future number of fatal cases, as in this sentence: 'Professor Hugh Pennington, president of the Society for General Microbiology, is even more pessimistic: he told *The Independent on Sunday* in March that **up to two million Britons** could perish'. The use of such statistical quotes can be interpreted as a further attempt to signal authority, in addition to the references to scientific experts per se. As Rundblad *et al.* (2006: 76) note:

> In a culture that incorporates specialized epistemic communities using numerical manipulation, the larger non-specialized population that gives credence to such communities may, without necessarily sharing its knowledge or methods, deploy limited or superficial numerical expressions, either (i) for limited numerical processing or (ii) for their connotations of authority.

It is time to take a closer look at the metaphors used in the above texts, asking the same questions: whether they have originated from public or scientific imagination, and what function they were intended to perform. Personification of the bird flu virus seems to be one of the most prominent metaphorical devices employed in the above media articles. In the first excerpt from *The Independent*, the linguistic expression 'knocking at our door', attributed to the WHO experts, refers to the personification based on conceptual mapping VIRUS IS A TRAVELLER, and the underlying metaphor of JOURNEY. According to the second text, some (unidentified) 'experts' are reported as saying that 'it is inevitable bird flu will **arrive** in Britain "within weeks"'. In the third text, the director of the National Institute for Medical Research is using the same journey metaphor to refer to the virus as an active agent: 'The fear is that all the virus that **comes** here might be resistant.'

Echoing the findings of studies examining earlier FMD and SARS outbreaks, in our texts the bird flu virus is also metaphorised as an enemy that can be human. Personification is frequent in reporting on infectious diseases and often serves as the basis of more elaborated metaphors using war-related terms such as armies, weapons, and battlefields as source domains (Larson *et al.*, 2005). It enables the conceptualisation of the virus as an adversary, and gives agency to the disease:

[…] if it is vicious enough it can **kill** tens of millions

[…] stockpiling Tamiflu to be used as the first **line of defence** against a flu pandemic

[…] when a great pandemic **carried off** 50 million people.

The texts also compare the bird flu virus to a natural force – and such a comparison again stems from the scientists' quotes. According to the opening of *The Independent* article, for example: 'Back in January, Professor John Oxford, one of the world's leading authorities on flu, likened it to 'a **tsunami** rushing towards us'. Here the virus is metaphorised as a powerful natural force in order to create a hyperbolic account of a situation and intensify readers' interpretations and possibly increase preparedness actions. Later on, we have a more novel comparison of an emerging disease virus to terrorism: 'Professor Michael Osterholm of the University of Minnesota, a key US government bioterrorism adviser, added: 'I cannot think of any other risk, terrorism or Mother Nature included, that could potentially pose any greater risk to society than this.' The reference to terrorism is related to an earlier statement by the leading British scientist Hugh Pennington who also made this link, when he stated in 2005 that avian flu 'is the biggest threat to the human race' and it 'far outweighs bioterrorism; this is natural terrorism' (*Daily Express*, 4 March 2005).

So what rhetorical advantages and disadvantages do these framing devices have in persuading audiences to act? On the one hand, the emotive lexis used along with militaristic metaphors can be a useful tool in media discourses where reporters and commentators search for novel and dramatic ways to sustain the readers' attention. Moreover, personification of viruses imbues them with agency, and this can then serve to justify a militaristic response by those who are engaged in the metaphorical fight with the enemy (Larson *et al.*, 2005). Similarly, the metaphor of terrorism invokes images of popular culture and in this way brings new dimensions to the virus commonly conceptualised in the media as an 'enemy' or 'invader'. The new contexts of use, however, can also amplify a message unintentionally, by triggering unforeseen associations. In the case of the bird flu virus, for example, the dramatisation with the help of the terrorism imaginary spawned various apocalyptic stories in subsequent media reports about how viruses can be 'weaponised' by terrorists (Furedi, 2010). At the same time, metaphors can also perform important structuring and explanatory roles. As a complex and abstract target domain, disease is often structured in our imagination through simpler concepts sourced from our everyday knowledge, such as war, journey, and natural forces, and emerging infectious diseases are not an exception in this regard.

On the other hand, however, the abundant use of war metaphors together with numerical quotes or 'scare statistics' can contribute to a fear-inducing effect, spawn accusations of sensationalism and fear-mongering, and as a result affect the relationships of trust that are so important in the emergency situations such as infectious disease outbreaks (Wallis *et al.*, 2005). In a single article excerpt from August 2005, for example, the readers learn that 'up to two million Britons could perish', one should 'prepare for up to 750,000 deaths in Britain' and that the virus could potentially 'kill tens of millions'. As mentioned earlier, some of these quotes come directly from scientific experts. This is accompanied by the use of such emotive lexis as *vicious* enough [pandemic], *deadly* bird flu, *bird flu panic* (headline) and references to historical events: 'That is what happened in 1918-19, when a great pandemic carried off 50 million people "including 250,000 in Britain" claiming more victims than the First World War'. Through the use of such statistics we can observe the strategy of linking current flu outbreaks to historic catastrophes, which can in turn contribute to a climate of fear. As Nerlich and Halliday point out, 'the shift of emphasis to past pandemics contributes to the rhetoric of fear by imbuing the as-yet minor flu outbreak with historical significance, which obscures the fact that the current strain of avian flu has, as yet, killed only a relatively small number of people who had direct contact with poultry' (2007: 2).

Overall, the analysis of the above excerpts has shown how warnings by scientists and public health authorities issued in scientific journals or interviews with journalists were recontextualised in the UK print media articles. In this process of recontextualisation, the illocutionary force of utterances was amplified in various ways. Whereas our example analysis is limited to three excerpts, a research project focussed on media framing of an event or phenomenon would explore a range of media reports published during a certain period to establish the frequencies with which selected words or expressions were used. The number of times such framing devices appear in media articles (through quotes or otherwise) is indicative of the potential amplification effects, as a repeated discursive citation or iteration can eventually alter perceptions of risk. In our analysis, informed by Nerlich and Halliday's work, a relatively moderate rhetoric of fear used by the scientists may have been enhanced through media articles that repeatedly covered the same topic and used emotive lexis and the rhetoric of blame to dramatise the story. At the same time, it is also clear that the UK print media cannot be blamed entirely for creating a climate of fear regarding a global influenza pandemic, at least as far as the coverage in the selected newspaper articles is concerned. Public health authorities and research communities turned out to be important actors in the construction of discourses about the disease.

According to Nerlich and Halliday (2007), the rhetoric of fear and blame created and circulated in such discourses can have profound consequences for the public understanding of science as well as for the policy-making process. Negative predictions and overstated expectations have direct implications in terms of allocation of resources such as vaccines and antivirals, and can lead to the distortion of policy priorities regarding human and animal health (ibid.). As the experience of the recent swine flu pandemic has shown, the UK government's decision to stockpile large quantities of swine flu vaccine came under scrutiny when it was revealed that 34 million of these jabs were left unused; and the government's chief medical officer had to defend accusations that he personally overreacted in his media interviews (Triggle, 2010). Finally, the use of sensationalist language has another, perhaps less immediately visible cost in terms of reputations, as accusations of hype can lead to the erosion of trust in authorities and the media.

Task 5.2 Framing devices in the reporting of swine flu

Practice identifying and analysing framing devices in media articles reporting on the 2009 swine flu pandemic. Select a newspaper of your choice and coverage period. Pay attention to metaphors referring to the disease itself, ways of transmission, and suggested solutions – measures of prevention and control. Who is quoted and how often? Can you identify militaristic metaphors? Are they used conventionally or in a new context? Which courses of actions and phenomena do these metaphors naturalise and what is marginalised?

Discourse and frame analysis of print media articles: theoretical underpinnings

Having explored the role of different linguistic frameworks in the study of journalistic texts earlier in this chapter, it is now time to dig deeper into the theoretical underpinnings of metaphor analysis and its value as an applied linguistic tool for interrogating health and illness discourses in the print media.

Metaphor is a rapidly developing area of study for applied linguists, who according to Gerard Steen can add 'an interventionist dimension to the more fundamental research on metaphor pursued in linguistics, psycholinguistics, and sociolinguistics' (2010: 91). Below we explore the theoretical grounding for one example of such an interventionist approach concerned with a critical interrogation of the use of metaphors in health communication. From the methodological point of view, such an analysis is situated at the intersection of three different domains. The first is concerned with the analysis of discourse understood as social practice (Fairclough, 2003), and a related domain of social constructionism (Lupton, 1998). The second is frame analysis, frequently applied in the studies of media and political texts (Entman, 1993). The third is that of cognitive linguistics studies, where the Lakoffian perspective and more recent discourse-based approaches to metaphor can be situated. The combination of these perspectives enables an approach that aims to provide a comprehensive in-depth analysis of the role of metaphors in the health and illness discourses. Below we will briefly discuss each of them in turn.

Critical Discourse Analysis

The analysis of lexical items that give prominence to certain assumptions has a long history in linguistic research. Since the publication of the influential work of critical linguists in the 1970s, numerous studies have examined how language is used by people to achieve certain communicative purposes rather than as an abstract system. More recently, proponents of Critical Discourse Analysis/ CDA (see Chapter 1) again drew attention to the ways language use can contribute to creating not only a propositional, but also an ideological message (Fairclough, 2003). Analysis of such ideological traits requires understanding of language as a formal system, and text analysis is therefore central to such CDA studies. A detailed study of linguistic features is used as a basis for inferring and reconstructing the ideology behind the text. One of the central tasks of such critical analyses of language use is to reveal how institutions produce and reproduce implicit and explicit social norms. It is therefore not surprising that proponents of CDA have a long interest in the language of the media, due to the media's role as an arena where various definitions and redefinitions of public issues take place. From this perspective, the media is one of the primary vehicles or mechanisms through which members of society encounter and share metaphors and other cognitive structures.

This concept of discourse is linked to the broader constructivist view of social reality postulating that social texts do not merely reflect phenomena and processes pre-existing in the social and natural world, such as health risks; rather, they actively construct them (Lupton, 1998). The constructionist approach helps to explicate the concept of authority used in our analysis of media reports earlier in this chapter. When we view reality as socially constructed, the authority of the textual source becomes crucial, as people have to rely on sources when making judgements. Authority is related to the category of 'legitimation', a process of making something acceptable to a group or audience; for example, through the process of claiming scientific authority by borrowing from the technical register of scientific articles. Critical studies of social texts therefore explore how different ways of institutional legitimation, for example, doctors with respect to patients or scientific experts with respect to 'lay' audiences, operate in society; as well as focus on the manner in which the media reporting can work to legitimise individuals, groups, and institutions. According to CDA theorists, such as Teun Van Dijk (1988), such legitimation processes work through the systematisation of the dominant ideas and values by the elite due to their position of control on media. Crucially, the elite formulate not merely the priorities, arguments, and evaluation parameters concerning the dominant discourses, but also the frames through which they must be structured, comprehended and communicated.

Discourse analysis therefore shares many analytical features with frame analysis, commonly used to analyse the reciprocal relationship between the news media and society. Reviews of the use of the term 'frame' in theoretical literature (Ensink and Sauer, 2003) show that it is used with different meanings in different fields of research, ranging from cognitive grammar and interactional linguistics to anthropology, communication studies and sociology. Due to our focus on the media framing of health and illness issues in this book, it is useful to approach frames from the social constructionist perspective, as suggested in the sociological literature on framing. In this theoretical camp, frames are seen as organising principles that are socially shared and durable, and which operate symbolically to structure our world (Reese, 2003). This constructionist take on the framing process locates frames within the larger culture rather than conceptualising them as a matter of individual cognition (Van Gorp, 2007).

Discourse metaphors

The idea that frames are part of culture is particularly relevant for the discursive study of media representations of medical and epidemiological claims. As discussed earlier, such media represent-ations are *recontextualisations* of specialised knowledge, and in order to study how such knowledge is recreated in a different communicative situation, we need to pay attention to the detailed structures of text and talk. Here the notion of 'discourse metaphors' as framing devices comes to the fore. Whereas from the cognitive linguistic point of view, metaphors are primarily motivated by experience, the discourse-based approach emphasises that 'participants of discourses on topics of social life tend to incorporate new events by interpreting them metaphorically as some culturally salient phenomenon, and not via projection of knowledge schemata abstracted from universal aspects of body experience' (Zinken, 2003: 508). Consequently, this strand of work investigates metaphors both as cognitive *and* social devices embedded in shared cultural, political and discursive formations (Nerlich *et al.*, 2002; Zinken *et al.*, 2008).

Similarly, in this book we draw from the insights of cognitive linguistics on the theory of metaphor, but adopt a discourse-pragmatic approach, in that our objective has been to explore the motivations underlying the choices of different types of metaphors in health-related media texts and explore implications for public understanding. According to this pragmatic view of metaphor use in discourse, we must study not only the processes of mapping sources and targets, as is common in cognitive linguistics, but also ask under what conditions particular models and structures are employed. As Charteris-Black states, 'A complete theory of metaphor must also incorporate a pragmatic perspective that interprets metaphor choice with reference to the purposes of use within specific discourse contexts' (2004: 247).

Here metaphors are seen as persuasive and performative in the sense of providing scenarios for thinking and acting, and metaphor use as pragmatic and ideological. Such culturally adapted metaphor as, for example, A VIRUS IS A KILLER or A VIRUS IS A TRAVELLER can be intentionally used to appeal to a general audience as they convey rich cultural knowledge in the source domain and tap into emotions. In other words, it can be argued that metaphors used in media texts reporting on the developments in health and medicine do not only serve to clarify complex scientific and medical phenomena and processes by rendering unfamiliar domains more accessible, but also:

> ...convey certain beliefs about the nature and importance of science and technology, and their limits, impacts and applications. Although people interpret scientific information and ascribe meaning to metaphors according to their personal experience and previous knowledge, metaphors are powerfully persuasive tools.
>
> (Nelkin, 2001: 556)

As we have seen in the case of the war metaphors employed by scientists and public officials during the FMD outbreak, they were consciously employed for specific political and ideological purposes. As Larson *et al.* suggested (2005: 257), such 'classic war metaphor framing' acted to 'mobilize, justify solutions, and exculpate government from responsibility and gave a focus and mode of operation' to the management of the outbreak.

Task 5.3 Metaphor and frame analysis   (TC)

The following articles from UK national newspaper texts deal with the issue of wake-promoting drugs (1) 'When sleep can be a killer' *The Times*, 12 February 2002; (2) 'Hypersomnia', *The Times*, 8 September 2003; (3) 'Say goodbye to sleep', *The Sunday Times*, 12 March 2006. Whole texts can be accessed via the electronic databases Factiva (www.global.factiva.com), LexisNexis (www.lexisnexis.co.uk) or *The Times* website (www.thetimes.co.uk). Read the texts and try to establish what metaphors and other framing devices are used to structure the newspaper discourse on modafinil and similar drugs. The following questions may be of help:

• What words are used to describe the drugs and their cognitive effects? Are the lexical choices similar or different in each text?
• How is narcolepsy described?
• What is the evaluative orientation of each text excerpt where the drugs are mentioned? (For example, if there are metaphorical expressions, are they used in a positive or negative way?)

After you have identified possible framing devices, the next step will be to analyse the implications of their use in the particular political and historical context. For each example of framing you have selected, think about and discuss the following:

• Does this framing enable the body and the use of drugs to be constructed in specific ways?
• Does this framing enable the portrayal of modafinil use as legitimate or illicit?
• Is the framing used to justify pharmaceutical intervention at the individual and/or societal levels?

Summary

The above discussion of theoretical points together with metaphor analyses performed earlier in this chapter intended to demonstrate that the use of metaphors in media and public health discourses is a multifaceted phenomenon. Metaphorical expressions are commonly used in the process of recontextualisation that accompanies any attempt to popularise specialised knowledge via newspaper discourse. Metaphors are rarely used alone but rather operate in chains to create coherence both on the level of the individual text and on broader intertextual level (Koteyko *et al.*, 2008; Koller, 2003). As a result, usually more than one metaphor is needed to represent medical knowledge, convey a sense of urgency, and structure a coherent argument when messages about health are communicated through the mass media channels. In this process, metaphors are employed to perform a range of discursive functions, such as explanation, creating and maintaining coherence, as well as deductive and persuasive functions. Some novel, colourful and culturally rich metaphors are well suited as attention-drawing devices in headlines, whereas others may be primarily used for their heuristic utility as explanatory shortcuts. By examining and critically evaluating these roles of metaphors, we can achieve a better understanding of the ways health and illness discourses circulating in society are formulated and (re-) constructed, as well as how they operate rhetorically. Such understanding is a prerequisite for devising effective public health communication strategies.

6 The patient information leaflet

Problems of interpretation: introducing the patient information leaflet

In the previous chapter we examined the role that the media plays in disseminating matters about health and illness to the public. Crucially, what we aimed to show was that, through the exercise of a range of linguistic and rhetorical devices, such information is never straightforwardly, transparently released into the public domain: it will inevitably undergo a transformation which simplifies and/or exaggerates it, making it, in a word, fit for popular digestion. Another ubiquitous source of health advice and information is that articulated in patient information leaflets, specifically the instructions that accompany both over-the-counter and prescription medication. Unlike media texts, which encode and reflect certain political biases and perspectives, patient information leaflets are functional texts designed to convey procedural information as directly and accurately as possible in order to help people make informed decisions about healthcare (Wright, 1999a: 85). However, as we shall shortly see, even healthcare documentation that purports to directly convey accurate procedural information may well be liable to communicate, even if extremely obliquely, more than what is seemingly articulated at face-value.

Patients, it goes without saying, are entitled to high quality information about their medications, and leaflets or packaging inserts are likely to be the only informational resource available to them when taking their medication (Raynor *et al.,* 2004). Consequently the information communicated in these texts needs to be accurate and accessible, as conducive to unimpeded comprehension as possible. Poorly constructed documentation, leaflets which are misleading or otherwise difficult for non-specialist readers to process, might result in harmful outcomes (Hirsh *et al.,* 2009). Conversely, documentation that is informative, accessible and straightforward to navigate can result in a clearer understanding of personal treatment regimens and extend the care provided by health practitioners (Clerehan *et al.,* 2009). Since effective communication in written documentation depends on messages being 'successfully and completely transferred' from writer to reader (Albert and Chadwick, 1992: 1266), with writers having to be precisely aware of how readers process and interpret printed information (Wright, 1999a: 85), we will consider the role of both text producers and consumers, examining some of the problems that writers and readers respectively face in the construction and comprehension of printed instructions.

In order to highlight some of the issues that face readers (and writers) of patient information texts, let us first consider a common type of text that accompanies everyday medication, namely the instructions for use printed on a bottle of aspirin. The following set of instructions is reproduced from Gee (1999), who argues that the text can be interpreted by readers in more ways than one.

> WARNINGS: *Children and teenagers should not use this medicine for chicken pox or flu symptoms before a doctor is consulted about Reye Syndrome, a rare but serious illness reported to be associated with aspirin.* Keep this and all drugs out of the reach of children. In case of accidental overdose, seek professional assistance or contact a poison control centre immediately. As with any drug, if you are pregnant or nursing a baby, seek the advice of a health professional before using this product. IT IS ESPECIALLY IMPORTANT NOT TO USE ASPIRIN DURING THE LAST 3 MONTHS OF PREGNANCY UNLESS SPECIFICALLY DIRECTED TO DO SO BY A DOCTOR BECAUSE IT MAY CAUSE PROBLEMS IN THE UNBORN CHILD OR COMPLICATIONS DURING DELIVERY. See carton for arthritis use and Important Notice.
>
> (Gee, 1999: 24)

As was mentioned at the beginning of this chapter, we would expect there to be little, if any, ambiguity or potential for multiple, competing readings in written information for patients and consumers, and indeed the above set of instructions looks unremarkable in this regard. However, close scrutiny of the text reveals that more is actually taking place besides the function of directing people how to use the medicine. The text appears to be heteroglossic, that is, it contains more than one voice or perspective. The information it presents, according to Gee (1999: 24), can be read in two ways, there being two interleaving 'who-doing-whats' in the text. The first voice or 'who-doing-what' is discernible in the following sentences:

> WARNINGS: *Children and teenagers should not use this medicine for chicken pox or flu symptoms before a doctor is consulted about Reye Syndrome, a rare but serious illness reported to be associated with aspirin* [...] IT IS ESPECIALLY IMPORTANT NOT TO USE ASPIRIN DURING THE LAST 3 MONTHS OF PREGNANCY

UNLESS SPECIFICALLY DIRECTED TO DO SO BY A DOCTOR BECAUSE IT MAY CAUSE PROBLEMS IN THE UNBORN CHILD OR COMPLICATIONS DURING DELIVERY.

As Gee points out, entities are referred to specifically, for example: '*this medicine*', '*chicken pox*', '*flu*', '*Reye Syndrome*', '*aspirin*', 'LAST 3 MONTHS', 'UNBORN CHILD', 'DELIVERY'. Medical staff are also referred to directly: doctors are labelled as 'doctors' and issues are highlighted by the use of capitals and italics: '*should not*', '*a rare but serious illness*', 'ESPECIALLY IMPORTANT', 'SPECIFICALLY DIRECTED'.

The second voice, or 'who-doing-what', is evident in the following sentences, which are interleaved with the sentences considered above:

Keep this and all drugs out of the reach of children. In case of accidental overdose, seek professional assistance or contact a poison control centre immediately. As with any drug, if you are pregnant or nursing a baby, seek the advice of a health professional before using this product.

In these non-italicised and capitalised sentences, items are depicted less specifically. For example, entities are referred to in rather general terms: 'this and all drugs', 'any drug' and 'this product' instead of the more specific '*this medication*' and '*aspirin*'; 'children' in place of '*children and teenagers*'; 'pregnant' rather than 'LAST 3 MONTHS OF PREGNANCY'. Further, doctors are not referred to as 'doctors' but more broadly as 'health professional[s]', while issues concerning the storage and use of the drug are treated with less urgent emphasis (with the exception of the single occurrence of the word 'immediately'): 'keep out of reach', 'accidental overdose', 'seek…assistance,' and 'seek advice' instead of the more strident '*should not*' and 'ESPECIALLY IMPORTANT NOT TO USE'.

Gee is right in his claim that these two voices 'feel' different. This difference is manifest in their carrying different weights of authority. The voices appear to serve different purposes, resulting in different effects. The first, more specific, more emphatic voice, 'speaks with a lawyerly voice responding to specific court cases; the second speaks with the official voice of a caring, but authoritatively knowledgeable company trying to avoid anyone thinking that aspirin in particular is a potentially harmful drug' (1999: 24-5).

The point is that, to some extent, one voice seemingly contradicts the other: the urgent caution articulated by the first is downplayed, perhaps even undermined, by the more relaxed and reassuring tone of its counterpart. Why is this? Well, according to Gee, the aspirin text reflects the 'history that has given rise to it'. The urgent tone of the first voice, the more emphatic 'who-doing-what', is in all likelihood a consequence of the company's (or other pharmaceutical company's) being sued over conditions such as Reye Syndrome and has thus been added to 'the more general and avuncular voice' (1999: 25).

For readers who both discern and fail to apprehend the subtle interplay of these voices, the apparent tension and contradiction in the aspirin text might ultimately not be too much of an issue. However, the presence of the two 'who-doing-whats' nevertheless confronts readers with potential problems of understanding and interpretation. The interplay of voices means that some readers might overlook the fact that they are being spoken to and addressed from two distinct positions. This, of course, might not be unduly troublesome in itself, but for readers obsessively alert to the finer shades of meaning, their responses to the text might undermine the import of the information the drug manufacturers are seeking to convey. For example, readers with knowledge of medical history might be particularly prone to misinterpretation, believing that the information has been communicated only to protect the drug manufacturer from any legal liability, that the information contained in the document is not relevant to them and their particular circumstances (Wright, 1999a: 91). What this illustrates is that in written health information materials, readers' inferences about writers' communicative purposes are a powerful determinant of whether written advice and instructions will be followed or not (ibid.).

Task 6.1 Reading household drug information

Examine the instructions of a common household drug such as aspirin or paracetamol. As with the aspirin text we have just considered, do you notice any potential conflicts of interest concerning the information provided?

Communicating side effects and frequency details (or the side effects of side effects information)

This example of the heteroglossic aspirin text demonstrates the difficulty that health providers have in presenting unambiguous information to consumers and patients and ensuring that readers will not misinterpret the information contained therein. Patient information leaflets are mandatory for all medicines (Raynor et al., 2004) and need to make patients aware of a number of details concerning the use of medications, including, eligibility criteria, directions for using the drug, and warnings concerning possible misuse or side effects (Wright, 1999a: 87). Given the range of these interleaving communicative functions, in particular the somewhat paradoxical activity of warning yet at the same time reassuring patients, the problem is likely to be even more acute when it comes to the matter of articulating side effects, since, for some readers, the mention of side effects will conjure unnecessary concern. This is borne out by research into the composition of, and reader responses to, healthcare materials, which has repeatedly documented the complex and ambiguous nature of side effects information (Albert and Chadwick, 1992).

According to Pander Maat and Klaassen (1994: 390), two kinds of problems are associated with conveying details of side effects. The first problem relates to patients being unduly worried: presenting side effects details might frighten patients to the extent that they do not take the medication at all or else fail to use it correctly. In addition, having been informed about the possibility of side effects while taking their medication, patients are liable to report side effects more frequently than they would if they were unaware of the possibility of unwanted complications.

A second problem arises as a result of the use of imprecise frequency descriptors (FDs for short). As Pander Maat and Klaassen point out, in many drug information leaflets the regularity or otherwise of side effects is communicated through the common use of a number of frequency descriptors, including terms such as *rarely, seldom, sometimes, infrequently, regularly, often*. Yet such frequency descriptors have been shown to be inaccurate in the sense that patients are liable to interpret them with irregular consistency. For example, Pander Maat and Klaassen refer to a study conducted by Toogood (1980) in which respondents were shown to ascribe remarkably divergent frequency rates to the FD *often*, with two thirds of people believing the term to indicate an occurrence rate of 43 to 75 per cent, and 5 per cent associating *often* with a frequency rate of either greater than 92 per cent or less than 28 per cent.

Moreover, evidence suggests that not only are patients liable to divergently evaluate frequency rates but, significantly, their appreciation of the value of frequency terms doesn't coincide with health professionals' assessments. Patients typically overestimate the occurrence rates of frequency descriptors (Pander Maat and Klaassen, 1994; Pander Maat, 1997), which, in turn, means that they overestimate the likelihood of side effects occurring during the course of their medication.

The significance of these and similar findings cannot be underestimated when it comes to communicating side effects information to patients clearly and accurately. As Wright (1999a: 87) observes, producers of drug information leaflets need 'to be sure that readers accord frequency terms similar meanings to those intended by professionals'. Yet frequency terms do not just relate to the occurrence of side effects. Patients may well experience problems accurately interpreting other frequency details, particularly instructions about dosages and timings. The canonical kind of directive that routinely features in patient information leaflets ('Take three tablets three times a day') will always be open to interpretation. Does this specific requirement, for example, involve taking a total of three or nine tablets daily? And even if such a directive is fortified with more concrete detail, dosage information is liable to remain unclear: 'Take this medication 3 times at mealtimes' introduces the seemingly transparent term 'mealtimes' into the instruction, but it still fails to rule out contrary interpretations. Readers might presume that the writer is directing them to take their medication at certain times of the day, whereas the author might have intended that the drug needs to be taken with food (Wright, 1999a: 91).

Composing and interpreting instructions successfully necessarily involves more than linguistic competence on the part of writers and readers (such as their ability to understand the meaning of specific lexical items). It also involves a range of literacy and problem-solving skills. Readers, for the most part, do not process functional texts such as patient information leaflets in a linear fashion, reading their entire contents in one long unbroken effort of concentration from beginning to end. Readers are necessarily selective in the passages they select for consumption: they approach texts with specific questions – such as 'What ages is this medication suitable for? Can I take it with alcohol? How long must I wait before I take another tablet?' – looking for answers to particular concerns that they may have (Wright, 1999a: 92).

In order to create effective, reader-friendly patient information leaflets, then, writers need to be sensitive to the various ways readers practically, actually search and consume written information and instructions, composing documents in light of such processing tendencies. Designing accessible, high-quality healthcare materials requires going beyond simply ensuring that specific linguistic features (such as vocabularies) are clear and accessible; effective document design involves the broader interplay among textual features, including the organisational and the generic structure (the format) of the leaflet. Likewise any approach to assessing the quality of written healthcare materials – at least if it is to offer a more reliable and comprehensive assessment of information provision – ideally needs to go beyond merely interrogating lexical and grammatical features, incorporating visual elements and the overall structure of the text, as well as taking into account the ways in which readers selectively process and navigate the contents of leaflets.

Linguistic interventions: unpacking the package insert

Since the 1990s there has been an increasing amount of research that has aimed to evaluate functional texts such as the patient information leaflet (Wright, 1999a: 89). Much of this work has focussed on statistical estimates of the readability of patient information leaflets (e.g. Mead and Smith, 1991; Albert and Chadwick, 1992; Payne *et al.*, 2000). Yet this type of statistical-based enquiry does not take into account the full context of communication, the non-textual elements of the communicative context, such as readers' prior knowledge, selective reading tendencies, cultural differences and visual layout (Clerehan and Buchbinder, 2006: 40). In other words such studies do not take into account the 'top down' elements involved in comprehending texts, including the overall organisation and structure of the document, along with its vocabulary and information density (Clerehan *et al.*, 2005). These are significant omissions for consideration since, as we have already noted, readers draw on a range of literacy skills and employ various cognitive strategies in order to make sense of textual information and find answers to the questions they ask of healthcare materials.

In order to address the statistical bias in healthcare documentation research, applied linguists have conducted analyses into, and designed frameworks for, appraising the readability and the communicative import of patient information leaflets. Arguably the most extensive and well established work in this area is research conducted Rosemary Clerehan and Rachelle Buchbinder, who, over a period of several years, have developed and refined a linguistic framework for assessing the quality of written healthcare materials (see Table 6.1). The framework, which is based on systemic functional linguistics (a linguistic theory which accounts for how grammatical choices are influenced by context) has been developed in order to ascertain whether there is a regular and fundamental text structure in medication instructions. One of the advantages of the framework is its universal applicability – it can be profitably applied to a range of functional documents (not just the type of medical text for which it was originally designed), affording analysts a rigorous and systematic tool for assessing the readability of written information.

The framework is resolved into nine elements, each of which evaluates a particular linguistic or structural component of the patient information leaflet. Although, for the sake of concision, the above table has been simplified, it nonetheless provides an overview of the framework and the range of textual themes that each element of the framework addresses. But so much for a theoretical overview; in order to demonstrate the practical utility of the framework, let us undertake a component-by-component analysis of the leaflet that accompanies paracetamol, a universally available, over-the-counter medication. The leaflet, in its original format, is reproduced in Figure 6.1.

Table 6.1 Framework for assessing patient information leaflets

---

Organisation/structure of the text (or generic structure)

This involves identifying what series of moves are present in a text.
Moves are distinct sections of a text that convey certain types of information such as the background on a drug, instructions about dosage, and details of side effects.

Rhetorical elements

What are the functions of each move in relation to the reader?

Technicality of vocabulary used in the text

How technical is the language that is used in the patient information leaflet and is this level of technicality appropriate?

Metadiscourse

Does the leaflet provide a description of the purpose or format of the text?

Role relationships communicated in the text

What is the nature of the roles articulated in the text between reader and writer (for example, expert to lay individual; doctor to patient)?

The use of headings

Does the text use headings for the purposes of signposting information for the reader?

Lexical density

What is the typical content density of the text (content-bearing words per clause)?

Factual content of the text

Is the factual information correct in the leaflet? Is the source of the information provided and the date of any revisions given?

Format

Considers the visual aspects of the text. What is the length, font size, layout of the text?

(adapted from Clerehan *et al.*, 2009: 119)

103120/1

PATIENT INFORMATION LEAFLET FOR PARACETAMOL TABLETS B.P. 500MG

This leaflet provides some important information about your medicine. Please read it carefully before you start taking Paracetamol Tablets B.P. 500mg. If you have any further questions, or if there is anything you do not understand, ask your Doctor or Pharmacist.

WHAT IS IN YOUR MEDICINE?

Your medicine is called Paracetamol Tablets B.P. 500mg and are white tablets. Each tablet contains the active ingredient Paracetamol B.P. 500mg. The tablet also contains the inactive ingredients Potato Starch, Pregelatinised Maize Starch, Talc, Povidone, Stearic Acid, Sodium Starch Glycollate, Nipasept (E214, E216, E218) and Magnesium Stearate. The Sodium content is less than 0.1mg per tablet. The active belongs to the following class of medicines: Paracetamol is a non-narcotic analgesic and antipyretic (a pain killer that also reduces fever).

PACK SIZE

Available in packs of 2, 4, 6, 8, 10, 12, 16 tablets. Packs of 20, 24, 25, 28, 30 and 32 tablets are only available from your Pharmacist. Packs of 48, 50, 96 and 100 tablets are only available on prescription from your Doctor. Packs of 240, 250, 252, 300, 500, 504, 1000 and 5000 are dispensing packs only.

PRODUCT LICENCE HOLDER/MANUFACTURER

The Wallis Laboratory Limited, Ash Road North, Wrexham, LL13 9UF, UK. (PL0211/5003R)

WHAT IS YOUR MEDICINE FOR?

Mild to moderate pain, such as headache, migraine, neuralgia, toothache, sore throat, period pains, aches and pains, muscle pains and backache. It can also relieve the symptoms of rheumatic aches and pains, influenza, feverishness and feverish colds.

BEFORE YOU TAKE YOUR MEDICINE:

If your answer to any of the following questions is YES, then you should ask your Pharmacist or Doctor before taking them.

- Are you pregnant or breastfeeding?
- Do you suffer from kidney problems or liver problems, including alcoholic liver disease?
- Are you or have you been allergic to Paracetamol and/or any of the ingredients listed above?
- Are you taking any other medicines - particularly other paracetamol-containing products; or other products containing non-steroidal anti-inflammatory agents (NSAID's), including aspirin and ibuprofen; or anticoagulants (drugs to thin the blood) such as warfarin; or drugs for nausea or vertigo such as metoclopramide and domperidone; or drugs for reducing cholesterol such as cholestyramine; or the antibiotic chloramphenicol?

TAKING YOUR MEDICINE:

Follow the instructions on the label about how to take your medicine. Your Pharmacist may also help you if you are not sure.
Dose: Unless otherwise directed by your Doctor-
Adults and children over 12 years: 1 to 2 Tablets (500mg - 1.0g) to be taken orally with water, every 4 hours up to a maximum of 8 tablets in 24 hours. **Maximum daily dose**: 8 Tablets (4.0g) in any 24 hour period in divided doses.
Children 6 to 12 years: $^1/_2$ to 1 tablet every 4 hours. The dose should not be given more frequently than every four hours and not more than 4 times in any 24 hour period.
DO NOT GIVE TO CHILDREN UNDER 6 YEARS OF AGE EXCEPT ON THE ADVICE OF A DOCTOR.

WARNING: DO NOT EXCEED THE STATED DOSE

If symptoms persist consult your Doctor. Do not take for more than three days without consulting your Doctor.

If you miss a single dose of Paracetamol Tablets B.P. 500mg, do not worry and take your next one at the normal time. DO NOT DOUBLE UP ON A DOSE TO MAKE UP FOR THE MISSING ONE.

WHAT SHOULD YOU DO IF YOU TAKE TOO MANY PARACETAMOL TABLETS B.P. 500MG?

If you accidentally take a large number of tablets (overdose) you should contact the nearest hospital casualty department or tell your Doctor immediately. Immediate medical advice should be sought in the event of an overdose, even if you feel well, because of the risk of delayed, serious liver damage.

WHILE TAKING YOUR MEDICINE:

Medicines may cause unwanted side effects in some people. If, after taking this medicine for the first time, you develop a rash or other allergic reaction - STOP taking Paracetamol Tablets BP 500mg and consult your doctor or pharmacist. Very occasionally it has been known for paracetamol to cause liver, kidney, pancreas (leading to stomach pain) and blood problems. If you experience these or any other unusual or unexpected symptoms, consult your Doctor or Pharmacist.

STORING YOUR MEDICINE:

Keep your medicine in a safe place where children cannot see or reach it. Paracetamol Tablets B.P. 500mg could be harmful to them. Store below 25°C in a dry place. Protect from light. Do not use these tablets after expiry date printed on the pack.

Date of leaflet preparation: September 2000
DD/DRUGS/DD-61

103120/1

Figure 6.1 Patient information leaflet for paracetamol tablets

Organisation/structure of the text

Patient information leaflets possess a typical overall generic organisation (Clerehan *et al.*, 2005). Although there will inevitably be a degree of variation among leaflets, an underlying structure, made up of identifiable moves, can be found to be at work in the documents. The organisation of the text consists of a sequence of moves (which may or may not correspond to section headings in the leaflet), such as information about dosages of medication, the likelihood and accounts of side effects, constraints on patient behaviour, and so forth. These moves are akin in predictability, Clerehan, Buchbinder and Moodie argue, to the set of moves one finds in a recipe book, for example: list of ingredients, method and serving suggestions. Thus whether appearing in an information leaflet or any other kind of functional text, moves help readers make sense of content and help them navigate their way through it.

With regard to the paracetamol leaflet, it is possible to locate at least nine moves which make up the generic structure of the text. The moves are readily identifiable since they broadly correspond to the nine capitalised, bold headings which introduce the various distinct sections that make up the document. The moves provide information about the background of the drug, a summary of its use, dosage instructions, an outline of the purpose of the drug, an account of potential side effects, information regarding monitoring, the constraints on user behaviour, storage instructions and contact information. In short, the leaflet would appear to contain all the possible moves that encompass the generic structure of the patient information leaflet.

Rhetorical elements

The two most common rhetorical elements employed in patient information leaflets are the speech acts of 'informing' and 'instructing' (Clerehan *et al.*, 2009: 121). These two speech acts recur throughout the paracetamol text. Instances of the informing element include statements such as 'Medicines may cause unwanted side effects in some people' and 'Packs of 48, 50, 96 and 100 tablets are only available on prescription from your doctor'; examples of instruction include unmitigated directions such as 'Do not take for more than three days without consulting your doctor' and 'Follow the instructions on the label about how to take your medicine'. Besides instructing and informing readers, the rhetorical elements of defining and describing are also present in the leaflet, specifically answers to heading questions, such as 'What is in your medicine?' and 'What is your medicine for?'

When assessing rhetorical elements it is important to see whether the grammar of such elements directly correlates with their rhetorical force. For example, with instructing elements (the most common rhetorical aspect in the paracetamol leaflet), the commands directed at readers will be clearer if they are compounded of imperative, rather than declarative or statement, forms. For example, an imperative direction 'Consult your pharmacist if you are unsure' is arguably clearer, and certainly more emphatic, than a declarative statement which ostensibly functions as a directive: 'Your pharmacist may also help you if you are unsure'.

Throughout the paracetamol text, the rhetorical elements, for the most part, consistently correspond with their appropriate grammatical forms, thus making clear which party (patient, pharmacist, doctor) is responsible for a particular action. There is, however, the odd occasion where, owing to a mismatch of rhetoric and grammar, the represent-ation of responsibility is not as explicitly encoded as it could be. For example, in the 'TAKING YOUR MEDICINE' section, the sentence 'The dose should not be given more frequently than every four hours' presumably functions foremost as explicit instruction rather than description. However, the message takes the grammatical form of a declarative statement: the instruction would have been more expressly communicated if it were formulated as an imperative.

Role relationships communicated in the text

The question to consider here is: Does the patient information leaflet make clear the role relations between writer and reader? For example, is the reader directly referred to and addressed by the writer and, if so, by what means is this achieved? This is an important consideration for writers of patient leaflets, since if they fail to make the role relations explicit, problems of interpretation might ensue for readers, such as their having difficulty in ascertaining exactly whom the information is intended for and directed at.

Applied linguistic research suggests that not all patient information leaflets articulate role relationships straightforwardly. Some documents have been found to be written purely for medical professionals rather than lay audiences, or else have communicated relations between writer and reader in a desultory fashion, with roles shifting from a relationship between equals to one in which the writer gives orders which the reader must follow (Clerehan *et al.,* 2005: 340).

The role relations in the paracetamol text appear to be less problematic: they make the intended audience of the document clear. Throughout the text, the reader is consistently referred to with the second person pronominal forms 'you' and 'your'. For example, 'If *you* have any further questions, or if there is anything *you* do not understand, ask your Doctor or Pharmacist'. In addition, the leaflet attempts to make clear that the document is for the patient to whom the medicine belongs: 'This leaflet provides some important information about your medicine' (although in this instance the possessive pronoun 'your' could also be read as multi-referential, potentially incorporating not only the taker of the medication but someone (such as a parent or guardian) reading the text on behalf of the patient).

The relationship between the writer/reader constructed by the text is that of an unspecified medical/pharmaceutical authority and patient. The exact identity (doctor? pharmacist?) of the writer (besides being someone representing the laboratory which produces the drug) is not made explicit. The writer adopts a position of clinical expertise and authority through which instructions are communicated to the reader, a number of which, as we have described previously, take the form of unmitigated directions, for instance: 'Follow the instructions on the label how to take your medicine'. This authority is also evinced through the use of the question headings 'WHAT IS IN YOUR MEDICINE?' and 'WHAT SHOULD YOU DO IF YOU TAKE TOO MANY PARACETAMOL TABLETS B.P. 500MG?'. These questions presume that the writer (as authority) possesses the information which the reader (as patient) lacks: questions that constitute an expert–patient relationship.

Metadiscourse and headings

Metadiscourse involves the use of language about language. In relation to health information materials, metadiscourse helps to explain the purpose of clinical documents as well as helping the reader to navigate their way around the text. One example of metadiscourse in the paracetamol text is contained in the opening paragraph where the general aim of the document is communicated directly to readers: 'This leaflet provides some important information your medication'. The main heading of the document (PATIENT INFORMATION LEAFLET FOR PARACETAMOL TABLETS B.P. 500 MG) also has a metadiscursive function, highlighting the status and purpose of the document overall, and the subheadings further down the page similarly help focus readers' attention on the content of the text.

Headings are a common feature of patient information leaflets and as such need to be considered in any evaluation of text quality (Clerehan et al., 2005: 338). Readers, as we have seen, do not process functional texts in a linear fashion, but are selective, asking questions of the document, trawling through it for answers (Wright, 1999: 90); answers which headings, standing out typographically from other parts of the text, conveniently provide. But despite their utility, headings can be inadequate due to their use of technical language and the presence of ambiguous phrasing. Headings can also be visually ambiguous, failing to stand out from the words in the main body of the document. However, the headings in the paracetamol text are shorn of technical lexis and stand out clearly in relief from surrounding text. In short, the headings throughout the document appear to be used appropriately, possessing a clear signposting function for readers.

Technicality of vocabulary used in the text

A common complaint of readers of medical texts is the complexity of the vocabulary they contain. The vocabulary choices a writer makes are not simply a matter of choosing the right word: they are based on the assumptions that writers have about their target readers' level of understanding of and familiarity with specific terms (Clerehan *et al.*, 2005: 336-7). As Wright (1999b: 192) argues, just because authors of healthcare materials are able to comprehend the technical jargon they employ in their writing does not mean that, as authors, they are sufficiently literate: the 'gold standard of literacy' involves mutual understanding between both reader and writer (ibid.). It goes without saying, then, that authors need sensitively to take into account the literacy levels of their audience, recognising that most readers will not be acutely familiar with clinical and technical lexis.

A number of specialist terms are present in the paracetamol leaflet: 'non-steroidal anti-inflammatory agents (NSAID's)', 'anti-coagulants', 'non-narcotic analgesic and antipyretic'. However, the use of these terms does not necessarily indicate, on the part of the writer, a lack of awareness of readers' appreciation of technical terminology. Most of these specialist terms are immediately paraphrased in accessible, non-technical language. For instance, 'non-narcotic analgesic and antipyretic' is glossed as 'a painkiller that also reduces fever', while 'anti-coagulants' is translated as 'drugs to thin the blood'. Indeed glosses are common throughout the text, qualifying specialist terms that might cause readers problems of interpretation. These glosses are useful, but there is one occasion where the use of an explanatory formulation potentially distorts rather than clarifies: 'If you accidentally take a large number of tablets (overdose) you should contact the nearest hospital casualty department or tell your Doctor immediately'. Here 'a large number of tablets' is deemed to constitute an overdose. However, the formulation arguably oversimplifies, for the obvious question one would wish to ask is: Just exactly what constitutes a 'large' amount? No qualifying details are provided and thus what precisely constitutes an overdose, an ingestion of tablets requiring medical attention, is not made clear.

Density of information (lexical density)

Lexical density is the ratio between lexical (or content) words and grammatical (functional) words. Lexical words provide informational content; some of the many examples that occur throughout the paracetamol leaflet include the words 'medicine', 'kidney', 'miss', 'taking'. Functional words are words that have a grammatical function: in themselves they provide no (or very little) informational content. Functional items belong to a closed class of words which includes prepositions ('in', 'of', 'out'), pronouns ('he', 'she', 'it'), auxiliary and modal verbs ('be', 'will'), determiners ('a', 'the'), and conjunctions ('and', 'but'). Lexical density relates to the average number of content words in a clause (or a given stretch of language). Approximately, the lexical density average for spoken English is between 1.5 and 2; for written English it is between 3 and 6 (although this will depend on the formality/ technicality of the writing: an email to a close friend is likely to be less lexically dense than an article written for a technical journal). The more lexically dense a piece of language, the more difficult it is to process it.

Lexical density is calculated by dividing the number of lexical words in a clause or sentence by the total number of words in that sentence, and then multiplying this score by 10. Thus if we take the following randomly selected sentence from the paracetamol leaflet: 'Immediate medical advice should be sought in the event of an overdose, even if you feel well, because of the risk of delayed, serious liver damage', the number of lexical words (underlined) is 13, and dividing this number by the total number of words in the sentence gives 0.5. Multiplying this number by 10 gives a lexical density score of 5, a rating which indicates, for this sentence at least, a relatively high lexical density level.

Now even if patients are familiar with the language forms associated with their illness, there is no reason why, Clerehan and Buchbinder argue, health professionals should not aim to make printed information as speech-like as possible (that is, possessing a relatively lower lexical density than writing). One way of realising this aim would simply be to use fewer lexical items in the first place or, as Clerehan and Buchbinder recommend, to extend the number of clauses in the document so as to distribute 'the information in a less concentrated manner' (2006: 55). However, such re-distribution would require judicious handling on the part of the author, since extending the word count of a written text may lead to the production of a less user-friendly document (owing to its undue size).

Validity of factual content

Although assessing the accuracy of the written information contained in the patient information leaflet is not strictly a linguistic concern, it is, of course, important that content should be valid and up to date. This means potentially signalling contentious issues and, where appropriate, identifying the source of the information provided or how that information was derived (Clerehan *et al.*, 2009: 120).

The paracetamol leaflet does not offer any quality assurance as to the reliability of the information: the detail contained in the document is presented as though it were indubitable fact. Moreover, there are omissions in the text, such as whether it is safe to consume alcohol while taking the drug. However the text does helpfully raise other contentious issues, providing advice, for instance, in the form of a series of questions about what patients need to consider before taking the medication: 'Are you pregnant or breastfeeding?', 'Do you suffer from kidney problems or liver problems, including alcoholic disease?' and so on.

Although the leaflet does not inform readers where they can obtain further information (apart from pointing out that they should consult their pharmacist or doctor if there is anything they do not understand), the document makes it clear to readers when it was last revised (September 2000) and thus how up to date it is.

Format

As with factual content, the format of the patient information leaflet is not strictly a linguistic consideration but is part of the broader semiotic structure and total communicative impact of the document. As we know, readers of written healthcare materials jump about, dart to and from, sections of the text and so the visual aspects of leaflets play an important part in how readers process and navigate them. Thus the length, format, layout and graphical aspects of how the information is presented in the text need to be considered.

The paracetamol leaflet makes consistent use of a range of visual features that visually sequence the text and prevent it from being one stretch of continuous print. For example, information is resolved into various sections introduced by headings, is sequenced by bullet points, and makes use of different font sizes and bold to highlight its significance. Overall, the format of the document is, for the most part, visually accessible. The only shortcoming is the average font size throughout the leaflet: it is relatively small – certainly smaller than the 12-14 point recommended by the Royal National Institute of Blind People (2006) – and therefore could cause problems for readers who are visually impaired.

(TC)

Task 6.2 The paracetamol text: more than one voice at work?

By now you should be familiar with the patient information leaflet for paracetamol (Figure 6.1), which we have scoured quite intensively. The linguistic assessment we conducted pointed an illuminating spotlight on the textual make up and function of the document. The analysis also provided insights into how readers might evaluate and respond to the text.

Now recall the intriguing notion of heteroglossia, the phenomenon of many voices, which we explored in relation to the aspirin text considered earlier in this chapter. Can you find similar instances of heteroglossia (distinct voices with different functions) at work in the paracetamol text – for instance the same 'lawyerly' and 'avuncular' voices that were present in the instructions for aspirin?

The patient information leaflet: theoretical underpinnings

The foregoing text-based analysis of the paracetamol document demonstrates some of the potential of an applied linguistic approach to evaluating written healthcare materials. Linguistic analyses of patient information leaflets are able to identify and describe potential generic structures in such documents. They are also able to tease out inconsistencies and the inappropriate use of textual features which might well undermine patients' comprehension of the specific meanings which authors intend to convey. Of course linguistic assessments of the patient information leaflet are not in themselves completely sufficient to appraise exhaustively the quality of written materials. Clerehan and Buchbinder (2006) suggest that document design approaches and a strategy for patient evaluation have an important role to play. For instance, concerning the latter, any design and assessment of leaflets should ideally involve users of written healthcare materials, allowing patients themselves to evaluate documents and make recommendations for improving the quality of medicinal information (Raynor *et al.*, 2004).

Yet for all their utility and potential, linguistic applications have been relatively neglected in the research context of designing and assessing professional–patient information leaflets. Such inconsistency perhaps reflects the variable quality of written healthcare materials and the lack of a standardised linguistic approach to health document design. This is surprising since the writing of patient information leaflets is universally regulated; leaflets, for instance, have to follow a template recommended by the European Commission (1998) which requires them to be uniform in content and structure. However, the European Union regulations have not necessarily resulted in the universal production of enhanced quality written health materials: they do not completely ensure high quality, accessible information and might even pose difficulties for readers (Pander Maat and Lentz, 2010: 118). For example, the extensive information requirements of the EU template have resulted in the production of leaflets in excess of 2000 words (ibid.), a not insubstantial word count whose size is hardly conducive to user-friendliness.

Such inconsistencies in the production of high-quality healthcare materials only reinforce the importance of submitting patient information leaflets to rigorous textual analyses in order to assess their usability. Applied linguistic approaches to document design, we argue, can facilitate the effective creation of written health information, affording professionals, at the very least, a more sensitive appreciation of the linguistic demands that processing the patient information leaflet places on readers. But what exactly are the theoretical foundations that underpin applied linguistic approaches to the patient information leaflet?

As mentioned earlier evaluative frameworks such as Clerehan, Hirsh and Buchbinder's approach are based on systemic functional linguistics (SFL for short). SFL is a theory of language which accounts for how lexico-grammatical choices in a text are functionally motivated by situation or context (Coffin *et al.*, 2004: 8). Context determines the production of any text (be it written or spoken) and how readers and listeners make sense of texts. The interplay, then, between text and context is crucial. For example, contextual variables (such as what is being communicated, the relationship between the participants involved, and the mode of language used for the process) determine the type of discourse used in a text and how readers make sense of it.

According to systemic theory, there are three situational factors that affect the language of a text (Halliday, 1978). They are the categories field, tenor and mode and can be defined, at a rather broad, abstract level, as follows:

Field: what is being written or spoken about between writer and reader, or speaker and listener; the ongoing communicative activity and the purpose of the activity;

Tenor: the interrelations among the participants;

Mode: the medium or mode of communication (for example, spoken or written language).

The interplay of tenor, field and mode give rise to certain kinds of text. Or, to put it another way, texts encode these three essential situational elements. As Butt *et al.* (1995: 12) note, it seems remarkable indeed that the three categories of field, tenor and mode alone account for the situational differences across all types of texts. But they do. And so inter-dependent are these three elements that altering just one of them would have a significant bearing on the language of a given text. Consider, for instance, the example of a face-to-face conversation between two close friends dedicated to the subject of health (with one of the speakers describing some recent medical problem from which he or she is suffering). The field of discourse would here relate to what is being discussed (i.e. health-themed interaction); the tenor of discourse would describe the close relationship between friends; and the mode of discourse would be that of face-to-face spoken conversation.

Now, if we were to change one of the three situational categories, a different type of text would result. Changing the tenor, substituting, say, a GP for one of the friends – so that now we have an interaction in which the speaker is offloading health problems to a clinician – would significantly affect the language used in the interaction. The presence of the medical professional (with their specialist status), and the concomitant increased social distance between the participants (let us assume that they are not intimates), would occasion the use of lexical and grammatical features different to those in a conversation between friends. We would expect, for example, the use of a more technical, specialist vocabulary (certainly on the part of the doctor) and, among other features, the increased use of politeness forms as the participants address each other as non-familiars and negotiate social relations.

The interplay of the situational factors of field, tenor and mode illustrates the importance of appreciating the context of culture in which texts are created. As language users, aware of practices and values in society, we will have expectations as to the way information is presented in, and can be efficiently recovered from, a particular text, along with a sense of the role relationships in a text and what kind of lexical features are expected to be in it (Clerehan and Buchbinder, 2006: 43). In order to produce and make sense of texts, language users need to be familiar with specific communicative practices and situations such as doctor–patient consultations, casual conversations and patient information leaflets (not to mention countless other communicative events). For some people, the conventions of these textual practices (such as patient information leaflets) might be unfamiliar, leading to difficulties interpreting written documentation and fully extracting the benefits from it. Writers of healthcare materials who neglect to take into account readers' knowledge and expectations are thus liable to produce documents which fail to achieve their principal purpose: helping guide patient behaviour and preventing any adverse events (Clerehan and Buchbinder, 2006: 42).

The systemic functional linguistic categories of field, tenor and mode, then, illuminate how meaning-making occurs in texts. Considering these categories when interrogating patient information leaflets (or indeed any kind of text) can help determine whether health information materials meet the aims of writers and readers. The comprehensive nine-stage linguistic framework we have explored in this chapter thoroughly appraises the categories of field, tenor and mode, an operation which enables us to determine the extent to which patient information leaflets are understandable to readers.

Summary

In this chapter we have looked at the way in which readers process and navigate their way through patient information leaflets, identifying a number of problems that readers experience interpreting such documents. Part of the reason for this is the knowledge differential between writers and readers. Writers of patient information leaflets possess a different level of understanding than the audience for whom they write, whether it be estimations of the rate of side effects associated with common frequency descriptors ('rarely', 'seldom', 'occasionally', etc.) or a familiarity with technical terminology that is likely to be possessed by non-specialist readers. Failure on the part of authors to address these knowledge imbalances can result in the production of variable quality health information that is liable to be misinterpreted or not fully understood by patients.

In response to the often ambiguous nature of written healthcare materials, applied linguists have designed frameworks for evaluating the readability of these functional texts. Applied linguistic approaches, such as the comprehensive nine-item framework developed by Clerehan *et al.* (2009), offer a novel way of assessing text quality, complementing non-linguistic approaches that depend purely on the statistical assessment of functional texts – approaches that overlook the full context of communication and so fail to take into account the 'top down' elements involved in processing texts, for example, the overall organisation and structure of documents (non-textual elements such as visual layout, font size and style.). Linguistic approaches to textual evaluation go beyond a mere de-contextualised, statistical focus, providing a rigorous and replicable framework for interrogating the textual construction of healthcare documents. The effectiveness of such frameworks, which take into account the broader communicative situation (unlike statistical readability measures), highlights the role of linguistic analysis within written medical information fields and the need to complement methods that solely utilise readability formulas to evaluate patient information.

Part III

Computer-mediated health communication

7 Electronic health communication

Peer-to-peer online interaction

Online peer-to-peer communication: challenges and opportunities

In this chapter we look at communication that takes place between people (peers) with different medical conditions when they join online support groups. Interactions with peers in self-management programmes offer people with different medical conditions the opportunity to share their concerns with similar others, in this way reducing the sense of isolation associated with many illnesses. Such interactions are typically a locus of social support defined as a 'transaction of empathy and concern, information and advice, or tangible aid (i.e., goods and services) between two or more individuals' and characterised by the use of verbal or nonverbal behaviours to seek or provide help (Mickelson, 1997: 157). Such support groups are particularly important for those who suffer from chronic illness as clinical research shows that interpersonal networks significantly impact on adaptation to the everyday management of disease. As the concept of supportive community is often deemed central to Internet-based interactions, it is not surprising that participation in online support communities has been hailed as holding a great potential for its therapeutic benefits. With the likely increase of such communications through dedicated websites and social networking possibilities in the modern era of the Internet, there is a growing need for health professionals and researchers to understand and evaluate such interactions.

In order to harness any potential therapeutic benefits of online interaction and networking, it is particularly important to understand the rhetorical challenges faced by those who decide to participate in such online groups, as well as the processes through which norms of particular online communities develop. In this chapter we will therefore review some of the current literature on online social support and then use different applied linguistic tools to explore the multitude of ways that people who have never met in person use the electronic medium to seek and offer support on physical and emotional health problems.

Personal reflection

What do you understand by the term 'online social support'? Can you think of the unique benefits that people with health problems can get from participation in online discussion groups (in contrast to the advantages found in traditional face-to-face support groups)? What about potential drawbacks, for example, the dangers commonly associated with anonymity on the Internet?

At present, virtual communities are recognised as a source of informational and emotional benefits which are often difficult to attain through face-to-face support groups. These groups have emerged around a broad spectrum of health-related topics and illnesses such as cancer, diabetes, AIDS, addictions (alcoholism, drugs), arthritis, chronic fatigue syndrome, depression, heart disease and a number of other conditions. Although clinical studies are yet to demonstrate pronounced health effects (Eysenbach *et al.,* 2004), there is a growing acknowledgement in the literature of such factors as the impact of writing and storytelling, expressions of emotions, self-disclosure and intimacy, collecting information and thereby improving understanding and knowledge. Access to online discussion groups offers adults with restricted mobility, speech and hearing difficulties, or caregiving responsibilities an opportunity not only to gather valuable information (which is abundant on a number of purpose-built non-interactional websites), but, crucially, also to receive emotional support and advice based on personal experience. Taken together, the opportunity of sharing information and feelings, the removal of geographical barriers, and the sense of solidarity involved in online groups can help individuals manage crises and generate a sense of personal empowerment (Barak *et al.,* 2008).

Clearly, the empowering and therapeutic nature of peer-to-peer communications depends on the health problem participants seek help for. Coping mechanisms and the verbal strategies of their expression will vary depending on whether the condition is terminal or chronic, and whether it is a disease well understood by the public. For example, Galegher *et al.* (1998) note that many discussions in the depression-related groups concern the stigma of these illnesses, as participants share the frustrations they experience in dealing with the expectations and criticisms of people surrounding them. The relative anonymity of Internet-based participation may facilitate discussion of potentially embarrassing topics and increase the possibilities for self-disclosure (a consideration we further pursue in Chapter 8). Also, as we explore later in this section, some online support groups can provide a number of benefits in cases when body image is part of a health concern.

However, online support groups are not without problems. Consequently, in addition to the above positive outcomes, studies of computer-mediated communication also describe online hostilities of variable intensity, such as disagreements, criticism or aggressive emotional outbursts (known as 'flaming' or 'trolling') that can cause stress and anxiety both for the interactants involved and other community members. There is also concern that peer-to-peer communities may promote misinformation and adoption of advice that runs contrary to clinical research. While other members may correct inaccurate information, in the case of large groups where there are long, and often archived, threads of conversations there is still a risk that some members may not read corrections in a timely manner. Other critics warn that participation in online groups rarely leads to transformation associated with the notion of 'empowerment' and that some conditions can actually become worse (Orgad, 2005). Such positive and negative outcomes of participation in online support groups have to be taken into account when setting up or moderating online communities.

Before we proceed to exploring particular communicative challenges faced by participants of online support groups, let us first outline the enabling and restricting aspects of Internet-based communication in general. Social media technologies provide opportunities for certain communicative phenomena such as relative anonymity, the opportunity to address others without being physically present, as well as the ability to choose between simply reading contributions of others and active posting. At the same time, however, other communicative opportunities are ruled out as one cannot observe their interlocutors' facial expressions and gestures; turn-taking and backchannel feedback are also precluded. These factors and properties of the electronic environment create a particular set of rhetorical challenges and opportunities that participants have to face regardless of the topic of discussion. Galegher *et al.* (1998) distil such challenges into two notions: establishing legitimacy, and establishing and maintaining authority through online interaction.

Whereas anybody can join an online support forum, there is no obligation to acknowledge one's presence, to reply to posts, and generally provide any kind of help. This means that in the context of an online group, there is always a risk that one's messages can be ignored. This is why Galegher *et al.* (1998) maintain that in order to obtain direct support and information from others in the group people must first demonstrate their legitimacy – in other words, they have to show that their requests for help are genuine and justified. This prerequisite for legitimacy does not usually pose communicative problems in face-to-face groups where a member's physical presence at a meeting is normally sufficient for them to make an indirect claim for the group's attention (ibid.). Other non-verbal actions such as following a particular dress-code and observing temporal and geographical requirements for a meeting can also contribute to and strengthen one's legitimacy within a group. Through observing these often implicit codes of behaviour individuals display a wish to belong to the group and in this way increase their chances of being granted some airtime during which their concerns will be considered and responded to.

For online participants, however, the situation is different. The behaviour codes signifying willingness to belong to the group are difficult or impossible to follow (for example, merely joining an online group and signalling one's presence is not enough), and conventions for demonstrating one's legitimacy have to take a different, and essentially verbal, form. This is no small task considering that first timers in an online environment usually do not have any relational ties to other members, and are often completely unaware of the composition and size of their potential audience. The example below written by a newcomer to an online group for people with arthritis illustrates this:

[1]
Hi. I've been reading/lurking here for a few months. I've been diagnosed with AS and have been taking anti-inflammatories since May. I am wondering what type of side effects others have had to these meds besides ulcers.

Currently I am taking Lodine 1200 mg/day. I am wondering if the swelling I've been having with my eyelids has anything to do with this drug. Any thoughts? Also, any other common side effects?

I also want to thank everyone who's responded about depression and relationships. Reading this newsgroup has really helped me – I don't feel like I'm the only one out here with this _thing_ you can't see, but can definitely feel. I'm 29 years old and I've had a hard time explaining to family and friends why I hurt, especially at a young age! The threads about depression and relationships have helped me explain to my husband what I'm going through. Thanks again everyone! (Galegher *et al.*, 1998: 495)

(TC)

Task 7.1 Identifying strategies of creating legitimacy and soliciting advice

Before you proceed any further, look at the above extract and note any features that you think make this post differ from a conversation in a face-to-face group. Can you link them to the rhetorical challenges discussed above? Next, comment on the author's strategies to create legitimacy in her post. How does the author reveal her commitment to the group?

Establishing legitimacy

How, then, does one stranger successfully seek social support from another stranger in an online environment? From the above extract, we can observe a number of discursive strategies that participants of online groups adopt in order to achieve legitimacy and simultaneously solicit support:

- Indicating one's condition by describing symptoms and/or mentioning the history of the disease. This is one of the most common opening moves, which is often used to articulate a relation with the shared problem of the group. At the same time, it serves as a proxy for personal introduction since a typical face-to-face introduction through stating one's name would not be relevant in the absence of audio-visual cues and knowledge about other participants.
- Making direct ('Any thoughts? Also, any other common side effects?'), or indirect requests for information ('I am wondering what type of side effects others have had to these meds besides ulcers.')
- Making references to shared experiences: 'I don't feel like I'm the only one out here with this _thing_ you can't see, but can definitely feel'. This is another common strategy of establishing one's legitimacy. Eichhorn (2008), for example, found that more than 50 per cent of the group members solicited social support by sharing experiences through statements of self-disclosure or description of an experience.
- Describing personal successes and elaborating on positive improvements, as in the following example: 'Hi guys, yesterday I went to the therapist for the first time and she was cool! I woke up this morning and didn't want to be dead' (Eichhorn, 2008: 71). As extract [1] demonstrates, this may be followed by statements expressing gratitude: 'The threads about depression and relationships have helped me explain to my husband what I'm going through. Thanks again everyone!'.

Eichhorn (2008) provides two additional strategies of soliciting support: providing self-deprecating comments, that is negative statements belittling oneself and/or one's problem ('I am a terrible person, I feel so fat, I even look fatter, a lot fatter and I'm not imagining it'), and statements of extreme behaviour referring to previous or planned activities that in some way exceed the range of 'normal' or 'acceptable' daily actions for a person with a medical condition, such as 'I just swallowed many pills with a beer!' (Eichhorn, 2008: 69). We will return to this strategy of making self-deprecating comments later in this chapter when we look into interactions on an eating-disorder forum.

It is also worth noting here that in their observation of existing group norms in order to make their contributions legitimate (for example, adhering to a set of topics highlighted by moderators or observing the unspoken rule of showing gratitude) participants are also co-constructing a safe communicative context. Indeed, as Armstrong *et al.* (in press) found in their study of conversations on a forum for people with diabetes, a particular type of rhetorical work, referred to as 'the rhetoric of gratitude' (Arminen 2001), functioned as an important social glue that facilitated participation in this online community from its inception onwards. The authors carried out a longitudinal study of this community from its very beginning and found that participants continuously emphasised the reciprocity of mutual help, which allowed them both to express their gratitude and demonstrate their own contribution in assisting others. This practice might have not only strengthened the feelings of solidarity among existing members, but also served as an indicator of a good-natured and 'flaming-free' atmosphere on the discussion board to those who were considering participation. One of the indicators pointing to the perceived safety effect was an increase of newcomers who, just like the author of the above post, had first 'lurked' for some time on the forum trying to learn the local interactional ropes before deciding to contribute. According to the authors, approximately a month after the start of the group, both existing and new members began to post more personal and potentially compromising questions. The following post, for example, belongs to a young female participant who, despite an opportunity to contribute to the discussion group from the beginning, withheld her participation for some time until she considered the environment 'safe'.

[2]
Hello. ... Ok! This has taken some gutts to start this, but i've got sooooo many questions that I would love answers to but always clam up when I start asking them when I go to clinic. So ... I'm hoping people on here can give me some answers etc. [...] Ok ... here goes (congratulate me on my bravery)

(Armstrong *et al.*, in press)

As we can see, apart from the explicit comment indicating awareness of potential risks that online posting might entail ('some gutts to start this', 'congratulate me on my bravery'), the author makes extensive use of three dots to signal hesitations and demonstrate her feelings of insecurity about participation and expectations of this group.

Conveying authority and giving advice

When participants move from asking questions to answering posts and providing emotional support and advice, their rhetorical strategies also change. Now they will need to convince their readers that they not only have a right to contribute but also that their answers should be believed. In other words, as Galegher *et al.* (1998) maintain, they have to convey authority in their posts. In this context, it is interesting to examine how users of online support groups may be displaying an awareness that they are in a position to supply advisory comments, given the fact that they are interacting with their peers rather than 'experts'. This awareness entails the possibility that one's comments and arguments can always be challenged, and the author might be asked to supply proof for any assertions he or she is making. As Ken Hyland warns, 'Claim-making is a risky practice' (2000: 93), to which we can add that it can be especially tricky if claims touch upon the area of medical expertise in a peer-to-peer discussion board.

In addition to demonstrating authority, answering online questions carries another rhetorical challenge for participants, namely handling the potentially conflicting demands of providing advice and simultaneously demonstrating emotional support that is often solicited in the opening posts. Furthermore, the act of giving advice, whether online or face to face, is in itself a linguistically complex endeavour. In this regard, Hutchby (1995: 221) points out that many studies from sociology and computer mediated interaction identify 'a distinctive and fundamental feature of advice-giving: In that it involves a speaker assuming some deficit in the knowledge state of a recipient.' Consequently, during participation in online discussions, the concern is not only whether one's posts will be believed, but also whether they can be perceived as potentially rude or imposing. Hence, provision of advice is often mitigated to avoid imposition or critique. In the field of pragmatics, this type of interactional business is referred to as 'face work' (Brown and Levinson, 1987), and advice giving is studied as a potentially face threatening act. Later on in this chapter, we illustrate how participants of online support groups find solutions to these challenges by using distinctive techniques and strategies to share advice and at the same time handle potential face threats in online exchanges.

To conclude, Internet communities can have a valuable role in engaging people with rare or long-term conditions in issues that affect their health and healthcare. These support groups have been found to provide certain benefits for users who may not be able to or simply do not wish to attend face-to-face sessions. For researchers and practitioners, such discussion groups constitute an important source of data on patient-to-patient communication and information sharing. Interactions taking place in this medium represent a window of opportunity to learn more about how participants articulate issues concerning well-being, physical and psychological needs, and trust – all of which have been singled out as important aspects in self-management of disease and doctor–patient interactions. We have also argued that the specific context of online support groups can help us learn more about the role advice plays in online peer-to-peer communities, and began to explore how we can study social behaviours in this online environment in order to inform future interventions to set up or moderate such communities. In the next section, we demonstrate how interrogation of online interactions with discourse analytic techniques can shed light on the linguistic structure and collaborative nature of 'cyber coping'.

Analysing discussions in online support communities: a micro-level approach

We hope to have shown in previous chapters how techniques of applied linguistics can provide a valuable framework for exploring the character of health communication (Sarangi, 2004). The large proportion of this research, however, continues to focus on face-to-face communication in the healthcare setting, whereas sociolinguistic explorations of online health-related encounters remain relatively rare. Although such research is undoubtedly theoretically and practically important, the focus on face-to-face interactions as part of structured interventions may preclude opportunities to examine the increasing volume of naturally occurring conversations initiated by patients online.

In this section we therefore want to demonstrate how linguistic approaches that so far have been mostly applied to analyse online interaction in non-health related discussion boards (such as fan and hobby communities studied by Nancy Baym (2000), for example) enable us to examine in detail how participants pursue 'cyber recovery' through peer-to-peer communication. In an environment where people create a social support community entirely through written text, applied linguistics offers a range of methods and tools for analysing social behaviours, for example, through the study of the linguistic expressions of status, negotiation, play and conflict (Herring, 2004). Such an analysis can bring new insights into the complex and negotiated nature of online social support, and can reveal dynamics that often go unnoticed by research that does not attend to micro-level aspects of communication, such as studies employing quantitative content analysis techniques. In particular, we focus on two frameworks that allow scholars and practitioners to examine online communications at such a micro-level: discourse analytical perspectives on narrative and politeness theory.

Since we have already covered the key tenets of narrative analysis in Chapter 3 of this book, here we only briefly draw on some of the concepts to situate this framework in the context of online support groups. Just like oral contributions in a face-to-face setting, posts written in online support groups often include an action which is experienced and recounted by the participant. Walstrom (2000) suggests that in this context it is useful to look at narrative as the presentation of self as a protagonist, including protagonist-doer and protagonist-experiencer positionings. The scholar illustrates these positionings with the help of statements produced by women narrating their experiences of an eating disorder. Thus, protagonist-doer positionings involve action, both behavioural ('I restricted last night') and discursive ('I keep telling myself...'), whereas protagonist-experiencer positionings include states of being ('I am sick' or 'I am anorexic') and stances of thinking ('I believe/think'), evaluating ('I deserve', 'I prefer'), and affect ('I feel happy') (Walstrom, 2000: 765).

As we have seen in Chapter 3, narratives can perform a range of functions, including constructing the identity of the narrator, establishing a common ground with the interlocutor(s), and serving as a catalyst for recovery. Walstrom (2000) draws on the latter therapeutic dimension of narrative to explore how the tool of narration is used to serve as a 'social process of coping' (2000: 264) in the online context. In addition, the scholar draws our attention to another function performed by narratives: that of problem-solving. In a group setting, problem solving often proceeds through the generation of hypotheses that are revised by co-narrators until a solution is produced. Walstrom notes that sometimes the process of co-narration, when fellow participants elaborate on a problem drawing on personal experience, may not yield a single solution or point. She draws on research on women's rap groups where this phenomenon is referred to as 'kernel storying' (Kalcik (1975) cited in Walstrom, 2000: 765). The importance of this phenomenon lies precisely in the process of co-narration itself, as each contribution enlarges collective understandings of a problem and in this way creates or strengthens solidarity among participants. Recalling our earlier discussion of advice exchanges in the online context, we may also add that such use of narratives enables provision of indirect advice, which in turn adds to the construction of a non-threatening environment.

The activity of co-narration brings us back to the socio-constructionist perspectives on language we discussed in the 'Written health communication' part of this book. Here an online narrative should be seen first and foremost as a joint and negotiated process. Politeness theory is therefore another framework that can be fruitfully applied to study communication in online support groups. The theory stems from Brown and Levinson's work (1987) which suggested that all interaction is guided by our concern over the interlocutor's autonomy needs and his or her desire to be liked. The various discursive strategies that demonstrate and attend to those needs result in politeness. Drawing on Goffman's (1981) concept of face, the authors proposed a model for such protective conversational interactions. Face 'is an image of self, delineated in terms of approved social attributes' (Goffman, 1981: 5), that is the public image that each person wants to portray in a social setting. We tend to take present or imaginary others into account as we craft our self-presentations, and in this way, in politeness theory terms, we strive to maintain or enhance our and/or others' face. This understanding of their mutual vulnerability can make interactants observe positive face through such politeness strategies as claiming common ground, for example; or attend to negative face by showing deference, using the passive voice, and in general emphasising the importance of one's independence in social interactions. You may also recall from our earlier discussion that acts that threaten one's positive self-image or autonomy such as advice-giving are called face threatening acts and require such politeness techniques as hedging and indirectness, for example, to avoid disruptions and awkwardness in social interactions (Brown and Levinson, 1987).

Politeness strategies in the online environment: soliciting support

Let us now apply the lens of politeness theory to the context of online social support where participants are creating relations through electronic text. If we revisit the rhetorical challenge of establishing legitimacy, it is clear that the difficulty of demonstrating legitimacy is related to what Walstrom calls the 'vulnerabilizing' nature of participation in online support groups (2000: 762). Looking at posting activity from the perspective of politeness theory, the scholar discusses the risk to face that an initial poster takes in requesting (through questions) particular types of information and support in order to cope with her problem. Here the risk lies in the possibility that other participants may refuse to address one's requests by withholding their answers. Another pitfall stems from the possibility that an online post may receive strongly negative replies and in this way be subjected to the practice of flaming. In addition to these threats to face conditioned by the online environment, participants have to deal with the overall challenge of posing a problem and soliciting support. Here the phenomenon of affective displays in situations of social accountability is particularly apposite. In this regard, Walstrom refers to the work of Buttny (1993) who drew attention to displays of affect as problem-posing devices and emphasised their vulnerabilising nature. Following this reasoning, negative affective stances can be used in the interaction to index problems: 'The uses of negative affect may be seen as a person's procedure for presenting an event as problematic—for showing the seriousness of the event—to mark it out of the ordinary as a way to intensify it' (Buttny (1993) cited in Walstrom, 2000: 766). The usefulness of this perspective on affective stances can be seen from Waltrom's commentary on the post below, where a participant is soliciting accounts from her online audience regarding her feelings.

[3]
I've been to this a few times—I always seems to feel extra self-conscious in groups, because I feel like everyone is judging the extent of my sickness on my appearance. If I feel fat one day, I feel guilty for claiming to have an eating disorder. If I restrict for a while, then I feel more sick and more eligible for the title of 'eating disordered.' I think I prefer individual therapy, but I've been having trouble calling my therapist lately. I don't feel like I'm skinny enough to deserve treatment. Why do I feel this way? Does anyone else have this problem? Karla (example cited in Walstrom, 2000: 768)

The participant (Karla) begins her post by outlining a problem through presentation of her negative feelings that involve a perception that others are evaluating the degree of her eating disorder based on her appearance (' … because I feel like everyone is judging the extent of my sickness on my appearance.'). In doing so, she uses one of the strategies to solicit support we have mentioned above, namely providing self-deprecating comments via negative statements about oneself. As Walstrom observes (2000: 768), Karla emphasises the force of her negative feelings in three ways—through an intensifier ('extra self-conscious'), use of temporality ('always'), and by referring to a perceived consensus ('everyone is judging'). After indexing a problem with these negative stances, she then evaluates her own appearance as fat ('If I feel fat one day') indicating the degree of her eating disorder condition and implicitly supplying a positive evaluation of a thin appearance. She also assesses her ability to claim she has an eating disorder as inadequate ('I feel guilty for claiming to have an eating disorder') and then proceeds to use negative evaluations to show that she has similar problems in one-to-one therapy ('just as in face-to-face groups'). Note that through affective stances and a state-of-being positioning ('I don't feel') Karla accomplishes a negative evaluation of her appearance linking it to another negative evaluation as being not qualified to seek treatment (' … to deserve treatment.'). In this way, Karla uses a short narrative not only to pose a problem but simultaneously to negotiate her identity of being eating-disordered. By linking the negative evaluation of her appearance to participant status she implicitly shows that she finds her eating disorder identity inadequate (ibid.).

In her final statement, the participant solicits informational and emotional support group resources through two questions. In the first question, Karla requests information by seeking an explanation for her feelings ('Why do I feel this way?'). The second question solicits support in the form of accounts by other group participants who might share her feelings. Note that at the same time Karla explicitly refers to her feelings, and the evaluations they index, as a problem ('Does anyone else have this problem?'). Walstrom (2000: 769) points to two face threats in this solicitation of support group resources. First, Karla uses the strategy of direct questions to ask for information ('Why do I feel this way?') and support ('Does anyone else have this problem?'). The risk to face in this solicitation is that respondents may dismiss Karla's specific requests. Analysis of replies to Karla's post would therefore consider if other participants strive to preserve the interactional order by supplying answers in the form of reasons for Karla's feelings and, following Karla's request, whether they offer accounts based on their personal experiences.

The other risk stems from the use of the affective stances as devices for negative evaluations (ibid.). Karla's use of these stances conveys negative evaluations of her appearance, her eating disorder identity, and her participant status in both therapy and face-to-face support groups. These evaluations may be seen as self-deprecations, and in using them Karla threatens her own face. Consequently, some form of redressive work is necessary on behalf of her respondents if they want to mitigate this face threat. According to Pomerantz (1984), a routine response to self-deprecations is disagreement, such as a compliment or negation. However, this is tricky online, as a statement such as 'you are not overweight' produced without seeing someone's appearance is unlikely to be perceived as credible or genuine (Walstrom, 2000: 770). As we will see from the extract we reproduce in Task 7.2 below, participants who respond to Karla's post devise other ways to attend to her threatened face and come up with statements that take into account the disembodied nature of online participation.

The micro-level analysis of Karla's post and the replies it generated made Walstrom conclude that the bodiless nature of the online support group is beneficial for women with eating disorders because it allows a flexible access to support group resources. The setting of the face-to-face support groups can be problematic because it reveals the physical appearances of its participants, which can jeopardise women's use of support resources in the context of coping with an eating disorder. From this perspective, online groups where women can share their negative feelings about their size and/or weight without automatically disclosing information about their physical appearance constitute a relatively risk-free context.

Politeness and peer-to-peer advice giving

Revisiting the challenges of advice-sharing outlined above, the politeness theory framework also allows us to explore how the face-threatening aspects of advice-giving are addressed in online peer-to-peer communication. In the following we analyse how female participants of an online diabetes group studied by Armstrong *et al.* (in press) tackle the delicate issue of advice provision. In particular, we will pay attention to how they use language to create legitimacy and authority within the broader rhetorical and interactional processes of eliciting, giving, and receiving practical advice and emotional support; and to jointly create and maintain norms for interaction in the discussion forum. The advice-soliciting message we reproduce below was posted under the subject 'Diabetes and pregnancy'.

[4]
Firstly, I'm in no rush to have children (but) my ultimate worry is diabetes affecting my ability to have 'healthy' babies, and the complications that I will incur etc etc. [...] I've just got sooo many questions and I just need anyone who has either gone through it, or knows any words of wisdom to put my little mind at rest. Thank you (phew). Participant 16, female

(from Armstrong *et al.,* in press)

[5]
Hi, just some input on this cos I have my own child and I work in a special care baby unit so see a lot of babies from IDDM (Insulin-Dependent Diabetes Mellitus) mothers. I found that the first 2 months of pregnancy were the worst and I couldn't believe how unstable and fragile I was, after that things just kinda fell into place and all went well until 35wks when I delivered [child], normally. Healthy and well. From a prof point the things to keep in mind are that the more stable your BGs are the less likely you will have problems. Diabetics always have bigger babies and it's no good keeping your BGs too low cos this can lead to problems with the baby. The other thing is when you do go into labour make sure you get to hospital ASAP as this can be the most dangerous time in any pregnancy esp when you are IDDM. Participant 15, female

(from Armstrong *et al.,* in press)

After outlining her problem, participant 16 is using justification ('I've just got sooo many questions and I just need anyone ... ') as a means of preserving her face as well as a mechanism of maintaining her peer status. As Kouper (2010) explains, when one discloses a need for advice, and, consequently, demonstrates a lack of knowledge and skills to deal with a situation or a problem, they can undermine their own position as a capable individual and a peer. Participants of online support communities therefore often resort to providing reasons for seeking advice – a technique that allows them to preserve their projected self-image and in this way minimise risk to face. After justifying her solicitation of advice, the participant then states she is explicitly interested in hearing from others who have 'gone through it' and in this way is seeking descriptive accounts rather than direct advice and evaluation (in other words, 'What was your experience?' rather than 'Is this the right thing to do?').

In response to such an interactional environment, participant 15 carefully manages her reply by using a softener ('just some input on this') followed by a short story drawing on her own experience as a mother but additionally highlighting her experience of working on a special care baby unit (note the use of both protagonist-doer and protagonist-experiencer positionings, e.g. 'how unstable and fragile I was'). Through this use of narration, she does not only provide the support that participant 16 is clearly seeking, but also manages the face-threatening aspect of advice-giving. As we can see, her advice is provided indirectly through a personal narrative, which also serves as a positive politeness strategy demonstrating shared concerns and experiences. As Harrison and Barlow (2009) observe, this technique is successful in enabling advice givers to avoid being prescriptive and at the same it allows them to express empathy and shared concerns with the recipient. In this way, as we can see from extract [5] there is no imposition for participant 16 to follow the advice. This is why Brown and Levinson maintain that positive politeness strategies can reduce the social distance between speaker and hearer (1987: 130).

In addition to functioning as a politeness strategy of demonstrating empathy and enabling indirect advice giving, the short one-sentence story ('I found that...') also helps to construct participant 15 as experientially knowledgeable. As Harrison and Barlow put it, such online narratives 'embody suggestions, while at the same time evidencing the writer's authority to make these suggestions' (2009: 107). Moreover, such advice giving has benefits for the narrator too, as through this act of storytelling participants can reflect on and make sense of their own experience, which, as we discuss in the next section, is an important aspect of their identity construction.

Of course, being shared in the context of an online group these narratives do not only address the person who is seeking support. Online solicitations of help and replies to them always have a larger audience, with the result that the use of positive politeness strategies contributes to reducing the social distance among all the group participants. Note also that the respondent in extract [5] engages in a problem-solving activity through co-narration, without providing a single solution. Instead, her reply together with responses of other women that now constitute the thread 'Diabetes and pregnancy' should be seen as a collective process of kernel storytelling, as other women join this process of co-narration by adding new stories which in some ways are tied to the preceding ones.

Earlier in this chapter we argued that there is a clear need to be aware of social processes that shape online communities. The analysis of discourse activities that are constitutive of an online group as outlined in this section might be one of the key steps towards achieving this goal. The examples examined above show how through their discursive exchanges online participants create and observe communicative norms, and in these processes co-construct a safe communicative context. By tracing these two processes within the frameworks of narrative theory and politeness theory, we aimed to shed light on how Internet-based support groups may serve as a viable alternative or at least a complement to face-to-face support initiatives. In particular, we hope to have demonstrated how politeness theory can allow us to deepen our analytical understanding of the legitimating and supportive functions of participants' exchanges.

Task 7.2 Providing emotional support online

Bearing in mind the multiple functions of online personal narratives, examine in more detail how a respondent to Karla's post provides informational and emotional support to help her cope with eating disorder related problems. Discuss how Tara protects Karla's face. Does she implicitly follow Karla's lead as we have hypothesised above?

karla,
I know exactly what you mean! I just started posting to this group recently, and its the most I've ever done to talk to anyone. The thought of talking to others (in person where they can see me and how fat I am) who are, in my opinion, are a lot sicker than me terrifies me. That's why I was glad to find this group (it is more private—no one can see me, they can only get a small window into my feelings). I am also afraid to talk to a therapist because they would probably laugh me out of the office. I'm not sure what causes this feeling, maybe self-doubt or low self esteem. I'm not an expert, but I can certainly relate with your feelings. Call your therapist, maybe one on one would be easier for you right now. Then, when you are ready to face others, you can give it a shot. Good luck :) tara

(cited in Walstrom, 2000: 776)

Theoretical and methodological frameworks for studying online peer-to-peer communication

In this final section we begin by reviewing some of the most important strands of research that explored how people communicate via computers and the Internet, a growing field that became known as computer mediated communication (CMC). This necessarily brief and incomplete review is focussed primarily on the insights these studies brought to light in terms of our knowledge about online interaction and online communities. We then look into the limitations of these theories and discuss the role of ethnographic and applied linguistic approaches in addressing some of the research gaps. Finally, we shall end this chapter by presenting a discourse-based approach to the analysis of communication in online social support groups.

Models of online behaviour and interaction

Over the last few decades, online social interactions have attracted much attention within psychology, sociology and anthropology. A number of theories in social psychology, for example, have looked at the possibilities and limitations offered by online interactions as discussed above. Within this body of theories, the Reduced Social Cues approach (Sproull and Kiesler, 1986) has been particularly influential. According to this model, the relative anonymity of online interactions makes people likely to engage in uninhibited and anti-social behaviour. This is a rather negative view of communication via the Internet whose proponents believed that due to certain fixed characteristics of CMC, such as lack of audio-visual cues, any interaction online is potentially dangerous because social and normative influences on groups and individuals are undermined. The notion of flaming, for example, was coined to refer to one type of extreme and uninhibited behaviour that was seen as a common outcome of online interactions. As social psychological research into CMC developed, however, a subsequent theory was proposed which tried to counter the predominantly negative view of CMC: the Social Identity De-individuation model, developed by Spears and Lea (1994). This theoretical model has put forward a more social perspective, rejecting the proposition that communication processes can be explained with reference to some fixed characteristics of the medium. In particular, Spears and Lea have drawn a distinction between social and personal identities and emphasised that computer mediated communication, even though participants are not physically present, does not preclude creation of social norms (Lamerichs, 2003).

You might have already guessed that despite these theoretical advances, the view of computer-mediated interaction put forward in both models remains rather mechanistic – it does not acknowledge or leave conceptual room for a well-established notion in discourse analytic research, namely that identities are fluid and dynamic. As much of our discussion in this book aimed to show, people can and do actively construct identities in their talks; and as they do so they display a sensitivity as to how they are expected to behave, accounting for their actions, and referring to what is 'normal' or 'proper'. Furthermore, on a general level, these models still come short of providing a comprehensive picture of online interaction. Lamerichs (2003), for example, argues that these perspectives have failed to present a 'truly social view of CMC' (2003: 18), partly because of methodological issues, such as reliance on experiments (which are essentially simulations and therefore do not represent actual uses of new technologies). This is where studies in ethnography and sociology come in, offering a more balanced view of communication via computers and the Internet, a view that is more in line with how people use this medium for various social purposes.

Research carried out within the field of ethnography is perhaps the closest to providing an in-depth picture of communication in online groups. An approach that aims to understand the nature of computer-mediated activities through qualitative analysis of electronic data is sometimes referred to as virtual ethnography or netnography (Hine, 2000). Like ethnographic methods applied in physical spaces, the main task of this type of ethnography is to provide a holistic study of the situated character of Internet practices, paying attention to their own structures and processes (ibid.). While these studies provide thorough and detailed accounts of actual online activities, they can and should be complemented by systematic analyses of participants' conversations that make up these activities.

A similar observation can be made regarding an array of sociological studies that focussed on social groups on the Internet-based medium. Some of these studies attempted to establish the extent to which different online groups represent 'authentic' communities or whether instances of 'real' communal attributes such as commitment can be traced online (Fernback, 2007). However, such studies tend to rely on theoretical assumptions and subsequently label online phenomena in broad terms, for example, in that all online gatherings are 'communities' or that the language of the Internet represents a single style or 'genre' (Herring, 2004). Furthermore, many studies mentioned at the beginning of this chapter (for details of the publications see reviews by Eysenbach *et al.*, 2004 and Orgad, 2005) apply a form of content analysis to analyse discussions in various condition-specific online groups. This type of analysis recruits a set of concepts defined by the analyst rather than participants themselves, and also involves classifying statements for what they are rather than what they do

(Lamerichs and te Molder, 2003); whereas, as we have emphasised throughout, people do a great variety of things with language, such as complaining, accusing, defending, constructing and maintaining authority and so on. This means that such analysis inevitably misses out on various kinds of local interactional business that participants attend to when they engage in conversational practices in these online spaces.

In contrast to the above studies, the approach to communication in online social support groups adopted in this chapter is informed by a linguistic perspective. This is to say that we look at online participation through the prism of language, and make our judgements on the basis of observations about language use. It is therefore not surprising that this perspective, termed by Herring (2004) as 'computer-mediated discourse analysis', draws on methodological paradigms that originated in the study of spoken and written communication, such as conversation analysis, pragmatics, discursive psychology, and critical discourse analysis. Such an approach does not look into isolated statements by individual participants but takes into account the interaction with other members of the online group, and in this way can illuminate different actions towards which participants' written descriptions may be oriented. From this point of view, online statements are not reflections of private mental states but social phenomena that are locally produced and attended to.

Personal reflection

Reflect on the way online communities can create and enforce their own rules of interaction and participation. Many groups have a Frequently Asked Questions section that provides basic information to newcomers. Some online forums have a moderator whose main goal is to make sure written contributions remain 'on-topic' and do not diverge too much from the purpose of the group. Discuss the implications of these social architectural features for encouraging and promoting (or otherwise) engagement and continuous exchange of social support.

Social norms in the online environment

If we now return to the issue of norms explored in our analysis of the extracts in preceding sections, we can see that the 'norms' characterising both online groups under study (the eating disorder group and an online community for people with diabetes) do not represent some rigid rules that guide participants' behaviour. Rather they can be best described as a set of interpretative resources that participants orient to, in order to make sense of their ongoing interaction with others (Lamerichs and te Molder, 2003). For example, revisiting the extracts from the online group for people with eating disorders, we can see how its participants observe two norms specific to this online community: not disclosing personal information and creating and maintaining a safe environment. This is done through an exchange of posts between the participants (see the initial post by Karla, and the reply by tara). This view of norms is in line with recent discourse-based studies of online social support (e.g. Stommel and Koole, 2010; Armstrong *et al.*, in press) that have stressed that online 'norms' do not constitute some predefined piece of information presented to participants when they join the group. Rather, as we have explored earlier, they should be seen and analysed as expectations that emerge and are continuously negotiated in online conversational practices.

So far our discussion has centred on positive and generally unproblematic aspects of communication in online support groups. While many studies have indeed documented various benefits stemming from participation in online health-related discussions, we are wary of painting a rose-tinted picture of online communities here. At a first glance, online groups seem to be open to everybody as people can drop in and drop out, they can refine each other's statements and challenge misinformation. However, we must be aware of the fact that the very issue of 'norms' implies construction of insiders and outsiders, and in this way has important implications in terms of access to online social support.

In this regard, Stommel and Koole (2010) discuss an interesting case when participation in an online community for people with eating disorders is not straightforward and low threshold. The authors studied such interactional phenomena as sequential organisation of online talk and membership categorisation (how people categorise themselves in relation to other people and phenomena) to reveal how certain normative requirements emerge in the course of discussion on this forum. In particular, they found that newcomers to this group were interactionally put in a position where they had to adopt a specific orientation on eating disorders, namely that an eating disorder is an illness that needs to be cured, not celebrated. To achieve this, established members of this group employed various strategies in order to orient newbies to what they saw as a 'not-glamorising' position, and did not grant full acceptance until this normative requirement was met. It follows from this that individuals who may not be (yet) ready to produce such statements are likely to be excluded. As a result of such discursive management of group talk, newcomers may be discouraged or even scared away from taking part in interactions in this and similar groups. This, in turn, made the authors question whether the key goal of an online social support group, namely to reach isolated people with a medical condition, is really met in such cases. As Stommel and Koole warn, 'although structural features such as geographic independence render OSGs a low threshold help and support service, other 'discursive' features seem to heighten the threshold' (2010: 375).

Communities of Practice

Having problematised the view of identity and group norms in online interaction, we shall now move on to examine possible frameworks for studying social interaction in online social support settings. To begin with, the negotiated and dynamic nature of norms necessitates a concept of online community that is not static (Stommel and Koole, 2010). According to this view, an Internet-based discussion forum should be seen and analysed as first and foremost a 'mutable construct, determined by social actors who create meaning about it' (Fernback, 2007: 66).

In this regard, it is useful to adopt Wenger's concept of Community of Practice in order to explore the phenomenon of online groups centred around discussions on health and illness-related topics. Wenger describes such communities as developing over time through 'the sustained pursuit of a shared enterprise' (1998: 45). This concept of community centres on active participation and is characterised by the practices members are engaged in. Consequently, participation norms are constructed and negotiated through discourse activities. This is one of the reasons that male-dominated forums are found to be hostile because flaming often constitutes a common practice in such groups, whereas female-dominated groups prioritise exchanges of support and intimacy. Similarly, the relevance of legitimacy as a requirement for newcomers can be understood when we look at online participants as a community of practice. As we saw in the above study by Stommel and Koole (2010), new participants were granted membership once they aligned to the practices that are constitutive of that community.

Within a community of practice, negotiation of norms and rules of participation constitutes an inseparable part of identity building – and here we refer to both individual and social identities theorised in social psychological research. Crucially for linguists, such negotiation is carried out through various discourse activities. Through daily online discussions that appear in the form of archived threads, participants create a shared repertoire of stories and histories. This is why an online community is primarily an online *discursive* community. Such online self-presentations through the use of language allow participants to craft their identities (manipulation of various technical features available in social networking sites, for instance, should also be taken into account). Just as offline, these online personal identities are intertwined with the identities of others. This is done through quoting, hyperlinking or referring to other participants, by following explicit and implicit rules for interaction, and generally indicating one's membership in the group.

In this way, online archives of conversations serve both as a reflection of collectivity and mutual engagement, and at the same time allow for the negotiation of personal meaning for each participating individual. In his account of participation in an online group for people with prostate cancer, Roos (2003) eloquently describes how this meaning-making process takes place in a community of practice:

> It was, and still is, a community in which I could learn my patientry, in which I could negotiate meaning and claim my new identity as a cancer patient. In this community, whilst my participation was reified as archived emails, the meaning learning and identity came out of my participation, and it was meaning for me, not for someone else. My responses may have provided meaning for others, but that resulted from their participation. (2003: 222)

A study of the interplay between participants' personal identities and the emergence and maintenance of the group's collective identity can profitably draw on Herring's classification of features characterising an online group as a community, namely *identity, sociability* and *support* (Herring, 2004). Active participation and the continuous exchange of messages (sociability) allows an online group to develop shared norms and values as well as create an awareness of its distinguishing features (identity). Participation in the form of creating content and consuming it (reading, commenting) is vital for the development of any group. By demonstrating solidarity and reciprocity and following any pre-existing as well as emerging social participation guidelines, members can then maintain the group (support). As discussed in the preceding section, this can be achieved through the use of different politeness strategies. Brown and Levinson (1987: 103) themselves refer to this role of positive politeness when they define it as:

> A kind of metaphorical extension of intimacy, to imply common ground or sharing of wants to a limited extent even between strangers who perceive themselves, for the purposes of the interaction, as somehow similar. For the same reason, positive-politeness techniques are usable not only for FTA redress, but in general as a kind of social accelerator, where S, in using them, indicates that he [sic] wants to 'come closer' to H.

Indeed, as we can see from extracts [4] and [5], instead of briefly outlining her position on the topic and giving direct advice through the use of imperatives ('do this ... but not that ... ', for example), which is a potentially viable action in a non-face-to-face setting, participant 15 chooses to state her views indirectly and takes time to elaborate on her background and experiences. This serves to create a common ground between herself and the advice-seeker, which in this online context is simultaneously extended to all those who not only contributed to this thread but simply read it while 'lurking' on this site.

We want to conclude this discussion with a note on practical applications that may stem from the discourse-based approach we have outlined. At the beginning of this chapter we argued that the proliferation of online communities will provide new challenges and opportunities for medical researchers and health educators if they want to understand the role of online social support in patients' self-management of their conditions. There is no doubt that continued research is needed to further examine the role of such groups in the promotion of beneficial health outcomes as well as their potential as an educational venue. However, before we focus on cultivating successful supportive relationships online, it is imperative to gain a greater understanding of the dynamics behind such behaviours. In this regard, a linguistic approach to CMC based on a micro-analysis of interactions elaborated here can yield relevant knowledge. Following Stommel and Koole (2010), such practical applications (informed by discourse analysis) as development of special sections for participants that cannot yet align to expectations of a particular online community may promote engagement, and in this way prevent emotionally vulnerable participants from falling back into social isolation.

Summary

We began this chapter by introducing the notion of online social support and outlining current research into how participants use Internet-based discussion forums as part of their coping processes. The discursive work thereby accomplished, and the linguistic tools applied to uncover it, became the centre of attention in the next section. We first focussed on participants' self-introductions when entering online support groups, and examined the kind of discursive work participants undertake when they present their problems and request information and support. It turned out that participants, when introducing themselves in these online spaces, do not merely enumerate some basic facts about their condition or diagnosis. Rather, their opening messages can be best described as acts of storytelling which take into account views of known or imaginary others and, in politeness theory terms, perform different types of face work.

We then examined how participants engaged in the provision of informational and emotional support, focussing on the face-threatening nature of advice-giving and revealing the ways in which participants used personal narratives to overcome it. It is noteworthy to emphasise here that interactions in online communities provide us with an opportunity to study support groups for peers, in which there are no predefined hierarchies that one can draw upon to display authority and expertise. This remains one of the relatively unexplored areas of CMC, as not many studies to date have systematically examined the ways in which advice is shared in online settings where participants are not caught up in different institutional ranks.

Finally, the last section explored a range of theoretical frameworks and positions that have been applied to study computer-mediated interactions. We hope to have demonstrated that, drawing on the framework of computer mediated discourse analysis, a study of how online social support is shared online requires understanding of both the electronic environment, that is technological affordances of the medium, and specific rules negotiated in group discussions.

8 Seeking online help from health professionals

Introducing computer-mediated health discourse: is it speech or writing?

In the parts of this book concerned with spoken and written health communication, we outlined some of the distinctive properties of speech and writing. Before we look in more detail at online health interaction, let us first consider some of the general linguistic characteristics of computer-mediated communication (CMC). A common conception of computer-mediated discourse is that it resembles either speech written down or speech by other means (Baron, 1998). Yet this is surely too hard and fast a division. CMC incorporates features common to both speech and writing; it is therefore more accurate to describe the medium as being 'Janus-faced – at once resembling and not resembling face-to-face speech' (Baron, 2003: 86). Whatever the case, such variability of form highlights the fact that linguistically classifying online communication is no straightforward task.

Despite its protean form, however, it is possible to identify some general truths about the expressive character of CMC. Electronic discourse formats such as email and instant messaging have wide stylistic potential, affording users considerable scope in formulating and responding to messages (Baron, 1998: 163). The following set of descriptors offers a useful overview of the linguistic profile of computer-mediated discourse, characterising the format in terms of four dimensions of human communication:

Social dynamics: **Predominantly like writing**
- interlocutors are physically separated
- physical separation fosters personal disclosure
- and helps level the conversational playing field

Format: **(Mixed) writing and speech**
- like writing, CMC is durable
- like speech, CMC is typically unedited

Grammar.

> LEXICON: predominantly like speech
> - heavy use of first- and second-person pronouns
>
> SYNTAX: (mixed) writing and speech
> - like writing, CMC has relatively high levels of lexical density
> - like speech, commonly uses present tense
> - contractions

Style: **Predominantly like speech**
- low level of formality
- expression of emotion not always self-monitored

(adapted from Baron, 2000: 251)

Although, as the above set of characteristics attests, computer-mediated discourse is likely to contain mixed elements of communication, it nevertheless constitutes a distinct mode of interaction, affording new communicative opportunities. As Crystal (2006: 126) observes, electronic discourse formats such as email have come to inhabit an interactive space not readily occupied by other forms of communication. For instance, the convenience and accessibility of email, as harnessed by interactive online health forums, connects patients with professionals separated from one another by time and space. Indeed, in the context of healthcare, online interaction is for many people a 'logical extension of communication with an already existing patient-physician relationship' (Spielberg, 1999: 730).

Task 8.1 Computer-mediated communication: a linguistically impoverished medium?   (TC)

Despite its potential for the delivery of healthcare, some language purists consider some forms of online communication to be linguistically impoverished, nothing less than stylistic free-for-alls. For example, as Herring (2001: 616) observes, computer-mediated discourse has been described as 'less correct, complex and coherent than standard written language'. But is this really the case? Are such informal and non-standard features of language insurmountable obstacles to communicating successfully with others online?

Consider the following brief emails. Despite their being replete with non-standard orthography, would you say they were ambiguous? And do any of these variant spellings produce certain deliberate expressive effects?

- Hav eyou got the tickets yet?
- i ham being bullied at school
- I AM LOSING MY MEMORY. . . !!! pleaaaaaaaaaaaaaase tell me what to do

Disembodied encounters: establishing credibility and professional identities online

As well as providing patients with convenient access to health information, the Internet has the potential to meet the widening gap between the need for transmitting information to patients and the relatively limited opportunities for face-to-face exchanges with doctors (Mandl *et al.*, 1998; Car and Sheikh, 2004). Moreover, the linking of patients and practitioners through online forms of communication potentially increases the involvement of patients in their treatment (Mandl *et al.*, 1998: 496). Some medical sociologists see this increased involvement of patients in the pursuit of cybermedicine (that is, online healthcare provision) as a threat to traditional healthcare services. Hardey (1999: 821), for example, refers to the phenomenon of 'proletarianisation', 'the process whereby organisational and managerial changes divest professions of the control they have enjoyed over their work'. In other words, the provision of healthcare is, to some extent, no longer considered to be the sole domain of health professionals. Patients are becoming increasingly active in their pursuit of healthcare, turning to the Internet for medical information rather than consulting their own doctors (Eysenbach and Diepgen, 1999). In the present era of choice and self-determination, where expert knowledge is freely available to anyone plugged into the World Wide Web, the passive term 'patient' no longer seems relevant. The dynamic term 'consumer', redolent of late capitalism, seems more appropriate.

Naturally the more active role taken by the cyber-surfing patient-consumer introduces new challenges for health professionals. Among the many reputable and evidence-based online health resources, the Internet is awash with disreputable and misleading websites run by mountebanks and a host of other self-styled authorities who, purporting to possess some level of clinical expertise, batten on the needy and vulnerable. The increasing ubiquity of such questionable 'services' puts health professionals under increasing pressure to produce more reliable and expertly informed provision. Yet although the Internet offers medical experts a new means of reaching people, interacting with patients online presents a unique set of rhetorical challenges. As we noted in Chapter 7, participants who exchange information electronically do so without recourse to non-verbal aspects of communication, such as gesture and facial expressions. Professionals and patients engaged in online exchanges, therefore, have to rely solely on words. Words alone are the conveyors of information, and, consequently, this places extra emphasis on the linguistic ability of practitioner and patient alike (Car and Sheikh, 2004).

During face-to-face medical encounters, the force and influence of practitioners' talk derives as much from the participants' communicative style and image as the content of their talk (Car and Sheikh, 2004: 437). Physical appearance, dress, movements, gestures and other paralinguistic traits are all, besides speech, integral to persona and identity. Practitioners who provide online services face the problem of not only having to provide effective health advice while being spatially and temporally separated from patients, but also having to construct an appropriate online identity. The problem becomes particularly acute if more than one advice-giver is involved. How, for instance, do a team of medical experts construct, and operate as, a single, unified persona whom advice seekers can trust and relate to? Little linguistic research has been conducted into how online advice-givers' identities emerge through the use of certain linguistic strategies and the way in which their advice is conveyed to patients: most discourse-analytic studies have focussed on peer-to-peer interaction.

One exception to this prevailing focus is the work of Miriam Locher (Locher, 2006; Locher and Hoffman, 2006). Locher's research examines the structure and content of advice offered to users of the web-based advice forum, 'Lucy Answers', an American Internet health column run by health professionals. 'Lucy' is the pseudonym given to the advisory collective, the name under which a team of health advisors respond to requests for help from online advice-seekers. Locher argues that, through the use of a range of linguistic strategies, 'Lucy', in her responses to help-seekers' problems, emerges with the identity of an expert advice-giver. Moreover, not only do these linguistic strategies construct a professional persona for Lucy, but they also help the advisors to negotiate the rhetorically delicate activity of providing counsel. As we observed in the previous chapter, giving advice is potentially a face-threatening activity (Morrow, 2006: 541), as well as being an activity that brings about an asymmetrical relationship between the advice-giver and the advice-seeker (experts possess knowledge; advice-givers have knowledge deficits). Providing effective advice, therefore, involves not only the production of dependable information on which advice-seekers can practically act, but also the skilful application of strategies to redress the face threat involved in giving advice.

Locher and Hoffman (2006: 78) identify seven linguistic strategies through which the identity of the health advisor emerges during postings to advice-seekers as follows:

1 Lucy's name itself, self-reference and other terms of address.
2 Lucy presents herself as a competent and knowledgeable source of accurate information.
3 Lucy makes readers think and gives options in her realization of advice.

4 Lucy chooses an easily accessible, informal, and non-offensive range of lexical choices.
5 Lucy has an opinion.
6 Lucy offers empathy.
7 Lucy uses humour.

It is worth noting that these features work collectively to produce a distinctive and expertly informed voice for Lucy. No one strategy is more significant than the others. Broadly the strategies incorporate aspects of personal image and expert identity projection (strategies 1-2); strategies for delivering linguistic advice and which further shape the advisor identity (3-4); and interpersonal strategies that contribute to advisor qualities (5-7). Examining all these elements in operation is beyond the scope of this chapter, so in order to demonstrate how the expert persona Lucy is brought into being, we confine our focus to a selection of these strategies. The following advice-giving sequence, prefaced by the help-seeker's problem letter, provides an illustration of how Lucy linguistically realises online counsel.

PANIC ATTACKS

Dear Lucy,

I need some information about panic attacks. My partner moved with me to NY and, at the time of moving, experienced several attacks of extreme fear.

This has paralyzed her to the extent that she no longer goes to work, her career is on hold, and she requires help traveling, if she travels at all. As well as being incredibly distressing for her, it's not helping our relationship either.

My question relates to my role in helping her recover from this. At present I frequently 'overlook' the problem by going everywhere with her and being as supportive as possible. Am I an 'enabler'? Should I make her 'tough it out,' or will she just get better?

Dear Reader,

Panic attacks are periods of heightened anxiety often coupled with an extreme fear of being in crowded or closed places. At first, these attacks are sudden and unexpected, but, if they continue, are often triggered by environment, like going through tunnels, traveling across bridges, or being in crowded elevators. Accompanying symptoms include a sense of chest pain, shallow breathing, lightheadedness, dizziness, sweating, a pounding heart, chills or flushes, nausea, and even tingling or numbness in the hands. A sense of impending doom is usually part of the experience.

Panic attacks are common, frequently linked to feelings of loss. Panic attacks vary in intensity and tend to be exacerbated by stressful periods. Psychotherapy, with and without medication, is effective for as many as 90 percent of people affected with panic attacks. Cutting back on caffeine may make a difference, too.

While your support may be comforting to your partner, it would be wise for her to get professional counseling, especially since her panic is affecting your relationship. With counseling for yourself as well, you may be better able to help your partner. If you are at AEI, call Counseling and Psychological Services (CPS) at [phone number].

Lucy

(Locher and Hoffman, 2006: 81-2)

Let us first consider the name 'Lucy' itself, the strategy of nomenclature. The questioner uses this proper noun to address the advice-giver, and the advice-giver, in turn, signs off her response with the name also. The choice of the proper noun, Lucy, is significant. Portraying the health advisor as a woman exploits a set of assumptions about the nature of advice-giving. The use of female names, Locher and Hoffman (2006: 79) observe, is connected with the longstanding tradition of women providing advice in problem pages. In the UK, for example, the agony aunt has been a staple of the tabloid newspaper and other popular publications. One well-known advisor was 'Rebecca Marjorie Proops', whose advice column, 'Dear Marje', coloured the pages of the *Daily Mirror* for over 30 years. Similar advice columns, featuring advice-givers with female personas, have been running for several centuries, reaching their zenith in the mid-nineteenth century, with the increase in mass literacy and the boom in popular journalism (Mangan, 2009). Thus, as Locher and Hoffman (2006: 79) argue, the name Lucy situates the online health advisor in a tradition for female advisors in the popular genre of the problem page.

Lucy is not the only term she uses to refer to herself. She also uses personal pronouns. However, where one might expect the presence of the first-person 'I' (arguably the most natural way for individuals to refer to themselves), Lucy generally sidesteps this indexing strategy, instead referring to herself in the third-person (Locher and Hoffman, 2006: 79). As the following examples attest:

(Response to question about drugs)
Lucy assumes that this is what you mean by contamination.

(Response to question about sexuality)
Lucy noticed that you signed your letter 'argh' and wondered about that.

(2006: 79-80)

According to multi-million word reference corpora (collections of text, such as the British National Corpus, designed to be representative of the language as a whole), the first-person form 'I' typically features as one of the most frequent words in general English. There is, accordingly, a high expectation of its recurring use in a wide range of English language varieties (including spoken and written genres). Lucy's relatively low use of the first-person pronoun (it occurs only 5 times in all of her 280 advice responses) is therefore significantly marked, not to mention intriguing. Locher and Hoffman suggest that there are two reasons why Lucy refers to herself by name. First, the frequent use of the third-person helps to point to the team of health professionals behind the Lucy pseudonym, a strategy which simultaneously cements her identity as an advice-giving expert while reminding advice-seekers that she is in fact not real. Secondly, the recurring appearance of the pseudonym actually 'talks Lucy into being' (2006: 80). This effect would be particularly discernible to those users who regularly access the website – users who, having harnessed its services over a period of time, are likely to perceive instances of the first-person as being slips in register rather than a deliberate index of personal identity.

Lucy's responses to advice-seekers' questions typically contain an address term, an assessment of the problem, an advice-giving section, and a signature (2006: 81). All of these features can be seen in Lucy's response to the problem letter above. Her answer opens with an address form ('Dear Reader'), followed by two paragraphs in which she provides background information about panic attacks. Locher and Hoffman note that, in displaying her encyclopaedic knowledge (presenting medical facts and describing symptoms), Lucy portrays herself as an expert, an advisor who is 'a competent and knowledgeable source of accurate information' (ibid.). This background assessment cues the advice itself, which is delivered in the concluding part of Lucy's response. To some extent, the orchestration of steps leading up to the advice reflects the 'Ideal Sequence' (ten Have, 1989) of the doctor–patient consultation, in which openings, complaint formulations and assessments all precede the delivery of treatment or advice. In adopting an advice-giving format not dissimilar to the Ideal Sequence of the face-to-face consultation, Lucy aligns herself to other practitioners, an alignment which, it is not unreasonable to suggest, adds to her professional legitimacy.

Linguistically, Lucy's advice is realised through three key syntactic devices: indicative statements, imperatives and questions (Locher and Hoffman, 2006: 83). In the example above, the advice is presented principally in the form of declarative statements ('it would be wise for her to get ... ', 'With counseling for yourself as well, you may be better able to help ... '). Constituting a series of suggestions rather than commands, the advice here is relatively low in directive force and hence adheres to the counselling ideal of non-directiveness. Rather than exhorting the advisee to future action, Lucy invites it. In offering advice in this fashion, Lucy simultaneously respects the autonomy of the advisee, their right to self-determination, while minimising the threat to their self-image. Lucy, in other words, exploits levels of indirectness: in using suggestions to convey advice, she presents the advisee with the opportunity of interpreting her statements as options (2006: 86).

In conjunction with the aforementioned strategies of self-reference and presenting herself as a reliable source of information, Lucy harnesses a particular set of lexical choices which Locher and Hoffman describe as 'accessible, informal, and non-offensive' (2006: 86). However, although informal, Lucy consistently uses Standard English, avoiding irregular spellings and any other non-standard forms of language that are common in modes of computer-mediated interaction. This standard-style approach differs from advice-giving in peer-to-peer online support forums, where using non-standard forms of English is not uncommon (Morrow, 2006) and certainly no bar to providing advice to others: delivering advice in such a fashion does not debase or otherwise invalidate it. However, Lucy's adoption of standard spelling, vocabulary and grammar, according to Locher and Hoffman, helps to emphasise her professional persona, contributing to an impression of competence and trustworthiness. This linguistic approach appears to be appreciated by the users of the website, for on the rare occasions when Lucy employs colloquial language she is liable to be upbraided. As one reader incensed by Lucy's use of the term 'whacking off' put it, 'GET SERIOUS – LOSE THE SLANG!' (2006: 90).

To sum up, then, it can be seen that Lucy emerges as an expert advice-giver through the use of a range of linguistic strategies. Not all of these seven strategies are harnessed in every one of Lucy's response letters. Yet the fact that not all of them are in operation at one time does not impede the discursive construction of Lucy's expert persona. Locher and Hoffman describe the emergence of her expert identity as a cumulative process: it emerges in readers' minds through repeated use of the website. Accordingly each reader will formulate a slightly different identity for the advice-giver but, whatever their impression, it will be determined, to a significant extent, by the rhetorical strategies discussed above.

Personal reflection

As we have seen, Lucy's use of Standard English is designed to construct her as a professional and trustworthy advice-giver. If her advice were couched in non-standard language (using, for example, colloquialisms, non-standard spelling and grammar) would this affect your perception of Lucy as a competent professional in any way?

Corpus linguistics: a novel approach to health communication

Having focussed our attention so far on how professionals provide online advice, let us now consider the problems submitted by advice-seekers to practitioners over the Internet. Here we draw on corpus linguistics, a method of analysis that is well suited to interrogating electronic texts and large quantities of linguistic information. Over the last decade, a number of researchers have begun to harness corpus methodologies in order to analyse substantially larger datasets than those that commonly feature in studies of health language. One of the advantages of using large collections of data – it is not unusual for a corpus to comprise many millions of words – is that it allows the analyst to account for a wide range of variation which might be present in the texts and therefore base generalisations about linguistic behaviour on more substantial and representative textual evidence (Stubbs, 1997).

A corpus (plural corpora) is a collection of naturally occurring linguistic texts which has been stored electronically. Corpora don't have to be compact of just one language type or variety. Corpora comprise linguistic data from many modes and genres, including: newspapers, magazines, radio broadcasts, fiction, interviews, casual conversations, websites and so on. What is key about the linguistic data that makes up a corpus is that it is naturally occurring (i.e. real language produced by people in various situations) and collected electronically. Thus one of the practical advantages of interrogating online health language is that, conveniently, it is already available electronically and therefore, unlike spoken and written texts, does not have to be rendered into a suitable electronic format.

The fact that corpora are stored electronically means that they are machine-readable and can therefore be subjected to the redoubtable processing power of computers. Corpus linguistics programs (a number of which are freely available and easy to use) enable researchers to undertake tasks which they would otherwise be unable to perform manually, including searching for every occurrence of a word or word combination, calculating the frequency of occurrence, and/or conveniently displaying contexts of use on one screen. In this way, corpus software can process vast amounts of textual material, revealing language patterns that a human interpreter would most certainly fail to notice (Butler, 1998). Devoid of human bias and computational imperfection, moreover, the analytical findings yielded by computers can be more reliable than other forms of manual linguistic interrogation (McEnery *et al.*, 2006).

However, this is not to suggest that corpus linguistics approaches trump every other mode and method of language analysis. Corpus approaches to health communication are not ends in themselves. Computers alone cannot provide explanations for the linguistic behaviour identified in a corpus. The frequent and salient features that corpus software is able to locate still need to be interpreted (Stubbs, 2005).

It is therefore important, we argue, to supplement quantitative approaches to analysing health communication data with qualitative analysis. Identifying the occurrence rates of linguistic features is an effective means of revealing the properties of a text (Widdowson, 2000: 7), but quantitative inquiries alone, which deprive linguistic data of context, are unlikely to be sufficient for providing an understanding of communication (Skelton and Hobbs, 1999a, 1999b). Conducting qualitative analysis (that is, scrutinising linguistic features in their original context of use) in conjunction with quantitative analysis is able to provide robust and sensitive insights into communication.

Task 8.2 Does (corpus) size matter?   (TC)

One of the criticisms of discourse analysis studies, including research into health communication, is that they often use small samples of data (such as fragments from practitioner–patient encounters). Indeed many of the studies we have considered throughout this book have harnessed relatively small collections of data (small enough, that is, so that they can be analysed without the aid of a computer). Do you think basing analytical claims on comparatively small collections of data weakens the validity of such research? How much data do you need to successfully conduct health communication research?

Using keywords and concordances to interrogate online health communication

One practical and reliable means of combining quantitative and qualitative approaches to analysing health communication is through the use of keywords. Keywords are an effective tool in the pursuit of discourse analysis (Baker, 2006), allowing researchers to identify salient themes in a corpus and then to interrogate those themes closely in context. Keywords are being used by an increasing number of researchers as a reliable method of identifying signal themes in health language corpora (e.g. Adolphs *et al.*, 2004; Harvey *et al.*, 2008; Atkins and Harvey, 2010). Keywords, according to McCarthy and Handford, are words which 'best define' (2004: 174) a text or texts – words that are an important indicator of both expression and content (Seale *et al.*, 2007).

Keywords are words which are key not by dint of their possessing social and cultural significance (words, that is, which the analyst deems to be worthy of critical attention, such as those interrogated in Raymond Williams' classic study (1983)), but words that have statistical significance. In corpus-based studies keywords are generated computationally. They are words that occur with a significantly higher frequency in one language variety in relation to another. To generate keywords, therefore, one has to compare one corpus with another. In order to illustrate this process, along with a subsequent contextual analysis of the keywords so generated, we will use a corpus of health emails submitted to a website dedicated to providing advice for young people: *Teenage Health Freak* (see Figure 8.1). Our analytical approach will follow that of Atkins and Harvey (2010). However, we will use a larger and more up-to-date corpus of adolescent health emails.

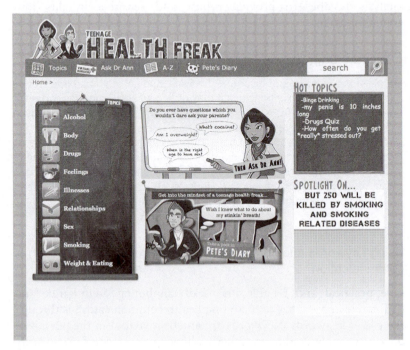

Figure 8.1 Homepage of *Teenage Health Freak* website

Operated by doctors specialising in adolescent health, the *Teenage Health Freak*, is a UK-based online advice column which launched in 2000. A key interactive feature of the website allows users to email their health-related questions in confidence to the online GP, 'Dr Ann' (a collective, virtual persona for the team of doctors who respond to the questions). These questions and requests for advice do not constitute emails in the traditional sense; they are not sent via the contributors' individual, personal email accounts, but communicated anonymously via a posting platform on the website. The corpus we use for our keyword analysis comprises 113,480 health emails submitted to the *Teenage Health Freak* website from 2004 to 2009, a total of just over two million words. It can be reasonably argued that the corpus provides a comprehensive picture of the health concerns communicated on a daily basis by the website's users.

It is worth noting here that, rather than directly extracting these messages from the website, we first sought permission to collect and use the email data from the practitioners who run the website. Accessing online data for the purposes of research raises questions about research ethics, not least whether investigators should, at the very least, consult with the operators of the domain from which they intend to gather and use data. That said, a number of health communication researchers, for example Seale (2006), argue that since online health forums provide open access, the messages posted therein are in the public domain and are therefore ethically suitable for collection. However, as we argued in Chapter 4, it is good practice to conduct, where possible, applied linguistic research as a joint enterprise, researching with, rather than purely on, participants. Accordingly, when it comes to collecting data from online health forums, researchers would be well advised to consult with the hosts of such websites.

What health issues trouble young people? Generating a keyword profile of concerns

As previously mentioned, keywords provide a reliable means of identifying salient items in a corpus, that is: words which characterise a particular language variety. Therefore, researchers wishing to survey a new domain of health language, to establish, for example, a profile of its thematic and expressive content, would do well to harness the facility of keywords. Table 8.1 lists a representative selection of lexical keywords that appear in the adolescent health email corpus. These keywords were generated by comparing the health emails from the *Teenage Health Freak* website with a ten-million-word collection of general spoken English from the British National Corpus (BNC), a corpus which contains a rich variety of authentic everyday spoken discourse formats, including informal conversations and more formal

Table 8.1 List of keywords (by theme) appearing in the health email corpus

Theme	Examples of keywords
Sexual health	Sex, sexual, penis, pregnant, period, orgasm, AIDS, infertile, STD, STI, sperm, contraception, HIV, clitoris, vagina, vulva, PMS, erection, condom, masturbate, abortion, foreplay, intercourse, virgin, unprotected, lesbian, oral, pill, ovulation, herpes, thrush, chlamydia, pregnancy, tampon, testicles, genitalia, viagra, scrotum, labia, ovaries, foreskin, balls, fanny, bisexual
Mental health	Depression, depressed, suicide, suicidal, die, overdose, cuts, [self] harm, [self] harming, scars, unhappy, upset, wrists, stress, stressed, anxiety, moods, crying
Body weight	Anorexia, anorexic, weight, size, overweight, fat, obese, underweight, skinny, thin, bulimia, BMI, exercise, diets, kilograms, kg, kgs, calories
Drugs/alcohol	Drugs, cannabis, cocaine, heroin, pills, addicted, alcohol, drunk, drinking, poppers, mushrooms, marijuana, crack, ecstasy, addict, stoned, LSD, cigarettes, dope
Serious conditions	Cancer, epilepsy, diabetes, diabetic, anthrax
Minor conditions	Spots, pimples, acne, zit, zits, blackhead, dandruff, worms, cystitis, warts
Medication	Medication, prescribed, antibiotics, tablets pill, pills

institutional talk. Ideally, when producing a list of keywords one should aim to compare like with like, that is, comparing one's target corpus with a similar set of texts. For example, comparing a collection of spoken medical interviews with a corpus of purely written texts will not produce a list of keywords that truly reflects what is salient in the clinical corpus. As Scott (2004) puts it, choose your comparison corpus in a principled way: 'compare apples with pears, or, better still, Coxes with Granny Smiths'. (For another useful discussion of how to generate and analyse keywords, see Baker (2006)).

Regarding our list of keywords, spoken language is an appropriate language variety with which to compare online discourse since, although the messages are written, they are in an informal language variety and are dialogic: thus speech is arguably their more appropriate point of comparison, rather than the more literary or technical styles commonly found in written language (Harvey *et al.*, 2008). In order to compare the corpora and yield a list of keywords, we have used the corpus software WordSmith Tools (Scott, 2004). However, a number of corpus programs are readily available (for readers interested in pursuing corpus-based health communication research, we provide a list of corpus software at the end of the book). The keywords in Table 8.1, resolved into categories of health themes, provide an overview of the kind of problems for which the *Teenage Health Freak* website users commonly seek advice. Given the size of the corpus (two million words) in which these keywords appear, it would have been extremely difficult to pinpoint these salient themes without recourse to computational means.

It should be noted that the keywords in Table 8.1 are all lexical (content) words. Functional or grammatical words are not reported here. This is not because words such as 'I', 'you', 'was', 'am', 'of', 'might', etc. are not and cannot be keywords; it is because functional words do not, in isolation at least, provide informational content and therefore are not, in themselves, indicative of themes and topics – in other words, what a corpus is about (Baker, 2006). However, functional words are, of course, essential conveyors of meaning and expression, connecting lexical words in phrases and clauses. Accordingly, when carrying out a close examination of lexical keywords, it is important to consider the surrounding context of keywords since the meaning of such items will be affected by the functional words to which they are attached.

The keywords in Table 8.1 reveal a range of adolescent health concerns, most prominent among them issues relating to sexual and mental health. Although informed by clearly defined general semantic areas (sexual and mental health, body weight, drugs/alcohol, etc.), the categories overlap and are to some extent arbitrary. For instance, issues relating to body image are potentially indicative of a mental health concern: dissatisfaction with bodily appearance is commonly linked to low self-esteem (Groesz et al., 2002).

Nevertheless, the keywords direct us to themes that are worthy of closer linguistic attention. Keywords in isolation, however, contribute little to a situational understanding of language use. Therefore, the next stage of our analysis involves a qualitative exploration of these salient items in context. Given the number of keywords that occur in the health email corpus, it is not possible to interrogate all of them in close detail. Here lies one of the limitations of corpus linguistics (a limitation, in fact, that also applies to other methods of linguistic analysis): Which specific analytical focus does the researcher pursue? All of the keywords in Table 8.1 – by dint of their being keywords – are justifiable points of qualitative entry into the corpus, but an exhaustive analysis of all the keywords is impractical, if not impossible (certainly in a book of this size). Some principled decision needs to be made.

Since lexical patterns clustering around the topic of sexual health predominate in the keyword list, we will examine lexis in this area, focussing specifically on the theme of sexually transmitted infection/disease (often abbreviated to STI/STD). As well as being a theme flagged up by a range of keywords (for example, 'AIDS', 'STD', 'STI', 'HIV', 'herpes', 'chlamydia'), the rates of sexually transmitted infections in young people are an international cause for concern (Health Protection Agency, 2010; Healthy People 2010, 2010). The prevalence of sexually transmitted infections (STIs) among young people is high, with, for example, 15 to 24 year olds having four times the chlamydia rate than the total population (Healthy People 2010, 2010). Young people are also affected by more serious infections such as HIV. Research indicates that, although often aware of the risks involved in taking part in sexual activity, adolescents are liable to have limited and erroneous understandings about reproductive health (Mason, 2005). Yet, tellingly, these negative constructions of adolescent sexual health are generated by an outsider perspective, prompted by what researchers deem to be the issues rather than young people themselves. According to Jackson (2005), a different perspective to that provided by much of the research literature emerges when young people are asked to formulate their own 'insider perspectives' concerning sexual health. The insider perspective allows researchers to see how young people themselves define their problems and, therefore, provides a more authentic picture of personal beliefs about health and illness.

Concordance analysis of HIV/AIDS related concerns

Table 8.2 lists the total frequencies of all the sexually transmitted infections and conditions referred to in the health email corpus. Intriguingly, 'HIV' and 'AIDS' make up 44 per cent of the total number of references to specific STIs, with mention of other infections being comparatively infrequent. Since they are the most common, we will closely examine the keywords 'AIDS' and 'HIV' in context shortly, but for the moment it is interesting to speculate why they appear so frequently.

With the advent of AIDS and HIV, it became apparent to many people that drug use and unprotected sexual behaviour carried 'connotations of health risk and death' (Woollett *et al.*, 1998: 370). Although it is not possible to ascertain whether the saliency of the terms 'HIV' and 'AIDS' in the email corpus is due to their seriousness, the lexical preference for 'HIV' and 'AIDS', the latter in particular, is revealing. Whatever the case, it is certain that practically all young people are aware of HIV/AIDS (Rosenthal and Moore, 1994).

Table 8.2: Frequencies of sexually transmitted infections and conditions

Rank	Word	Frequency	%
1	AIDS	437	28
2	HIV	243	16
3	thrush	225	15
4	crabs	203	13
5	genital warts	146	9
6	herpes	132	9
7	chlamydia	129	8
8	gonorrhoea	19	1
9	syphilis	14	1

However, as the concordance analysis below reveals, awareness is not the same as understanding. Many of the messages concerning HIV/AIDS expose some profound misconceptions and entrenched folk beliefs about sexual health.

Concordance analysis involves examining keywords as they appear in their original contexts of use. More specifically, concordances are lines of data featuring a particular keyword (or what is also sometimes referred to as a 'node') presented within the context they occur in (known as the 'span'). In the following concordance examples, the keywords 'HIV' and 'AIDS' are highlighted in bold. Since the emails in which these two keywords appear are relatively small (sixteen words on average), we here reproduce the entire messages themselves. The following extended concordances (replete with original spelling, punctuation and capitalisation) illustrate some of the types of questions which young people have about HIV/AIDS. In concordance lines, the key terms under consideration (in our case HIV and AIDS) are typically highlighted for ease of processing and making sense of the text that surrounds them (the co-text).

- i heard that drug users can get **hiv/aids** from using needles. is this true?
- can you get **Aids or HIV** from being touching (down there)
- what are the syptoms of **AIDS/HIV**
- i wanna get a tatoo but i'm worried i could get HIV/AIDS from the needle. Am i right to be concerned?
- is there a way to absolutly stop yourself from **getting hiv/aids**
- how does **hiv/aids** affect you

One way of making sense of these concordance lines is to consider how, if at all, the questioners relate HIV to AIDS, whether they conflate these two in any way. In the foregoing messages at least the questioners clearly distinguish HIV and AIDS, conceiving them as separate entities which are also connected in some way (given the oblique (/) or conjuncts ('and', 'or') that co-ordinate them). However, of the remaining 192 occurrences of the keyword 'AIDS' in the corpus, 92 per cent) appear in isolation, that is, with no mention of HIV, the virus that can cause AIDS (UNESCO, 2006). This in itself doesn't necessarily indicate that the adolescents do not perceive any relation between HIV and AIDS. That said these AIDS-themed messages potentially expose some revealing insights about the questioners' knowledge and understanding of the syndrome. The following concordances are typical of the range of contexts in which 'AIDS' in isolation is used:

- how do you get **aids**?
- If a women with **Aids** gives you oral sex can you catch it from her?

- What does **AIDS** stand for?
- do you need a condom to protect you from **aids** if you are having a blowjob
- I received oral sex about 6 months ago, now i am noticing some pimple on my penis, I don't know if it is from masturbating or if it is herpes, could you help me. And also can you get genital warts, or **AIDs** from oral sex.
- dear anne! my friend had unprotected sex! might she have aids?
- I think a girl in my class has aids. She cut her finger by accident and i got blood on my hand. Does this mean i have **aids** too?
- can you get **aids** from a toilet seat
- Can you get **AIDS** by being fingered?
- I had unprotected sex with a girl and ejaculated inside her. she has had many sexual partners and im not sure if she had always practiced safe sex. im worried i may have **aids**. is the risk that great?
- my penis has been itching me but i am scared to scratch it because i don't want to catch **aids**

Atkins and Harvey (2010) observe that, with regard to AIDS-related questions such as these, the absence of any reference to 'HIV', and the foregrounding of 'AIDS', potentially suggest a terminological conflation of the two concepts, a misconception that may well influence how the adolescents conceive of and understand 'HIV' and 'AIDS'. For instance, in a number of the concordances, there is the underlying belief that AIDS itself is a communicable infection, not a syndrome or range of conditions (UNESCO, 2006), with its being constructed as, and confused with, a virus or disease, something that can be transmitted with or without sexual activity: 'can you get aids from a toilet seat', 'can you get ... AIDS from oral sex.', 'Can you get AIDS by being fingered?' and so on.

Collapsing the distinction between HIV and AIDS in this way inevitably results in confusion, reinforcing 'unrealistic and unfounded fears' (Watney, 1989: 184) on the part of the adolescents who may mistakenly believe themselves to be at risk of AIDS but not HIV. Such extreme worse case scenarios conceive of AIDS as something that sets in immediately after infection, a unitary phenomenon rather than a collection of different medical conditions – beliefs which obscure, if not efface altogether, the existence of HIV, the virus which is indeed infectious. Such erroneous conflation of HIV infection with AIDS (by definition, the stage of HIV infection 'when a person's immune system can no longer cope' (Terrence Higgins Trust, 2007: 1)) potentially recycles some of the early and fundamental misconceptions about AIDS that were widespread during the 1980s and 1990s (Helman, 2007).

For example, Warwick, Aggleton and Homans' (1988) in-depth study into youth beliefs about AIDS revealed that a significant number of young people, as with many adults, were unable to distinguish between HIV infection and AIDS, a finding which they attributed to the media's consistent failure to provide the public with accurate information. This fundamental misunderstanding (identifying AIDS as a transmissible disease) was related to the 'public terror about 'catching' AIDS from people in public places or during casual contact' (Grover, 1990: 145) such as through cutlery or toilet seats. These beliefs (and the emotive linguistic choices encoding them) which were prevalent during that period appear to be evident in the adolescent health emails communicated over twenty years later. For instance, one of the central ways in which adolescents describe becoming infected with HIV or developing AIDS is through use of the verb 'catch'. This use of 'catch' as a verb to describe the transmission of HIV/AIDS is telling, suggesting a particular set of beliefs about disease contraction:

- Can you **catch** HIV through rubbing the penis around the pelvic area?
- Can you **catch** HIV from a person who has never had sex with anyone else before and only if any sexual fluids or blood get into your body.
- can you **catch** aids if havnt had sex?
- how do you prevent **catching** h. i. v
- I am very worried about **catching** HIV
- Is it possible you can **catch** HIV from a sponge?
- is the aids virus difficult to **catch**?
- Can you **catch** HIV if you wear a earring that might have been worn by somebody else before?
- my boyfriend went down on me the other night and i came on my period while he was. . . ya know. all abit embarassing . but can he **catch** aids, HIV etc etc
- out of ten what is the average to **catch** aids when having sex
- can your catch **aids** by kissing
- if i have sex with someone with aids without protection can i **cath** it
- can you **catch** aids if someone masterbates you
- Can you be born with HIV or AIDs or do have to **catch** it ?
- the other day i had sex without using a condom i am going to take a test but i am also worried i could have **caught** an STI or AIDS or sumthing wot shall i do ????!!!!!
- how do i **catch** HIV?

Many commentators and public health bodies stress that neither HIV nor AIDS can be 'caught' (Watney, 1989: 184). Indeed contemporary health promotion literature produced by standard-setting organisations such as UNESCO continually warns against the use of this verb to signify the way that people might become HIV positive, since it only helps to reproduce myths about HIV and AIDS (UNESCO, 2006). In the health emails above, for example, the appearances of 'catch' unavoidably conjure notions of the common cold and influenza, as evidence from the British National Corpus (BNC) attests. Consulting the 110 million word British National Corpus, a corpus designed to be representative of both spoken and written English language as a whole, Atkins and Harvey (2010) note that, as a transitive verb, 'catch' commonly co-occurs (collocates) with the direct objects 'cold', 'chill', 'bug' and 'colds'. As this collocational profile suggests, a common use of the verb 'catch' in general English is to describe the acquiring of relatively minor infections, in the sense of their being widespread and comparatively less serious. With regard to more serious viruses and illnesses, other less euphemistic constructions are used in the BNC to describe the process of infection and the onset of morbidity: HIV is typically 'contracted', 'got', 'acquired', while AIDS is 'got', 'developed', 'contracted'.

Given this association, a consequence of using 'catch' to describe infection with HIV/AIDS is perhaps to assume that the virus can be acquired via casual contact, that it possesses a transmission efficacy similar to both colds and influenza. As such, talk of 'catching' HIV/AIDS metaphorically transforms the virus from something which is, in reality, difficult to transmit and is only communicable via specific routes (Terrence Higgins Trust, 2007: 2) to something highly contagious, liable to spread easily and diffusively. This underlying metaphor of HIV/AIDS as 'invisible contagion' (Helman, 2007: 395) and attacking, engulfing from without (Weiss, 1997), still appears to inform some young people's understanding of the virus.

To sum up, then, the concordance analysis of the keywords 'HIV' and 'AIDS' exposes some potential misunderstandings that young people may have regarding sexual health. As we have argued throughout this book, language reflects people's understanding of and attitudes towards health and disease, and the corpus approach affords an effective means of identifying the 'incremental effect' (Baker, 2006: 13) of discursive patterns and commonalities in collections of health discourse. With regard to the HIV/AIDS questions posed by the users of the *Teenage Health Freak* website, it was possible that these young people displayed some potential misconceptions about HIV and AIDS, among which perhaps the most striking was the apparent tendency to conflate the two concepts, reinforcing the idea that HIV and AIDS are identical. Such a conflation may well obscure awareness of the ways in which the virus is actually transmitted.

However, it is important to realise that these findings cannot simply be generalised to the adolescent population at large. The young people who contribute to the *Teenage Health Freak* website constitute a specific group of users who articulate certain feelings and thoughts, and therefore their potential knowledge gaps cannot be said to be representative of adolescents more widely. Many young people are well informed about matters of sexual health and have no need to seek online health advice. Not all young people have questions about HIV and AIDS.

That said, a corpus analysis of naturally occurring language data, such as the *Teenage Health Freak* email corpus, has the potential for highlighting some of the folk conceptualisations which people may well possess about health and illness. Identifying these beliefs has practical implications for health education. Responding to lay beliefs like those described in the foregoing commentary is crucial since people filter official health education messages through their own pre-existing beliefs about health (Helman, 2007), reinterpreting them to suit their own needs (Aggleton and Homans, 1987: 25). If educational initiatives are to be successful, then language, as Cameron and Kulick (2003: 154) argue, must not simply be regarded as 'a medium for sex and health education but something that must be discussed explicitly as part of the process', a contestation for which our corpus analysis provides further support.

As the foregoing analysis has sought to demonstrate, a corpus linguistics approach to health communication is able to provide insights into people's understandings of and beliefs about health and illness. Yet it is important to realise that this analysis was principally confined to a small number of prominent keywords. Consequently many other analytical avenues were, unavoidably, left unexplored. Returning to the keyword list in Table 8.1, for instance, we could have pursued any number of these salient items. The fact that we had to confine our analysis to an examination of the keywords 'HIV' and 'AIDS' points up the selective nature of corpus analysis and that, like other forms of textual analysis, a corpus linguistics approach can never be exhaustive.

Task 8.3 Explicating HIV and AIDS metaphors   (TC)

The foregoing corpus-based analysis revealed how young people conceive HIV and AIDS as a form of contagion, something that appears relatively easy to contract or acquire. Examine the following concordances and identify any underlying metaphor or metaphors that characterise the adolescents' questions. What does the use of metaphor potentially betray about the advice-seekers' understanding of and beliefs about HIV and AIDS?

- my girfreind as already kissed a boy and she wants to kiss me would I get aids?
- i want to know if AIDS can gotten through kissing?
- Can you get aids from dogs?
- does anyone who has aids have to be quarantied
- can you get hiv from somebody who doesn't have it?
- Hi im 14 (duh) and i have never had sex or used injection drugs (or drugs at all) but from a toothbrush is it possible for me to get HIV?
- Dr Ann, I am food for nats and mosquitoes, they absolutly love me, but if they have bitten someone that has AIDS, then I am bitten, Can i be at risk of getting AIDS? Thanks Ann
- can i get aids off my cat?
- i know you said that you cant get hiv from kissing. but we were told in sex education that if you are french kissing and swallow the persons spit you can get hiv. is this true? please tell me bacause i hav been put off kissing now.

Theoretical accounts of expressive behaviour: the online disinhibition effect

Having examined methodological and analytical approaches to online health communication, we dedicate the final part of this chapter to theoretically accounting for some of the factors that give rise to the distinctively candid character of electronic health communication. In the previous chapter we noted that the relative anonymity of Internet-based health forums facilitates self-disclosure and, in some instances, uninhibited and even anti-social behaviour (flaming). The theoretical questions we address here are: How exactly does this candidness arise? What are its consequences for health interaction online?

A number of the adolescent health emails that featured in our earlier corpus analysis were characterised by the use of non-euphemistic language, with the website users articulating their questions and concerns in direct and non-euphemistic detail. This level of directness is not confined to matters concerning HIV and AIDS, but a whole range of health issues in which the website users formulate problems in typically frank terms. Whether these adolescents would have displayed the same directness in other communicative contexts remains to be seen, but it is unlikely. For instance, research into sexual health has described the communicative difficulties that people experience when discussing sensitive topics face-to-face (Weijts *et al.*, 1993). Speaking about sexual issues by both doctors and patients appears to be frequently conducted through euphemisms, vague language and omissions rather than through explicit references. In cyberspace, however, sensitive issues are broached much more directly. According to Suler (2004), this is a consequence of the 'online disinhibition effect', the phenomenon whereby people 'loosen up, feel less restrained, and express themselves more openly' when interacting online (2004: 321).

The effect of disinhibition is brought about by six factors, namely anonymity, invisibility, asynchronicity, solipsistic introjection, dissociative imagination, and minimisation of authority. Although Suler observes that these factors interact with and supplement each other, one or two of them produce the 'lion's share of the disinhibition effect' (2004: 322). Accordingly, we will here devote our attention to anonymity, invisibility and asynchronicity – the key disinhibition factors that are most likely to determine the expressive texture of health problems online.

Anonymity is, according to Suler, the principle reason for the online disinhibition effect. Being anonymous involves altering one's identity or effacing it altogether, allowing, in either case, people to dissociate themselves from their own behaviour and activities. Possessing online anonymity is akin to wearing a protective cloak: people are able to hide their online activities, separating them from their actual (i.e. offline) identities, and, as a consequence, whatever they do or say online cannot be 'directly linked to the rest of their lives' (2004: 322). This is an important consideration for people seeking health advice online, particularly young and vulnerable individuals. To approach others for help is potentially to validate any sense of failure and weakness experienced by help-seekers, for, in the eyes of other people, seeking assistance 'could be perceived as a shameful act' (Scourfield *et al.*, 2007: 252). However, whatever information advice-seekers communicate to others (at least online) cannot be linked directly to their lives: when obtaining advice over the Internet, no one need know that they have sought professional assistance.

With regard to reducing inhibition online, invisibility works in a similar way to anonymity. As we noted in Chapter 7, users of online health forums are most likely unable to see each other. Their exchanges are conducted through typed words alone. Concealing one's physical presence, Suler notes, 'gives people the courage to go to places and do things that they otherwise wouldn't' (2004: 322). Being invisible produces a reduced sense of public awareness and, with this, a propensity for increased self-disclosure (Joinson, 2001). For example, people seeking advice from health professionals over the Internet do not have to concern themselves with how they look or sound. Nor do they have to worry about their messages being received with a sigh or frown. In this sense, disclosing problems to health professionals online reflects, according to Suler, the traditional psychoanalytical practice of analysts sitting behind their clients in order to remain distant, physically removed figures. Able to apprehend neither the body language nor the facial responses of therapists, clients are free to express whatever they wish 'without feeling inhibited by how the analyst is physically reacting' (Suler, 2004: 322). While communicating health problems to professionals online, advisors' gazes remain constantly averted. As Griffiths observes, 'Words that are originated from within ourselves are received by the computer without contest or contempt' and so 'may produce the feelings that tell us we are being accommodated' (2004: 157).

Most professional online health forums (such as the *Teenage Health Freak* website) are asynchronous, that is, they are not conducted in real-time. Not having to interact with correspondents in real-time, and not having to deal with any immediate reactions from others, further contributes to communicative candour. Requesting advice online typically involves help-seekers having to wait for a response to their questions. After sending a message that is personal, emotional or otherwise revealing, advice-seekers may experience asynchronous communication as a kind of 'running away' or escape (Suler, 2004: 323). Knowing that they are not involved in real-time, moment-by-moment interaction with others, they are more likely, according to Suler, to feel safe 'putting their messages 'out there' in cyberspace where they can be left behind' (ibid.).

As can be seen, then, the disinhibition effect has important consequences for the way in which people communicate their health concerns to professionals and what personal information they reveal about themselves. The disassociative anonymity, invisibility and asynchronicity that characterise much online health communication make it an attractive channel for reaching out to people who are reluctant to seek medical advice from professionals face-to-face.

Summary

The Internet hosts an ever-increasing number of websites dedicated to providing health advice and information. Although the quality and reliability of much health provision is open to question, many websites are professionally operated, affording reliable, evidence-based advice which allows people to make informed choices about their health.

As we observed at the beginning of this chapter, for professionals providing online services, a key challenge is to establish a credible expert persona, one whom advice-seekers can trust and one to whom they can relate. Online advisors, such as 'Lucy', are able to emerge through a range of carefully chosen linguistic strategies, strategies that not only construct an expert status but also imbue a fictional, virtual persona with interpersonal qualities.

Another appealing feature of the Lucy persona is the non-directive nature of her advice: the information provided to help-seekers is designed to facilitate independent decision-making rather than prescribe it. This strategy works by presenting help-seekers with the opportunity of interpreting advice statements as options. Help-seekers, therefore, have to decide for themselves how best to act on this information.

In the second part of the chapter, we focussed on advice-seekers' requests for help, exploring patterns and commonalities in young people's health concerns submitted to a website specialising in adolescent health. We considered the utility of a corpus linguistic approach to interrogating large collections of health language, harnessing the staple corpus tools of keywords and concordances to first identify salient lexical items in the corpus before closely examining these terms in their original context. Combining these two techniques allowed us to uncover some intricate patterns and commonalities in young people's questions about health issues, specifically HIV and AIDS; and it was also possible to relate individuals' linguistic choices to their personal beliefs about disease. For example, the relatively common use of the emotive verb 'catch', which was used to describe the contraction of HIV, pointed to a set of lay beliefs about infectious disease, reflecting perhaps the widespread circulation of irrational myths about AIDS.

Yet for all the findings that a corpus-based analysis of health communication is able to produce, it is important not to overstate the utility of computational analysis. Corpus tools such as keywords usefully indicate what is salient and frequent in a corpus, but such words have to be analysed closely in context and selected for analysis in the first place. Corpus linguistics, though an invaluable method for interrogating large amounts of language, is therefore not an end in itself but rather a means (and one means at that) to an analytical end. Such limitations apart, it is becoming increasingly evident that corpus-based approaches are powerfully able to explicate various modes of health communication, offering researchers new opportunities for discovering patterns of language that would otherwise be difficult to locate in large collections of linguistic data.

Commentary on selected tasks

Chapter 1

Task 1.2 The egalitarian medical encounter

Defining what constitutes an egalitarian medical encounter is a difficult, if not impossible, endeavour. Consultations (even the most equitable) will always exhibit some degree of interactional asymmetry and involve various levels of 'conflict, cooperation, authority and subordination' (Heritage and Maynard, 2006: 1). However, a number of researchers concerned with interrogating the language of doctor–patient exchanges have, as we note in Chapter 1, consistently identified and described discursive practices (along with the institutional exigencies giving rise to them) that contribute to marginalisation of the patient and the interruption of the voice of the lifeworld. In order to maximise the patient's voice and remedy the problems of the clinical encounter, Fisher outlines a linguistic, cultural and ethical ideal. As follows:

> If patients are treated as whole people rather than sick body parts, if the medical and social, the pathological and the psychological are valued equally, if the emphasis on diagnosis and treatment is extended to include education and prevention, if patients are recognised as the experts on their own lives, if doctors ask open-ended questions, if they share medical information, if they listen to what patients have to tell them and if they encourage patients to participate, then an asymmetrical relationship could become more equalitarian.
>
> (Fisher 1991: 160)

The rather extensive list of conditional clauses betrays the fact that realising such an ideal is not a straightforward prospect. However, Fisher's suggestions for humane and effective healthcare effectively draw attention to many of the key concerns that applied linguists have sought to address when interrogating doctor–patient communication. Fisher's checklist echoes the recommendations of Mishler (1984), who similarly advocates the use of open-ended questions and the negotiation of power between doctor and patient, as well as the rendering of any technical language into the more familiar voice of the lifeworld.

Task 1.3 A further look at footings in the consultation

Goffman (1981: 128) notes that footings can be held across a strip of verbal activity ranging from less than the length of a sentence to anything above and beyond. This means that a footing can be maintained over several turns at talk. Although it is not possible to account for every potential change of footing in the doctor–patient consultation, the opening sequence of the encounter is likely to feature a notable shift in participant alignment as the parties (particularly if they are known to each other) emerge from small talk into the main business of the consultation. Consider again the opening exchange we examined earlier in Chapter 1 between Jeremy (the patient) and his doctor, Ben.

1	L	P:	Hello Ben
2	L	D:	Hello
3	L	P:	[How are you
4	L	D:	[How are- er how- ((laughs))
5	L	P:	((laughs))
6	L	D:	I'm okay
7	L	P:	Okay?
–	L		*Doctor and patient chat about the patient's previous GP who the doctor knows*
8	L	D:	Right. (0.9) Right. What are we talking about?

In this opening phase of the consultation both participants engage in a bout of small talk, an interpersonal exchange which includes both phatic enquiries about the other's general well-being and reciprocal laughter. It is only at line 8, some way into the conversation, that the doctor eventually steers the talk into the business of the consultation proper: 'Right. What are we talking about?' Up until this point, the participants have occupied the footing of social intimates. The terms of address used by Jeremy further bear out this personal footing: he refers to his fellow interlocutor as 'Ben', not as 'Doctor'. Addressing the GP as 'Doctor' would most likely encode another kind of alignment, a more official footing intimating the participant statuses of doctor and patient.

This kind of verbal conduct is not unusual in the opening phase of primary care encounters. Indeed it recalls the experience of one of the authors (KH) when in consultation with his own GP. Having known his doctor for several years, the author typically engages in not unsubstantial stretches of preliminary social talk, enquiring about the general well-being of the medic and the present rating of his golf handicap. In return the GP broaches the subject of the author's preparation for some forthcoming long(ish) distance running event, and both participants inevitably lament, as if for mutual comfort and support, the parlous divisional position of their local football team. This small talk occurs at the preface and postface of the consultation, during which times the participants occupy a personal rather than an institutional footing.

Does this experience similarly reflect the reader's?

Chapter 2

Task 2.2 Patient empowerment or nurse control?

On the face of it, it would appear that the patient exhibits a substantial degree of power, and the nurse, to some degree, facilitates this empowerment. For example, in both extracts she encourages the patient to openly disclose his feelings, giving him substantial access to the conversational floor: 'How did you feel in yourself when all this was happening' (lines 1-2: Extract 1) as well as validating his feelings and encouraging further disclosures: 'yeah it must have been very hard for you that happening and then getting sick yourself' (lines 6-8: Extract 2). The patient, in response to the nurse's elicitations, takes extensive turns at talk, providing a detailed and highly personal (not to mention painful) account of his life situation. He appears to be able to fashion his responses very much in his own terms.

Yet is this a truly accurate assessment? Although the nurse, in her desire to elicit disclosures from the patient, cedes control of the floor to him, she nevertheless sets the parameters of the discussion: despite the seemingly open, unbounded nature of the interaction, the participants still follow an agenda: the talk is restricted to the patient and his concerns and, as Candlin (2000: 235) points out, neither participant deviates from these parameters.

Moreover, just how empowering is the patient's account of himself? Candlin argues that, for all the autonomy and self-determination the interaction affords him, he is effectively powerless. Consider, for example, the way he represents himself linguistically. Lexically and grammatically the patient positions himself in a passive way, a linguistic encoding which reflects his lack of control over his situation: 'I still couldn't see it happening to me', 'I suppose there's nothing I could do', 'I suppose that's the lot that's dealt out to you'. Here, the recurring use of the verb 'suppose' conveys a relatively low modality (commitment to an utterance). The patient appears to be uncertain about what he is saying and accordingly hedges his statements. Rarely does he present himself in a dynamic way. Note, for instance, his use of the passive voice which emphasises that things are done to him rather than his performing actions or taking control, e.g. 'But it was after I was retrenched'.

Candlin argues that, for all the current emphasis on patient-empowerment in healthcare policy, the asymmetry which has traditionally characterised much practitioner–patient talk still obtains in the nurse–patient relationship, but is manifested in far more subtle ways. Following Fairclough (1992), Candlin refers to this linguistic phenomenon as the 'democratization of discourse'. A feature of much contemporary institutional talk (not just talk confined to the context of healthcare), the democratisation of discourse involves the

> removal of inequalities and asymmetries in the discursive and linguistic rights, obligations and prestige of groups of people. Democratization in discourse, like democratization more generally, has been a major parameter of change...but in both cases...there are questions about how real or how cosmetic the changes have been.
>
> (Fairclough, 1992 cited in Candlin, 2000: 234)

Readers interested in pursuing the notion of the democratisation of discourse in greater detail, particularly in relation to recent changes in healthcare, might wish to consult Fairclough's (1992) *Discourse and Social Change*, a seminal text which has had a significant influence on critical studies of contemporary discourse.

Task 2.3 Patient-empowerment in physiotherapy: the problem of goal-setting

The interactional exchange illustrates the difficulty of actively involving patients in goal-setting processes during physiotherapy sessions. For example, the first part of the session commences with the physiotherapist asking the patient an open question that allows him a not insubstantial amount of interactional room to formulate his troubles: 'What would you say your biggest problems are?'. As Parry (2004: 672) notes in her commentary on this encounter, the patient at this point casts his gaze away from the physiotherapist's face down to the floor and does not respond to this specific question. There appears to be some difficulty on the part of the patient in formulating a response.

After a pause of two seconds – a not inconsiderable amount of time in the moment-by-moment flow of interaction – the therapist further prompts the patient to respond to her original question: 'whilst you're here in hospital'. After another long pause, the patient offers a response: 'My left and right arm'. The therapist, in a questioning voice, repeats the patient's words, a turn which is evidently designed to encourage the patient to elaborate on his statement, which he subsequently does: 'when I fell I hit both the elbows here they're very painful'. The therapist, Parry observes, acknowledges the patient's description of pain but does not pursue it, eliciting instead further problems from him through the use of a specific set of questions (lines 18-20), questions which narrow down the range of topically relevant responses.

What is striking about the first part of this encounter is that the patient is evidently reluctant to respond to the therapist's problem-seeking questions. Parry attributes this resistance to a more general reluctance on the part of physiotherapy patients to offer personal judgements about their problems and performance (2004: 674). The difficulty of eliciting patient responses is also testament to the difficulty of obtaining information from patients which is relevant to physiotherapy. Only certain issues are deemed to be amenable to the goal-setting process and thus, though the patient has indicated that pain in his arms is his main trouble, the therapist does not pursue this concern since it is not relevant to the goal-setting agenda she proposes.

In the second half of the session, the therapist, during lines 45-49, formulates the patient's goals on his behalf: 'that you can reach and put yer socks on maybe we should say within two weeks'. Once the therapist has set the goals, she seeks confirmation from the patient: 'd'you think that's fair enough', a leading question which invites an affirmative response. The patient, however, does not respond to this question, instead detailing his proficiency at already being able to dress himself. Yet rather than amend the goal in light of the patient's account of this proficiency, the therapist persists in setting the same original goal, only varying it slightly: 'so we'll try and look at ways of doing it in sitting', a goal that doesn't seem to accord with the patient's own assessment of his physical abilities.

So what is the significance of these goal-setting difficulties? Parry relates the tension to broader social constraints in physiotherapy. Setting goals takes time. Therefore some therapists, despite professional recommendations that encourage them to involve patients in goal-setting routines, may set goals on their patients' behalf, doing so in order to devote more time to physical treatment than verbal negotiation (2004: 679). Moreover, eliciting details from patients about their problems is, as we have seen, a fraught and complex interactional activity. Consequently some therapists may spend little time on goal-setting episodes or, indeed, sidestep the process altogether.

Although, as we noted in Chapter 2, a patient empowerment ethos pervades contemporary healthcare, it is not always practicable to actively involve patients in the delivery of care (at least to the extent desired by policymakers). Not all patients want to be empowered and to take responsibility for goal-setting and other treatment decisions.

Consequently, practitioners often have to manage the irreconcilable: the will of the patient and the injunction of policy.

Interrogating naturally occurring practitioner–patient talk presents an altogether different kind of reality than that depicted in healthcare policy and professional standards. As we have seen in Chapters 1 and 2, notions of patient choice and empowerment translate rather less ideally into practice. For many patients, making decisions about treatment, actively involving themselves in care, simply means coming to terms with their conditions and acquiescing to the recommendations of medical experts, on whom they rely to provide the appropriate treatment (Salmon and Hall, 2004: 53).

Chapter 3

Task 3.1 Identity construction in narratives of illness

Burt's account is a striking example of the use of personal narrative as a resource for making sense of illness and presenting a certain image of oneself. In his narrative, he attempts to communicate that he is not to blame for his illness and disability and that therefore he has a right to be relieved from certain social, occupational responsibilities and roles. As Riesmann observes, sickness relieves him of personal blame for his present situation. He does not deny the severity of his illness, but nor is his narrative a portrait of victimisation and dependency: his account, Riessman (1990) argues, preserves essential aspects of his masculinity – he creates a social self that is competent and controlled.

Chapter 4

Task 4.1 Narrating the case report

One of the most striking features of this case report is its consistently impersonal tone. As Hunter (1991: 98) observes, the account is written 'by an almost wholly effaced narrator' to the extent that the 'the narrative of the patient's illness and medical care were telling itself'. This impersonal effect is mainly due to the pervasive use of the passive voice and the absence of an agent, or agents, responsible for the actions depicted in the text. For example, in the clause 'He was therefore sent in 1964 to Strong Memorial Hospital' the emphasis is purely on the process undergone by the patient (his being sent to hospital), not on the person or persons responsible for sending him to the hospital.

The absence of the narrator, the person (and, by extension, the personality) behind the report, is symptomatic of 'the commitment to the rational scrutiny of detail' (Hunter, 1991: 99). In other words, although the report is presented in a colourless and one-sided way, it nonetheless achieves consistency: this is exactly the type of report,

Hunter notes, that another doctor, presenting a similar case, would also produce. The authors of case reports seek to establish medical facts so that the causes of patients' pathologies can be identified and treated, and this endeavour is best realised by adopting a style of communication that approximates to scientific objectivity, leaving little room for the overt presence of narrators. Such an objective style serves the practical interests of the clinicians treating patients but – and this is an issue we address throughout Chapter 4 – it is a detached mode of presentation that represents flesh and blood patients with little degree of singularity or humanity.

Chapter 5

5.3 Metaphor and frame analysis

The texts suggested for analysis allow us to explore the role of the media in relation to the sociological debates on the medicalisation of everyday life (Conrad, 2007) and social representations of pharmaceuticals. Although there is a large market for wakefulness drugs as a treatment for various disorders such as sleep apnoea and narcolepsy, it is their potential 'lifestyle' market that attracts the attention of critical scholars. Along with many other pharmaceuticals, the drug modafinil belongs to an array of so-called 'enhancement' technologies designed to 'improve' various aspects of our lives. Sociologists therefore point out that these waking aids raise a number of social and ethical questions, and call for a debate on the implications of our present and future ability to manufacture wakefulness on demand (Williams *et al.*, 2008).

Note how all three media articles begin by weaving medical conditions into their storylines. A variety of rhetorical devices and moves are used to achieve that, from relatively straightforward accounts peppered with scientific terms focussing on how the drugs can be used to treat narcolepsy (texts 1 and 3) to more celebratory stories of the transforming power of these 'revolutionary' pills that are told on behalf of either well-known or anonymous sufferers (texts 2 and 3). In the former case, different scientific experts are quoted to legitimate particular uses of the drug. However, the reports do not stop at the description of medical symptoms and their treatment but extend into discussion of the everyday use of these drugs, in this way placing them in the recreational context (text 3). Apart from brief cautionary notes on possible side effects, the articles are uncritical in tone, ranging from neutral to highly optimistic.

The use of metaphors of course plays an important part both in how the positive effects of these drugs are foregrounded and how the seamless transition from the medical to the everyday is achieved. In terms of metaphorical expressions, war metaphors (e.g. in text 2, 'Those who suffer from narcolepsy are doomed to lose the fight to keep their eyes open, and the battle is lost more rapidly if they are already tired or bored') are used to construct the treatment of narcolepsy with the drug as something positive; an action that allows the sufferers from narcolepsy to win the battle of 'keeping their eyes open' and restore the normal patterns of sleep and wakefulness. If we now recall the four functions of frames suggested by Entman (1993), namely, defining a problem, diagnosing causes, making moral judgements, and suggesting solutions, it becomes clear that in our examples the metaphorical war frame is used to justify pharmaceutical intervention because it enables the articulation of moral reasoning (Coveney et al., 2009). Note also the surrounding lexis describing the use of modafinil as a technological solution that will enable individuals to 'control' and 'abolish' sleep and fatigue (texts 1 and 3), and in this process enhance and promote one's capabilities (e.g. the drug as a 'cognitive booster' and 'wakefulness promoter' in text 3). As Coveney et al. (2009) observe, such pharmaceutical properties can be seen as outcomes of winning a metaphorical race against the need to sleep, suggesting the use of a competition frame to legitimise the recreational use of these drugs.

For a detailed study of the social construction of sleep drugs in the media see Williams et al. (2008) and Coveney et al. (2009).

Chapter 6

6.2 The paracetamol text: more than one voice at work?

If we take Gee's (1999: 24) notion of a voice to correspond with particular 'who-doing-whats', then it is indeed possible to discern different voices in the paracetamol leaflet. On the one hand there is a voice that appears to speak in an (to borrow Gee's term) 'avuncular' fashion, personalising the information communicated to the reader and referring to the drug in a more general way: 'This leaflet provides some important information about your medicine'. On the other hand, there is a more urgent, hortatory voice which is emphatically precise in the details it communicates: 'If after taking this medicine for the first time, you develop a rash or other allergic reaction – STOP taking Paracetamol Tablets BP 500mg and consult your doctor or pharmacist'. Unlike the former voice, this more emphatic voice refers to specific entities: 'this medicine', 'Paracetamol Tablets BP 500mg', 'for the first time', as well as drawing attention to, through the use of capital letters, the unmitigated commands it directs at readers: 'STOP taking Paracetamol Tablets BP 500mg'.

The first voice, then, appears to be less urgent than the second, while the second voice is consecrated to alerting readers about possible side effects and ensuring that they cease taking paracetamol and seek medical assistance, in the precise person of their pharmacist or doctor. However, there is evidently some overlap between the two voices throughout the document, for they both, in their unique ways, function to inform and instruct readers, making it clear, for instance, how the drug is to be taken properly and for which patients it is suitable and unsuitable.

Chapter 7

Task 7.1 Identifying strategies of creating legitimacy and soliciting advice

The first thing we can observe about this message is that the author expresses her request for help in an elaborate manner. In a single post, we can find several questions and requests for opinion, and each of them is accompanied by other structural elements. As a result, the post in itself resembles a story where personal disclosures are skilfully mixed with questions rather than a request or a short speech act. To analyse its composition in more detail it is useful to draw on Kouper's (2010) model consisting of the following structural elements: *orientation*, *justification*, and *appreciation*. The scholar identified these elements as systematically occurring in the data consisting of live journal posts where participants solicited and provided different kinds of advice. Orientation clauses, for example, were found to be used in order to present additional information and help to describe the time, place, persons, or the situation itself. While this additional information may not be necessary for the development of the story, Kouper argues that it provides details that make the story more interesting or realistic.

In our example, the participant mentions that she had read posted notices and conversations for a month ('lurking'), in this way indicating her familiarity with the site and the rules of the group. As Kouper explains, in contrast to background information, the goal of which is to provide information relevant to the issue (discussed by Locher (2006)), orientation information is not always directly relevant to the problem about which advice was being sought. Rather it may serve other functions such as establishing rapport with potential readers of the post, and/or creating legitimacy. The second element of justification is commonly employed to provide various reasons for soliciting advice or information, and, in Kouper's study (2010), these included such reasons as being scared or worried. In our post, the author provides an indirect justification for her previous request of information (regarding 'depression and relationships') by alluding to potential feelings of isolation and confusion 'I've had a hard time explaining to family and friends why I hurt, especially at a young age'. The third element – appreciation – concerns appreciation in advance. Whereas Kouper found that when asking for advice or opinion participants frequently expressed their appreciation for advice to be provided (e.g., 'i'd appreciate your help'), in our example the participant goes back to her earlier activity on the forum and thanks other members for the feedback she had received then.

Chapter 8

Task 8.2 Does (corpus) size matter?

The question about the size of the dataset can only be answered with regard to the research question that the analyst is pursuing. Given the difficulties associated with gathering health communication data because of privacy, confidentiality and ethical issues that often arise from such an endeavour, it is reassuring to know that the analysis of even very small data sets, both in terms of qualitative and quantitative approaches, can be very revealing and lead to new insights about a particular domain of discourse. Using small data sets does not invalidate the findings of any analysis. Indeed as O'Keeffe *et al.* (2011) point out, patterns of communication are likely to emerge even from very small collections of data, especially if such collections are concentrated around a specific area of discourse.

Researchers interested in examining the occurrence and behaviour of an individual word or small set of words will most likely need to use a large corpus. This is for the simple reason that a corpus comprising many millions of words is much more likely to have numerous occurrences of the specific items the researcher wishes to investigate. If, however, the researcher is interested in examining many words or themes in a corpus, or wishes to identify and explicate a range themes present therein, then a much smaller corpus will be suitable. Such specialist corpora (smaller collections of language that focus on one communicative domain, such as health language) are more manageable and may be subject to qualitative investigation. The analysis of the health email corpus we conduct in Chapter 8 illustrates how a specialist corpus can be interrogated in this way.

But what, in the final analysis, is most likely to determine corpus size is the actuality of data collection. Researchers may intend to construct a corpus of a certain ideal size, aiming for a large, multi-million word collection of data. But issues such as time constraints, the availability of and access to linguistic data may well result in a corpus smaller in size than one desired. However, this is not, by any means, the end of the world. Falling short of one's intended total, not having a corpus as balanced as scientifically as possible, is by no means a bar to using a corpus. Corpora are to be used. It is surely better to use a corpus as soon as practicable rather than assembling it, perhaps indefinitely, in pursuit of some dream end.

In this regard, the collection of special purpose corpora from online sources allows linguists and discourse analysts to engage with 'real-world problems' (Cook, 2003: 5) as they emerge – not a long time later when they have changed or been superseded by new ones (Koteyko, 2010).

Task 8.3 Explicating HIV and AIDS metaphors

As with the other messages evoking notions of 'catching' HIV/AIDS, these questioners' concerns similarly communicate a fear of contagion and pollution. Here ambiguity over the transmission of HIV and AIDS is related not just to sexual activity but to a wide and common range of circumstances, with, for instance, even toothbrushes and household pets considered to be potential contaminants and sources of the virus.

This perceived infiltration by HIV/AIDS of routine aspects of everyday and domestic life potentially resonates with folk beliefs common in the first years of the AIDS epidemic when the virus was believed to be 'transmitted by virtually any contact with an infected person' (Helman, 2007: 395). Such a conception of the virus draws on the notion of the 'miasma' theory of disease (Lupton, 2003), the folk model of infection which conceives of infected persons as being surrounded as if by a miasma or highly contagious cloud of poisonous air liable to spread disease at the slightest contact (Helman, 2007: 395).

Appendix

Transcription system

The notation used to represent spoken discourse throughout this book is based on Gail Jefferson's model of transcription (as set out in Atkinson and Heritage, 1984), a model which is commonly used in conversation analysis research. Transcription systems vary with regard to how they represent interactional phenomena such as pauses, interruptions and connected speech. For the sake of consistency, the original transcript notations of a number of the extracts have been altered in order to correspond with the Jeffersonian system. However, where we have standardised transcripts, we have lost none of the interactional subtleties denoted by the original rendering: one type of symbol or device has merely replaced another.

[ ]	–	square brackets indicate overlapping talk: the point where one utterance begins to overlap another utterance is marked by a left-hand bracket
=	–	latching speech: two utterances where there is no interval between them such that they 'latch' on to each other
_	–	words that are underlined carry extra stress and emphasis
:	–	denotes an extension of the sound or syllable that follows
hh	–	audible exhalation
.hh	–	audible inhalation
(.)	–	a short untimed pause
(1.5)	–	a timed pause measured in tenths of a second
( )	–	words that appear in single brackets are in doubt; empty parentheses indicate inaudible words
(( ))	–	double brackets are used to indicate paralinguistic features, such as laughter ((laughs)) or coughing ((coughs))

Glossary

Active voice
a form of grammatical representation whereby the action of a verb is attributed to a particular person or thing. In the active voice, the agent is present and therefore responsibility for an action is clear. For instance, in the following example, the nurse is the agent of the active verb 'take': 'the nurse took the patient's temperature'. Compare **passive voice**.

Adjacency pairs
central to conversational organisation, adjacency pairs are sequences of paired utterances that are bound together, the first part of the pair cueing the second part. Adjacency pairs perform a range of functions, such as question-answer, greeting-greeting, invitation-acceptance, blame-denial, and so forth.

Agent
the person or thing responsible for an action or process, the 'doer' of a verb.

Backchannelling
minimal tokens such as hm, mm, uhuh produced by hearers to indicate that they are actively listening to a fellow interlocutor, encouraging further verbal traffic. Backchannelling can also be realised by certain gestures, such as nods of the head.

Backstage
see **frontstage.**

Community of practice
is a term created by cognitive anthropologists Jean Lave and Etienne Wenger (Wenger, 1998) to refer to a group of people who have a common interest in a particular domain or area. In the process of sharing information and their experiences, group members can learn from each other, and in this way have an opportunity to develop themselves personally and professionally.

Content/lexical words
are words that provide informational content, such as injection, disease, suffer, recovery. Content words are always being added to the language and as such form an open class of words. The total number of content words appearing in a text in relation to the number of functional words is a measure of lexical density – a means of evaluating the readability of a stretch of discourse. See **functional/grammatical words**.

Concordances/concordance lines
are lines of text from a corpus that present all the occurrences of a particular (node) word. Concordance lines present the surrounding linguistic context in which the node word is situated, allowing the analyst to identify what patterns it is part of and how it relates to other words.

Cooperative Principle
the principle formulated by Paul Grice (1991: 78-79) which accounts for verbal cooperation between speakers. The Cooperative Principle is resolved into four maxims: quantity, quality, manner and relevance. Language users observe these maxims if they wish to communicate meaning. Cooperation in this sense relates to understanding, making sense of each other's talk, not to verbal concord.

Corpus/corpora
a corpus is a collection of texts (spoken, written or both) that are stored electronically. These texts are made up of naturally occurring language and can be subjected to a range of computational analyses (such as frequency, keyword, concordance and collocation analyses).

Discourse marker
is a word or phrase (okay, right then, now, etc.) that is used to signal some phase or change in spoken discourse. Discourse markers 'mark' out stages in interaction, for example the beginning or end of a particular sequence of talk.

Disease
is a technical, medical formulation that refers to biological malfunctioning. Disease, in this sense, is rather a narrow notion; it is objective, purely biomedical in scope – something that is both defined and treated by health practitioners. Disease is divorced from personal experience of suffering. Compare with **illness**.

Face
with regard to politeness theory, face relates to the projection of one's self-image to others. Face can be considered from two angles: positive and negative. Positive face concerns one's desire to be appreciated, to a feel a sense of belonging to others, whereas negative face concerns one's desire to be free from imposition. In order to promote positive face people use politeness strategies such as claiming common ground. When attending to negative face, linguistic strategies involve showing deference to others, and mitigating the burden involved in making requests of others.

Face-threatening acts
acts that threaten one's positive self-image (positive face) or autonomy (negative face) are called face threatening acts. Face threatening acts require politeness techniques (such as hedging and indirectness) in order to avoid disruptions and awkwardness during social encounters.

Fishing
an interactional device whereby a participant in conversation indirectly solicits information from a fellow interlocutor. Fishing is a subtle activity: instead of expressly putting a question to someone, a speaker offers a statement (about a co-participant's personal state of affairs, for example), provoking a response. In the context of medical encounters (psychiatric interview and counselling sessions

especially), fishing invites (rather than overtly obliges) patients and clients to disclose private feelings and discuss their predicaments.

Flaming
is the activity of sending rude, abusive or threatening messages to other Internet users, particularly in chat rooms and forums.

Footing
are alignments that speakers step in and out of during interaction. Participants in talk adopt various social roles, the occupation of which affects the direction and nature of talk. For example, at the beginning of a medical interview (before the official business of the consultation proper) both doctor and patient might adopt an informal footing and engage in small talk. These footings will change once the consultation progresses past the opening phase and the participants align themselves to the formal roles of doctor and patient.

Frontstage/backstage
the term frontstage and its counterpart, backstage, are concepts conceived by Goffman (1959). Used to describe a region from which social activities (such as interaction) can be analysed, the two concepts are based on the dramaturgical metaphor of performance. Frontstage activities involve some kind of public display (in the sense that they involve, or are visible to, an audience). For example, the doctor–patient encounter, a particular realisation of the public face of medicine, is a frontstage encounter. Conversely, interaction between medics during tea breaks (where there is no public audience to perceive events) constitutes a backstage activity. Needless to say, backstage activities involve different uses of language than frontstage activities. Goffman (1959: 129) provides a long, near-breathless, list of attributes that comprise backstage discourse, including, to name but several: 'reciprocal first-naming, cooperative decision-making, profanity, open sexual remarks, elaborate griping, smoking, rough informal dress, 'sloppy' sitting and standing posture, use of dialect or sub-standard speech ... '. If these and many other traits constitute backstage behaviour, then their absence, according to Goffman, can be taken to characterise frontstage discourse.

Functional/grammatical words
are words that belong to a closed class. Rather than conveying discrete information (like content/lexical words), they have a grammatical function. We speak of such words as being part of a closed class because they belong to fixed, finite categories, categories such as prepositions, pronouns, auxiliary and modal verbs, determiners, and conjunctions. The higher the proportion of functional words in a text, the lower the lexical density will be. See **content/lexical words**.

Heteroglossia
a term coined by the literary critic Mikhail Bakhtin (1981) to describe the presence of two or more distinct voices in a text – voices potentially in conflict with one another. The presence of such plurality voices might not be readily apparent: only close textual scrutiny reveals their presence and operation.

Idiolect
an individual's particular language habits, their unique 'thumbprint' of linguistic style and behaviour.

Illness
whereas disease describes objective biomedical entities, illness is an innately human phenomenon that relates to an individual's personal experience of suffering. Illness accounts for how sick people respond to disease and the common sense ways in which they try to make sense of disease, such as the personal judgements they make about symptoms and ailments. Illness, therefore, takes into account the personal, social and cultural context of disability and suffering. Compare **disease**.

Illocutionary act
in contrast to a perlocutionary act, an illocutionary act refers to intended meaning regardless of the resulting effect. For example, 'Do not drink this wine' is a warning to an addressee not to drink the wine (an illocutionary act). If this warning is heeded then the speaker is successful in persuading the interlocutor not to drink the wine (a perlocutionary act).

Implicature
an implied meaning produced by speakers (and writers). An implicature is an additional unstated meaning which is different from the literal meaning of an utterance. Implicatures arise when language users flout one or more of the conversational maxims (quantity, quality, manner or relevance).

Keywords
are words that are statistically significant. They are words that appear in one corpus with a significantly higher frequency when compared with another corpus. Keywords indicate saliency and are therefore words that can be seen to characterise a particular language variety, offering researchers a useful point of analytical entry into a corpus.

Lexical density
see **content/lexical words.**

Lifeworld/voice of medicine
lifeworld issues relate to patients' personal and social attitudes towards health and illness. The lifeworld encapsulates natural attitudes of everyday life and, according to Mishler (1984), is often in conflict with technical, biomedical formulations of illness (the voice of medicine).

Lurking
is the activity (or rather lack of it) of spending time in an Internet health forum without contributing to the discussion at hand or otherwise failing to interact with other forum users.

Locutionary act
is the basic action of uttering, writing or making public by other means a meaningful sequence of words. It is part of a speech act theory that places emphasis on the perfomative role of language according to which to say something (locutionary act) is to do something. **See illocutionary and perlocutionary act**.

Metaphor
is a contested and variously defined term. It refers to non-literal meaning, signalling to the reader or listener that they should treat something as something else (make links between, say, a house and a battlefield). Previously seen as a mere figure of

speech and an ornament to language, metaphors are now increasingly recognised as discursively powerful tools used by people to make sense of the world.

Modality

concerns a speaker's or writer's commitment to, or certainty about, an utterance. Modality formulations encode opinions about likelihood and obligation through the use of dedicated modal verbs (may, can, will, shall, etc.). Modality can also be expressed in other ways, for example, through the use of adverbs (certainly, possibly, maybe) and verb phrases (think, believe, suggest).

Narrative turn

is used to refer to a widespread adoption of narrative and narrative analysis (originating from literary studies) across a range of social science disciplines, as well as in law, health studies and theology.

Passive voice

a form of representation whereby the grammatical subject receives or suffers the action of a verb. For instance, '*He* was removed from the ward'. In this example, 'He' is the subject who suffers or experiences the action of the verb 'remove'. The passive voice provides the option of deleting the agent (the entity responsible for performing an action). In the aforementioned example, for instance, the agent is not present and hence it is not clear who performs the act of removing the patient. Compare **active voice**.

Perlocutionary act

is a speech act performed *by* saying something, and not *in* saying something, for example, comforting, persuading, annoying or inspiring. In other words, such acts are performed to produce a further effect.

Personification

refers to the act of ascribing human qualities to animals or objects, for example, when talking about 'dancing sun rays' or 'smiling cats'.

Phatic (talk)

involves language being used for sociability purposes rather than for meaningful information exchange. Phatic talk is commonly used to build and maintain social relations, to establish rapport between speakers. Common, classic examples of small talk include questions and statements about the weather and enquiring after fellow interlocutors' general well-being.

Pragmatics

an area of linguistic study that investigates speaker meaning. Pragmatics is concerned with the context in which language is produced and the background knowledge that speakers draw on in order to infer meaning. Politeness, Relevance Theory, cooperation and speech acts are, among others, all aspects of language study that fall under the concern of pragmatics.

Primary care

refers to a level of medical care first accessed by patients. Primary care services are provided by general practitioners (GPs), dentists, community pharmacies and optometrists. Most people's contact with healthcare providers is with these services.

Relevance
a cognitive theory of communication that considers language in terms of relevance. Relevance Theory overhauls all four of Grice's conversational maxims (1991: 78-9), subsuming them under the one principle of relevance. Language users look for the relevance in one another's utterances and, accordingly, aim to make their utterances as relevant as possible. See **weak and strong communication**.

Sick role
a socially sanctioned role that legitimates illness. Broadly speaking, the sick role involves ill people complying with certain obligations, for example: their recognising that they cannot recover by themselves and their accessing professional medical care in order to get better.

Speech act
the function performed by a particular utterance, such as requesting, complaining, instructing and apologising.. See **locutionary, illocutionary and perlocutionary act**.

Strong communication
with regard to Relevance Theory, strong acts of communication involve instances of language use which require little processing effort on the part of hearers. The less effort required to make sense of an utterance, the more relevant it is. Strong communication enables listeners to readily identify speakers' intentions concerning the meaning of an utterance. Compare **weak communication**.

Syntax
the arrangement of words in a sentence – the componential structure of sentences.

Vague language
is language which is purposely vague. Vague language is not unhandy, sloppy language but has a deliberate communicative function. For instance, vague language plays an important interpersonal role in social interaction, allowing language users to mitigate speech acts such as requests and directives.

Weak communication
a concept in Relevance Theory relating to language use that requires significant processing effort on the part of hearers. In contrast to strong communication, which is comparatively clear, weak communication is vague and open to interpretation, involving speakers presenting listeners with a range of inferences to choose from. Compare **strong communication**.

Further reading

We hope that readers, as part of their continuing journey into the fascinating realm of health communication, will endeavour to pursue the various references that appear throughout this book. Alternatively, readers seeking a starting point with which to begin their further reading might wish to pursue the titles in the following list. We have given attention to some of these publications already, but our consideration of these texts is certainly no substitute for an intimate consultation with the original source.

Books

Baker, P. (2006) *Using Corpora in Discourse Analysis*. London, UK: Continuum.
   A practical and accessible introduction to using corpus linguistic tools in the pursuit of discourse analysis, a text teeming with ideas about how to conduct one's own analysis. An essential text for researchers interested in using corpus techniques to interrogate health discourse.

Brown, B., Crawford, P. and Carter, R. (2006) *Evidence-Based Health Communication*. Berkshire, UK: Open University Press.
   An illuminating text that adopts a multidisciplinary perspective in exploring a wide range of health communication issues.

Cameron, D. (2001) *Working with Spoken Discourse*. London, UK: Sage.
   Provides an excellent and practical guide to using and analysing spoken language. Covers a range of themes and approaches to discourse analysis.

Carter, R. and McCarthy, M. J. (1997) *Exploring Spoken English*. Cambridge, UK: Cambridge University Press.
   An accessible book that examines language use in a range of interactive contexts. Among other linguistic themes, contains insightful commentaries on narrative and vague language.

Charteris-Black, J. (2004) *Corpus Approaches to Critical Metaphor Analysis*. London, UK: Palgrave Macmillan.
   One of the first book-length discussions on the study of metaphor use within the framework of corpus linguistics.

Conrad, P. (2007) *The Medicalization of Society*. Baltimore, USA: John Hopkins University Press.
An insightful sociological work investigating how human conditions and problems come to be defined and treated as medical phenomena and disorders.

Cook, G. (2000) *Language Play, Language Learning*. Oxford, UK: Oxford University Press.
A book that highlights the significance of language play, particularly with regard to applied linguistics and language learning.

Crystal, D. (2011) *Internet Linguistics: A Student Guide*. London, UK: Routledge.
A highly accessible text that examines the linguistic properties of a range of online modes of communication. Also explores the differences and distinctions between speech and writing and the hybrid nature of iInternet discourse.

Fairclough, N. (1992) *Discourse and Social Change*. Cambridge, UK: Polity Press.
An engaging and persuasive manifesto for critical discourse analysis that also presents some extremely insightful analyses of medical discourse.

Gwyn, R. (2002) *Communicating Health and Illness*. London, UK: Sage.
Placing a firm emphasis on the role of discourse, this text serves as an elegantly accessible and informative introduction to health communication.

Heritage, J. and Maynard, D. (eds) (2006) *Communication in Medical Care: Interaction between Primary Care Physicians and Patients*. Cambridge, UK: Cambridge University Press.
A comprehensive collection of in-depth conversation analysis studies that examine doctor–patient consultations in the primary care setting.

Hunter, K. M (1991) *Doctor's Stories: The Narrative Structure of Medical Knowledge*. Princeton, USA: Princeton University Press.
Considers the types of texts that doctors produce when communicating information about patients. Contains a detailed chapter about the linguistic content of patient records.

Iedema, R. (ed.) (2007) *The Discourse of Hospital Communication: Tracing Complexities in Contemporary Healthcare Organizations*. Hampshire, UK: Palgrave Macmillan.
An enlightening collection of innovative and inter-disciplinary articles that explores a number of under-researched themes in the hospital setting.

Karp, D. (1996) *Speaking of Sadness: Depression, Disconnection and the Meaning of Illness*. Oxford, UK: Oxford University Press.
An excellent, sustained analysis of personal narratives of depression which effectively integrates linguistic and social science insights.

Kleinman, A. (1988) *The Illness Narratives: Suffering and the Human Condition*. New York, USA: Basic Books.

A classic treatise on personal narratives of illness: one of the first texts to give due consideration to patients' personal experiences of suffering and illness.

Mishler, E. (1984) *The Discourse of Medicine: Dialectics of Medical Interviews*. Norwood, NJ, USA: Ablex.

This is a classic and still influential study of the doctor–patient consultation. Now sadly, pointlessly, out of print, we nevertheless recommend it to anyone interested in knowing more about the interactional dynamics of the practitioner–patient relationship.

Sarangi, S. and Roberts, C. (eds) (1999) *Talk, Work and Institutional Order*. Berlin, Germany: Mouton de Gruyter.

Brings together a range of insightful chapters concerning language and the workplace, a number of which examine medical discourse.

Journal articles and book chapters

Adolphs, S., Brown, B., Carter, R., Crawford, P. and Sahota, O. (2004) 'Applied clinical linguistics: corpus linguistics in healthcare settings', *Journal of Applied Linguistics*, 1: 9-28.

One of the first studies to demonstrate the facility of keywords as an analytical resource in health communication. The research also offers insights into combining quantitative and qualitative discourse analysis.

Brown, B., Nerlich, B., Crawford, P., Koteyko, N. and Carter, R. (2009) 'Hygiene and biosecurity: The language and politics of risk in an era of emerging infectious diseases', *Sociology Compass*, 2: 1–13.

The article reports on research based on metaphor analysis and corpus linguistics, revealing how metaphorical concepts were used as framing devices by different groups to advocate disease management.

Candlin, C. and Candlin, S. (2003) 'Healthcare communication: A problematic site for applied linguistic research', *Annual Review of Applied Linguistics*, 23: 134-54.

Provides a succinct and detailed review of health communication from an applied linguistic perspective. The issues it raises are still extremely pertinent, particularly the discussion of intercultural research in healthcare settings.

Clerehan, R. and Buchbinder, R. (2006) 'Toward a more valid account of functional text quality: The case of the patient information leaflet', *Text & Talk*, 26: 39-68.

This article systematically sets out a linguistic framework for examining the text of the patient information leaflet.

Drew, P., Chatwin, J. and Collins, S. (2000) 'Conversation analysis: a method for research into interactions between patients and health-care professionals', *Health Expectations*, 4: 58-70.

Presents a practical account of how conversation analysis can be used to interrogate practitioner–patient interaction.

Morrow, P. (2006) 'Telling about problems and giving advice in an internet discussion forum: some discourse features', *Discourse Studies,* 8: 531-548.
  Focussing on emotional health issues, this article is a succinct and insightful analysis of online problem and advice messages.

Pilnick, A. and Dingwall, R. (2011) 'On the remarkable persistence of asymmetry in doctor/patient interaction: A critical review', *Social Science & Medicine,* 72: 1374-1382.
  Provides a fascinatingly penetrating up-to-date interactional assessment of the doctor–patient consultation.

Segal, J. (1997) 'Public Discourse and Public Policy: Some Ways That Metaphor Constrains Health (Care)', *Journal of Medical Humanities,* 18: 217– 31.
  The author provides an insightful analysis of metaphor use in the health policy discourse, calling for more attention to rhetoric work done by metaphors and the ways in which they constrain what can be argued at the outset.

Skelton, J. and Hobbs, F. (1999a) 'Descriptive study of cooperative language in primary care consultations by male and female doctors', *British Medical Journal,* 318: 576-579.
  This article presents a useful illustration of how corpus tools can facilitate analysis of doctor–patient encounters.

Corpus software

WordSmith Tools http://www.lexically.net/wordsmith/
  An accessible and easy to use program which has been widely employed in discourse analytic corpus-based research.

AntConc http://www.antlab.sci.waseda.ac.jp/index.html
  Another extremely accessible program which features all the staple corpus tools. Can be downloaded and used free of charge.

Wmatrix http://ucrel.lancs.ac.uk/wmatrix/
  Allows users to conduct a range of corpus operations. The program will also tag data into semantic themes and parts of speech. Comes with a useful tutorial which provides an effective introduction to the software. The program is free to use for the first month.

BNCweb http://bncweb.info/
  Like AntConc this is a freely available and easy to use piece of software which gives access to the British National Corpus (BNC). It also has a useful tutorial for beginners.

References

Adolphs, S., Brown, B., Carter, R., Crawford, P. and Sahota, O. (2004) 'Applied clinical linguistics: corpus linguistics in healthcare settings', *Journal of Applied Linguistics*, 1: 9–28.

Aggleton, P. and Homans, H. (1987) 'Teaching about AIDS', *Social Science Teacher*, 17: 24–8.

Ainsworth-Vaughn, N. (1998) 'Claiming Power in Doctor–Patient Talk.' (Oxford Studies in Sociolinguistics.) Oxford, UK and New York, USA: Oxford University Press.

Ainsworth-Vaughn, N. (2001) 'The discourse of medical encounters', in D. Schiffrin, D. Tannen and H. Ehernberger Hamilton (eds) *The Handbook of Discourse Analysis*. Malden, MA, USA: Blackwell Publishing.

Airhihenbuwa, C. O., Makinwa, B. and Obregon, R. (2000) 'Towards a new communication framework for HIV/AIDS', *Journal of Health Communication*, 5: 101–11.

Albert, T. and Chadwick, S. (1992) 'How readable are practice leaflets?' *British Medical Journal*, 305: 1266–8.

Annandale, E. (2004) 'Working on the front-line: Risk culture and nursing in the new NHS', in M. Bury and J. Gabe (eds) *The Sociology of Health and Illness: A Reader*. London, UK: Routledge.

Annas, G. (1995) 'Reframing the debate on healthcare reform by replacing our metaphors', *New England Journal of Medicine* 332: 744–7.

Anspach, R. (1988) 'Notes on the sociology of medical discourse: The language of case presentation', *Journal of Health and Social Behaviour*, 29: 357–75.

Arminen, I. (2001). 'Closings of turns in the meetings of Alcoholics Anonymous'. *Research on Language and Social Interaction*, 34, 211–52.

Armstrong, N., Koteyko, N. and Powell J. (in press) 'Oh dear, should I really be saying that on here?' Issues of identity and authority in an online diabetes community', *Health: An Interdisciplinary Journal for the Social Study of Health, Illness and Medicine*.

Atkins, S. and Harvey, K. (2010) 'How to use corpus linguistics in the study of health communication'. In M. McCarthy and A. O'Keeffe (eds), *The Routledge Handbook of Corpus Linguistics*. Abingdon, UK: Routledge

Atkinson, J. and Heritage, J. (eds) (1984) *Structures of Social Action: Studies in Conversation Analysis*. Cambridge, UK: Cambridge University Press.

Atkinson, P. (1997) 'Narrative turn or blind alley?' *Qualitative Health Research*, 7: 325–344.

Atkinson, P. and Delamont, S. (2006) 'Rescuing narrative from qualitative research', *Narrative Inquiry*, 16: 164–72.

Austin, J. (1962) *How to Do Things with Words*. Cambridge, MA, USA: Harvard University Press.

Baker, P. (2006) *Using Corpora in Discourse Analysis*. London, UK: Continuum.

Bakhtin, M. (1981) 'Discourse in the novel', in M. Holquis (ed.) *The Dialogic Imagination*. Austin, TX, USA: University of Texas Press.

Barak, A., Boniel-Nissim, M. and Suler, J. (2008) 'Internet use and personal empowerment of hearing-impaired adolescents', *Computers in Human Behaviour*, 24: 1867–83.

Baron, N. (1998) 'Letters by phone or speech by other means: the linguistics of email', *Language and Communication*, 18: 133–70.

Baron, N. (2000) *Alphabet to Email: How Written English Evolved and Where It's Heading*. London, UK and New York, USA: Routledge.

Baron, N. (2003) 'Why email looks like speech', in J. Aitchison and D. Lewis (eds) *New Media Language*. London, UK: Routledge.

Barrett, R. (1996) *The Psychiatric Team and the Social Definition of Schizophrenia: An Anthropological Study of Person and Illness*. Cambridge, UK: Cambridge University Press.

Barrett, R. (1999) 'The writing-talking cure: An ethnography of record-speech events in a psychiatric hospital', in C. Candlin and K. Hyland (eds) *Writing: Texts, Processes and Practices*. London, UK: Longman.

Barry, C., Stevenson, F., Britten, N., Barber, N. and Bradley, C. (2001) 'Giving voice to the lifeworld. More humane, more effective medical care? A qualitative study of doctor–patient communication in general practice', *Social Science & Medicine*, 53: 487–505.

Baym, N. K. (2000) *Tune In, Log On: Soaps, Fandom, and Online Community*. London, UK: Sage.

Benwell, B. and Stokoe, E. (2006) *Discourse and Identity*. Edinburgh, UK: Edinburgh University Press.

Berg, M. (1996) 'Practices of reading and writing: the constitutive role of the patient record in medical work', *Sociology of Health & Illness*, 4: 499–524.

Berger, J. and Mohr, J. (1976) *A Fortunate Man*. London, UK: Writers and Readers Publishing Cooperative.

Bergmann, J. (1992) 'Veiled morality: notes on discretion in psychiatry', in P. Drew and J. Heritage (eds) *Talk at Work: Interaction in Institutional Settings*. Cambridge, UK: Cambridge University Press.

Bloor, M. and Horobin, G. (1975) 'Conflict and conflict resolution in doctor/patient interactions', in C. Cox and A. Mead (eds) *A Sociology of Medical Practice*. London, UK: Collier-Macmillan.

Bosher, S. and Smalkoski, K. (2002) 'From needs analysis to curriculum development: designing a course in health-care communication for immigrant students in the USA', *English for Specific Purposes*, 21: 59–79.

Brown, B., Crawford, P. and Carter, R. (2006) *Evidence-Based Health Communication*. Berkshire, UK: Open University Press.

Brown, P., and Levinson, S. C. (1987) *Politeness: Some universals in language usage*. Cambridge, UK and New York, USA: Cambridge University Press.

Brown, B., Nerlich, B., Crawford, P., Koteyko, N. and Carter, R. (2009) 'Hygiene and biosecurity: The language and politics of risk in an era of emerging infectious diseases', *Sociology Compass*, 2: 1–13.

Bruner, J. (1990) *Acts of Meaning*. Cambridge, USA: Harvard University Press.

Bruthiaux, P. (1996) *The Discourse of Classified Advertising*. Oxford, UK: Oxford University Press.

Bury, M. (2001) Illness narratives: Fact or fiction? *Sociology of Health & Illness*, 23, (3): 263–85.

Butler, C. (1998) 'Using computers to study texts', in A. Wray, K. Trott and A. Bloomer (eds) *Projects in Linguistics: A Practical Guide to Researching Language*. London, UK: Arnold.

Butt, D., Fahey, R., Spinks, S. and C. Yallop (1995) *Using Functional Grammar: An Explorer's Guide*. Sydney, Australia: National Centre for English Language Teaching and Research.

Buttny, R. (1993) *Social accountability in communication*. London, UK: Sage.

Buus, N. (2008) 'Negotiating clinical knowledge: a field study of psychiatric nurses' everyday communication', *Nursing Inquiry*, 15: 189–98.

Byrne, P. and Long, B. (1976) *Doctors Talking to Patients*. London, UK: DHSS.

Calsamiglia, H. and Van Dijk, T. A. (2004) 'Popularization discourse and knowledge about the genome', *Discourse and Society*, 15: 369–89. Special issue: *Genetic and genomic discourses at the dawn of the 21st century*, guest edited by B. Nerlich, R. Dingwall and P. Martin.

Cameron, D. (2001) *Working with Spoken Discourse*. London, UK: Sage.

Cameron, D. (2008) 'Talk from the top down', *Language & Communication*, 28: 143–55.

Cameron, D. and Kulick, D. (2003) *Language and Sexuality*. Cambridge, UK: Cambridge University Press.

Cameron, R. and Williams, J. (1997) 'Sentence to ten cents: A case study of relevance and communicative success in nonnative-native speaker interactions in a medical setting', *Applied Linguistics*, 18: 415–45.

Candlin, S. (2000) 'New dynamics in the nurse–patient relationship?', in S. Sarangi and M. Coulthard (eds) *Discourse and Social Life*. London, UK: Longman.

Candlin, C. and Candlin, S. (2003) 'Healthcare communication: A problematic site for applied linguistic research', *Annual Review of Applied Linguistics*, 23: 134–54.

Candlin, C. and Sarangi, S. (2004) 'Making applied linguistics matter', *Journal of Applied Linguistics*, 1: 1–8.

Car, J. and Sheikh, A. (2004) 'Email consultations in healthcare: 1 – scope and effectiveness'. *British Medical Journal*, 329: 435–8.

Carey, J. T. (2009) *Communication as Culture,: Essays on Media and Society*. (Revised Edition) London, UK: Routledge.

Carter, R. and McCarthy, M. J. (2006) *Cambridge Grammar of English: A Comprehensive Guide*. Cambridge, UK: Cambridge University Press.

Charon, R. (1986) 'To render the lives of patients', *Literature & Medicine*, 5: 58–74.

Charon, R. (1992) 'To build a case: medical histories as traditions in conflict', *Literature and Medicine*, 11: 115–32.

Charteris-Black, J. (2004) *Corpus Approaches to Critical Metaphor Analysis*. London, UK: Palgrave Macmillan.

Cicourel, A. (1992) 'The interpenetration of communicative contexts: examples from medical encounters', in A. Duranti and C. Goodwin (eds) *Rethinking Context: Language as an Interactive Phenomenon*. Cambridge, UK: Cambridge University Press.

Clerehan, R., Buchbinder, R. and Moodie, J. (2005) 'A linguistic framework for assessing the quality of written patient information: Its use in assessing methotrexate information for rheumatoid arthritis', *Health Education Research*, 20: 334–44.

Clerehan, R. and Buchbinder, R. (2006) 'Toward a more valid account of functional text quality: The case of the patient information leaflet', *Text & Talk*, 26: 39–68.

Clerehan, R., Hirsh, D. and Buchbinder, R. (2009) 'Medication information leaflets for patients: The further validation of an analytic linguistic framework', *Communication & Medicine*, 6: 117–28.

Cobb, M. (2001) 'Walking on water? The moral foundations of chaplaincy', in H. Orchard (ed.) *Spirituality in Healthcare Contexts*. London, UK and Philadelphia, USA: Jessica Kingsley Publishers.

Coffin, C., Hewings, A. and O'Halloran, K. (2004) 'General introduction', in C. Coffin, A. Hewings and K. O'Halloran (eds) *Applying English Grammar: Functional and Corpus Approaches*. London, UK: Arnold Publishers.

Collins, S. (2005) 'Explanations in consultations: the combined effectiveness of doctors' and nurses' communication with patients', *Medical Education*, 39: 785–96.

Cook, G. (2003) *Applied Linguistics*. Oxford, UK: Oxford University Press.

Cook-Gumperz, J. and Messerman, L. (1999) 'Local identities and institutional practices: Constructing the record of professional collaboration', in S. Sarangi and C. Roberts (eds) *Talk, Work and Institutional Order*. Berlin, Germany: Mouton de Gruyter.

Conrad, P. (2007) *The Medicalization of Society*. Baltimore, USA: John Hopkins University Press.

Coulter, J. (1994) 'Is contextualising necessarily interpretive?' *Journal of Pragmatics*, 21: 689–98.

Coveney, C., Nerlich, B. and Martin, P. (2009) 'Modafinil in the media: Metaphors, medicalisation and the body', *Social Science & Medicine*, 68: 487–495.

Crawford, P., Nolan, P. and Brown, B. (1995) 'Linguistic entrapment: medico-nursing biographies as fictions', *Journal of Advanced Nursing*, 22: 1141–8.

Crawford, P., Johnson, A., Brown, B. and Nolan, P. (1998) 'The language of mental health nursing reports: firing paper bullets?' *Journal of Advanced Nursing*, 29: 331–40.

Crowe, M. (2000) 'Constructing normality: a discourse analysis of the *DSM-IV*', *Journal of Psychiatric and Mental Health Nursing*, 7: 69–77.

Crystal, D. (2006) *Language and the Internet* (Second Edition). Cambridge, UK: Cambridge University Press.

DEFRA/Department for Environment, Farming and Rural Affairs (2011) Foot and mouth. http://www.defra.gov.uk/animal-diseases/a-z/foot-and-mouth (accessed November 2011).

Department for Environment, Farming and Rural Affairs (2003) *About foot and mouth disease.* http://www.defra.gov.uk/footandmouth/about/index. htm (accessed January 2010).

Donnelly, W. (1997) 'The language of medical case histories', *Annals of Internal Medicine*, 127: 1045–8.

Dougherty, L. and Lister, S. (eds) (2004) *The Royal Marsden Manual of Clinical Nursing Procedures.* Oxford, UK: Blackwell Science.

Doyal, L. and Cameron, A. (2000) 'Reshaping the NHS workforce', *British Medical Journal*, 320: 1023–4.

Drew, P. (2001) 'Conversation analysis', in R. Mesthrie (ed.) *Concise Enyclopedia of Sociolinguistics.* Oxford, UK. Elsevier.

Drew, P., Chatwin, J. and Collins, S. (2000) 'Conversation analysis: a method for research into interactions between patients and health-care professionals', *Health Expectations*, 4: 58–70.

Eichhorn, K. C. (2008) Soliciting and providing social support over the Internet: An investigation of online eating disorder support groups. *Journal of Computer-Mediated Communication*, 14(1), 67–78.

Ensink, T. and Sauer C. (eds) (2003) *Framing and Perspectivising in Discourse.* Amsterdam, The Netherlands and Philadelphia, PA, USA: John Benjamins.

Entman, R. (1993) 'Framing: Toward clarification of a fractured paradigm', *Journal of Communication*, 43: 51–8.

European Commission (1998) *A guideline on the readability of the label and package leaflet of medicinal products for human use.* Brussels, Belgium: European Commission Enterprise and Industry Directorate-General.

Evans, R. G. and Stoddart, G. L (1990) 'Producing health, consuming healthcare', *Social Science and Medicine*, 31: 1347–63.

Eysenbach, G. and Diepgen, T. (1999) 'Patients looking for information on the Internet and seeking teleadvice: Motivation, expectations, and misconceptions as expressed in e-mails sent to physicians', *Archives of dermatology*, 135: 151–6.

Eysenbach, G., Powell, J., Englesakis, M., Rizo, C. and Stern A. (2004) Health related virtual communities and electronic support groups: systematic review of the effects of online peer to peer interactions. *British Medical Journal*, 328: 1166.

Fairclough, N. (1992) *Discourse and Social Change.* Cambridge, UK: Polity Press.

Fairclough, N. (2001) *Language and Power* (Second Edition). London, UK: Longman.

Fairclough, N. (2003) *Analysing Discourse: Textual Analysis for Social Research.* London, UK: Routledge

Fernback, J. (2007) Beyond the diluted community concept: A symbolic interactionist perspective on online social relations. *New Media & Society*, 9(1) 49–69.

Fisher, S. (1991) 'A discourse of the social: medical talk/power talk/ oppositional talk?' *Discourse & Society*, 2: 157–82.

Fitzgerald, M. (2002) 'Meeting the needs of individuals', in J. Daly, S. Speedy, D. Jackson and P. Darbyshire (eds) *Contexts of Nursing: An Introduction.* Oxford, UK: Blackwell Publishing.

Fleischman, S. (1999) 'A linguist on illness and disease', *Journal of Medical Humanities*, 20: 3–31.

Fleischman, S. (2001) 'Language and medicine', in D. Schiffrin, D. Tannen, and H. Ehernberger Hamilton (eds) *The Handbook of Discourse Analysis.* Malden, MA, USA: Blackwell Publishing.

Frank, A. (1997) 'Illness as moral occasion: Restoring agency to ill people', *Health*, 1: 131–48.

Furedi, F. (2010) *Swine flu and the dramatisation of disease.* http://www.frankfuredi.com/index.php/site/article/302/ (accessed 15 January 2012).

Galegher, J. L. Sproull and S. Kiesler. (1998). 'Legitimacy, authority, and community in electronic support groups' *Written Communication*, 15: 493–530.

Garfinkel, H. and Bittner, E. (1967) 'Good organizational reasons for 'bad' clinic records', in H. Garfinkel (ed.) *Studies in Ethnomethodology.* Englewood Cliffs, New Jersey, USA: Prentice-Hall.

Gee, J. (1999) *An Introduction to Discourse Analysis: Theory and Method.* London, UK and New York, USA: Routledge.

Gibbs, R. W. (2002) 'A new look at literal meaning in understanding what is said and implicated'. *Journal of Pragmatics*, 34, 457–86.

Goffman, E. (1959) *The Presentation of Self in Everyday Life.* New York, USA: Doubleday Anchor.

Goffman, E. (1961) *Asylums: Essays on the Social Situations of Mental Patients.* New York, USA: Doubleday Anchor.

Goffman, E. (1981) *Forms of Talk.* Philadelphia, USA: University of Pennsylvania Press.

Gowers, E. (1954) *The Complete Plain Words.* London, UK: Her Majesty's Stationery Office.

Grainger, K. (2002) 'Politeness or Impoliteness? Verbal Play on the Hospital Ward', *Sheffield Hallam Working Papers: Linguistic Politeness and Context.* http://extra.shu.ac.uk/wpw/politeness/grainger.htm (accessed 26 October 2011).

Greenhalgh, T. and Hurwitz, B. (1999) 'Why study narrative?', *British Medical Journal*, 318: 48–50.

Greenhalgh, T. and Wessely, S. (2004) '"Health for me": A sociocultural analysis of healthism in the middle classes', *British Medical Bulletin*, 69: 197–213.

Grice, P. (1975) 'Logic and conversation', in P. Cole and J. Morgan (eds) *Syntax and Semantics 3: Speech Acts.* New York, USA: Academic Press.

Grice, P. (1991 [1967]) 'Logic and Conversation', in P. Grice, *Studies in the Way of Words.* Cambridge, MA, USA and London, UK: Harvard University Press.

Grice, P. (1999) 'Logic and conversation', in A. Jaworski, and N. Coupland, (eds) *The Discourse Reader.* London, UK: Routledge.

Griffiths, L. (2004) 'Electronic text-based communication – assumptions and illusions created by the transference phenomena', in G. Bolton, S. Howlett,

C. Lago and J. Wright (eds) *Writing Cures: An Introductory Handbook of Writing in Counselling and Therapy*. London, UK: Routledge.

Groesz, L., Levine, P. and Murnen, S. (2002) 'The effect of experimental presentation of thin media images on body satisfaction', *International Journal of Eating Disorders*, 31: 1–16.

Grover, J. (1990) 'AIDS: Keywords', in C. Ricks and L. Michaels (eds) *The State of the Language: 1990s Edition*. London, UK and Boston, USA: Faber & Faber.

Gumperz, J. (1999) 'On interactional sociolinguistic method', in S. Sarangi and C. Roberts (eds) *Talk, Work and Institutional Order*. Berlin, Germany: Mouton de Gruyter.

Gwyn, R. (2002) *Communicating Health and Illness*. London, UK: Sage.

Hak, T. (1999) '"Text" and "con-text": Talk bias in studies of healthcare work', in S. Sarangi and C. Roberts (eds) *Talk, Work and Institutional Order*. Berlin, Germany: Mouton de Gruyter.

Hak, T. (1992) 'Psychiatric records as transformations of other texts', in G. Watson and R. Seiler (eds) *Text in Context: Contributions to Ethnomethodology*. London, UK: Sage.

Halliday, M. (1978) *Language as Social Semiotic*. London, UK: London Edward Arnold.

Halliday, M. (1985) *Spoken and Written Language*. Victoria, Australia: Deaking University.

Hardey, M. (1999) 'Doctor in the house: The Internet as a source of lay health knowledge and the challenge to expertise', *Sociology of Health & Illness*, 21: 820–35.

Harrison, S. and Barlow, J. (2009) 'Politeness strategies and advice-giving in an online arthritis workshop', *Journal of Politeness Research: Language, Behavior, Culture*, 5: 93–111.

Harvey, K., Churchill, D., Crawford, P., Brown, B., Mullany, L. Macfarlane, A. and McPherson, A. (2008) 'Health communication and adolescents: What do their emails tell us?', *Family Practice*, 25: 304–11.

Hassan, I., McCabe, R. and Priebe, S. (2007) 'Professional–patient communication in the treatment of mental illness: A review' *Communication & Medicine*, 4: 141–52.

Healthy People 2010 (2010) *Health Communication*. Office of Disease Prevention and Health Promotion, USA: U.S. Department of Health and Human Services.

Health Protection Agency (2010) *STI Annual Data*. London, UK: Health Protection Agency.

Heffer, S. (2010) *Strictly English: The Correct Way To Write...And Why It Matters*. London. UK: Random House.

Helman, C. (2007) *Culture, Health and Illness* (Fifth Edition). London, UK: Hodder Arnold.

Heritage, J. (1984) 'A change-of-state token and aspects of its sequential placement', in J. Maxwell Atkinson and J. Heritage (eds) *Structures of Social Action: Studies in Conversation Analysis*. Cambridge, UK: Cambridge University Press.

Heritage, J. (2004) 'Conversation analysis and institutional talk: Analysing data', in D. Silverman (ed) *Qualitative Research: Theory, Method and Practice* London, UK: Sage.

Heritage, J. and Maynard, D. (eds) (2006) *Communication in Medical Care: Interaction between Primary Care Physicians and Patients*. Cambridge, UK: Cambridge University Press.

Herring, S. (2001) 'Computer-mediated discourse', in D. Schiffrin, D. Tannen and H. Hamilton (eds) *The handbook of discourse analysis*. Oxford, UK: Blackwell.

Herring, S. C. (2004) 'Computer-mediated discourse analysis: An approach to researching online communities', in S. A. Barab, R. Kling. and J. H. Gray (eds) *Designing for virtual communities in the service of learning*. Cambridge, UK and New York, USA: Cambridge University Press.

Hewett, D., Watson, B., Gallois, C., Ward, M. and Leggett, B. (2009) 'Communication in medical records', *Journal of Language and Social Psychology*, 28: 119–38.

Hine, C. (2000) *Virtual Ethnography*. London, UK: Sage.

Hirsh, D., Clerehan, R., Staples, M., Osborne, R. and Buchbinder, R. (2009) 'Patient assessment of medication information leaflets and validation of the Evaluative Linguistic Framework (ELF)', *Patient Education and Counseling*, 77: 248–54.

Hobbs, P. (2003) 'The use of evidentiality in physician's progress notes', *Discourse Studies*, 5: 451–78.

Hobbs, P. (2007) 'Managing the division of labour: the discursive construction of treatment in two hospital obstetrical units', *Journal of Applied Linguistics*, 2: 273–98.

Hodgkin P. (1985) 'Medicine is war: And other medical metaphors', *British Medical Journal*, 291: 1820–1821.

Hunter, K. M (1991) *Doctors' Stories. The Narrative Structure of Medical Knowledge*, Princeton, USA: Princeton University Press.

Hutchby, I. (1995) Aspects of recipient design in expert advice-giving on call-in radio. *Discourse Processes*, 19 (2): 219–38.

Hyden, M. (1992) *Woman battering as marital act: The construction of a violent marriage*. PhD thesis: Department of Social Work, University of Stockholm, Sweden.

Hyden, L-C. (1997) 'Illness and narrative', *Sociology of Health & Illness*, 19: 48–69.

Hyland, K. (2000) *Disciplinary discourses: social interactions in academic writing*. London, UK: Longman.

Iedema, R. and Scheeres, H. (2003) 'From doing work to talking work: Renegotiating knowing, doing, and identity', *Applied Linguistics*, 24: 316–37.

Iedema, R. (2007) 'Communicating hospital work', in R. Iedema (ed.) *The Discourse of Hospital Communication: Tracing Complexities in Contemporary Healthcare Organizations*. Hampshire, UK: Palgrave Macmillan.

Iyer, P., Levin, B. and Shea, M. (2004) *Medical Legal Aspects of Medical Records*. Tuscon, USA: Lawyers and Judges Publishing Company.

Jackson, S. (2005) '"Dear girlfriend ... ": Constructions of sexual health problems and sexual identities in letters to a teenage magazine'. *Sexualities*, 8: 282–305.

Jackson, L. D. and Duffy, B. K. (eds) (1998) *Health Communication Research*. Westport, CT, USA: Greenwood.

Jaworski, A. and Coupland, N. (1999) 'Perspectives on discourse analysis', in A. Jaworski and N. Coupland, (eds) *The Discourse Reader*. London, UK: Routledge.

Joinson, A. (2001) 'Self-disclosure in computer-mediated communication: the role of self-awareness and visual anonymity'. *European Journal of Social Psychology*, 31: 177–92.

Jones, A. (2007) 'Admitting hospital patients: A qualitative study of an everyday nursing task', *Nursing Inquiry*, 14: 212–23.

Jones, A. (2003) 'Nurses talking to patients: Exploring conversation analysis as a means of researching nurse–patient communication', *International Journal of Nursing Studies*, 40: 609–18.

Karp, D. (1993) 'Taking anti-depressant medications: resistance, trial, commitment, conversion, disenchantment, *Qualitative Sociology*, 16: 337–59.

Karp, D. (1996) *Speaking of Sadness: Depression, Disconnection and the Meaning of Illness*. Oxford, UK: Oxford University Press.

Kasperson, J., Kasperson, R., Pidgeon, N. and Slovic (2003) 'The social amplification of risk: assessing fifteen years of research and theory', in N. Pidgeon, R. Kasperson and P. Slovic (eds) *The Social Amplification of Risk*. Cambridge, UK: Cambridge University Press.

Kemp, M. (2003) 'Hearts and minds: agency and discourse on distress', *Anthropology and Medicine*, 10: 187–205.

Kleinman, A. (1988) *The Illness Narratives: Suffering and the Human Condition*. New York, USA: Basic Books.

Kohr, W. (1999) 'Deconstructing the language of psychiatric hospitalization'. *Journal of Advanced Nursing*, 29: 1052–9.

Koller, V. (2003) 'Metaphor clusters, metaphor chains: Analyzing the multifunctionality of metaphor in text' *Metaphorik.de*, 5, 115–34.

Koteyko, N. (2010) 'Balancing the good, the bad and the better: A discursive perspective on healthy eating and probiotics', *Health: An Interdisciplinary Journal for the Social Study of Health, Illness and Medicine*, 14: 585–602.

Koteyko, N. (2010) 'Mining the Internet for linguistic and social data: An analysis of 'carbon compounds' in web feeds', *Discourse & Society*, 21: 655–74.

Koteyko, N. and R. Carter. (2008) 'Discourse of "transformational leadership" in infection control' *Health: An Interdisciplinary Journal for the Social Study of Health, Illness and Medicine*, 12: 479–99.

Koteyko, N., Brown, B. and P. Crawford. (2008) 'The dead parrot and the dying swan: The role of metaphor scenarios in UK press coverage of avian flu in the UK in 2005–2006', *Metaphor and Symbol*, 23(4), 242–261.

Kouper, I. (2010) 'The pragmatics of peer advice in a LiveJournal community', *Language@Internet*, 7: article 1.

Labov, W. (ed.) (1972) *Language in the Inner City: Studies in the Black English vernacular*. Philadelphia, USA: University of Pennsylvania Press.

Lakoff, G. and M. Johnson (1980) *Metaphors We Live By*. Chicago, USA: University of Chicago Press.

Lakoff, G. (1993) 'The contemporary theory of metaphor', in A. Ortony (ed.) *Metaphor and Thought*. Cambridge, UK: Cambridge University Press.

Lamerichs, J. (2003) *Discourse of support: Exploring online discussions on depression*. PhD thesis. Wageningen University, The Netherlands.

Lamerichs, J. and te Molder, H. (2003) 'Computer-mediated Communication: From a Cognitive to a Discursive Model', *New Media and Society*, 5: 451–73.

Larson, B., Nerlich, B. and Wallis, P. (2005) 'Metaphors and Biorisks', *Science Communication*, 26: 243–68.

Lewison, G. (2008) 'The reporting of the risks from severe acute respiratory syndrome (SARS) in the news media 2003–2004', *Health, Risk and Society* 10(3): 241–62.

Locher, M. (2006) *Advice Online: Advice-Giving in an American Internet Health Column*, Philadelphia, USA: John Benjamins.

Locher, M. and Hoffman, S. (2006) 'The emergence of the identity of a fictional expert advice-giver in an American advice column', *Text and Talk*, 26: 69–106.

Lupton, D. (1998) *Risk*. London, UK: Routledge.

Lupton, D. (2003) *Medicine as Culture* (Second Edition). London, UK: Sage.

Lycan, G. (2008) *Philosophy of Language: A Contemporary Introduction* (Second Edition). New York, USA and London, UK: Routledge.

Mandl, K., Kohane, I. and Brandt, A. (1998) 'Electronic patient-physician communication: Problems and promise', *Annals of Internal Medicine*, 129: 495–500.

Mangan, L. (2009) 'A brief history of agony aunts', http://www.guardian.co.uk/lifeandstyle/2009/nov/13/agony-aunts (accessed 15 October 2011).

Mason, L. (2005) ' "They haven't a clue!" A qualitative study of the self-perceptions of 11-14-year old clinic attenders', *Primary Healthcare Research and Development*, 6: 199–207.

McCarthy, M. and Handford, M. (2004) ' "Invisible to us": A preliminary corpus-based study of spoken business English', in U. Connor and T. Upton (eds) *Discourse in the Professions: Perspectives from Corpus Linguistics*. Amsterdam The Netherlands: John Benjamins.

McEnery, A., Xiao, R. and Tono, Y. (2006) *Corpus-Based Language Studies*. London, UK: Routledge.

McKay, S. and Bonner, F. (2002) Evaluating illness in women's magazines. *Journal of Language and Social Psychology*, 21: 53–67.

Mead, C. and Smith, C. (1991) 'Readability formulas: Cautions and criteria', *Patient Education and Counselling*, 17: 153–8.

Melia, K. M. (1978) 'A sociological approach to the analysis of nursing work', *Journal of Advanced Nursing*, 4: 57–67.

Mickelson, K. D. (1997) 'Seeking social support: Parents in electronic support groups', in S. Kiesler (ed.) *Culture of the internet*. NJ, USA: Lawrence Erlbaum Associates.

Mishler, E. (1984) *The Discourse of Medicine: Dialectics of Medical Interviews*. Norwood, NJ, USA: Ablex.

Monzoni, C. and M. Reuber (2009) 'Conversational displays of coping resources in clinical encounters between patients with epilepsy and neurologists: A pilot study', *Epilepsy & Behavior*, 16: 652–9.

Moore, R. and J. Hallenbeck (2010) 'Narrative empathy and how dealing with stories helps: creating a space for empathy in culturally diverse care settings', *Journal of Pain and Symptom Management*, 40: 471–6.

Morrow, P. (2006) 'Telling about problems and giving advice in an internet discussion forum: some discourse features', *Discourse Studies*, 8: 531–48.

Nathanson, C. (1999) 'Social movements as catalysts for policy change: The case of smoking and guns', *Journal of Health Politics and Law* 24(3): 421–88.

Nelkin, D. (2001) 'Molecular metaphors: The gene in popular discourse' *Nature Reviews Genetics*, 2: 555–559.

Nerlich, B. and Halliday, C. (2007) 'Avian Flu: the creation of expectations in the interplay between science and the media', *Sociology of Health and Illness*, 29: 46–65.

Nerlich, B., Hamilton, C. and Rowe V. (2002) 'Conceptualising foot and Mouth disease: The socio-cultural role of metaphors, frames and narratives', *Metaphorik.de*.http://www.metaphorik.de/02/nerlich.htm (accessed 12 November 2002).

O'Keeffe, A., Clancy, B. and Adolphs, S. (2011) *Introducing Pragmatics in Use*. Abingdon, UK, Routledge.

Ong, L., De Haes, A., Hoos, A. and Lammes, F. (1995) 'Doctor–patient communication: A review of the literature', *Social Science & Medicine*, 40: 903–18.

Orgad, S. (2005) *Storytelling Online: Talking Breast Cancer on the Internet*. New York, USA: Peter Lang.

Pander Maat, H. (1997) 'What authors and readers do with side effects information on drugs', in L. Lentz and H. Pander Maat (eds) *Discourse analysis and evaluation: functional approaches*. Amsterdam, The Netherlands: Rodopi

Pander Maat, H. and Klaassen, R. (1994) 'Side effects of side effects information in drug information leaflets', *Journal of Technical Writing and Communication*, 24: 389–404.

Pander Maat, H. and Lentz, L. (2010) 'Improving the usability of patient information leaflets', *Patient Education and Counseling*, 80: 113–19.

Parry, R. (2004) 'Communication during goal-setting in physiotherapy treatment settings', *Clinical Rehabilitation*, 18: 668–82.

Parsons, T. (1987) 'Illness and the role of the physicians: A sociological perspective', in J. D Stoeckle (ed.) *Encounters between Patients and Doctors: An Anthology*. Cambridge, MA, USA: MIT Press.

Payne, S., Large, S., Jarrett, N. and Turner, P. (2000) 'Written information given to patients and families by palliative care units: A national survey', *The Lancet*, 355: 1792.

Phythian, B. (1979) *A Concise Dictionary of Correct English*. London, UK: Hodder and Stoughton.

Pilnick, A. (2001) 'The interactional organization of pharmacist consultations in a hospital setting: A putative structure', *Journal of Pragmatics*, 33: 1927–45.

Pilnick, A. (2003) ' "Patient counselling" by pharmacists: four approaches to the delivery of counselling sequences and their interactional reception', *Social Science & Medicine*, 56: 835–49.

Pilnick, A. and Dingwall, R. (2011) 'On the remarkable persistence of asymmetry in doctor/patient interaction: A critical review', *Social Science & Medicine*, 72: 1374–82.

Pomerantz, A. (1980) 'Telling my side: "limited access" as a "fishing" device', *Sociological Inquiry*, 50: 186–98.

Pomerantz, A. (1984) 'Agreeing and disagreeing with assessments: Some features of preferred/dispreferred turn shapes', in J. Maxwell Atkinson and J. Heritage (eds) *Structures of Social Action: Studies in Conversation Analysis*. Cambridge, UK: Cambridge University Press.

Porter, K. (2005) *The frequency and function of passive voice use in nurses' notes*. Unpublished dissertation: University of North Carolina Wilmington, USA.

Potter, J. (2000) 'Post Cognitivist Psychology', *Theory and Psychology*, 10: 31–7.

Potter, J. and Wetherell, M. (1987) *Discourse and social psychology*. London, UK: Sage.

Pragglejaz Group (2007) 'MIP: A method for identifying metaphorically used words in discourse', *Metaphor and Symbol*, 22: 1–39.

Prince, G. (1982) *Narratology: The Form and Functioning of Narrative*. Berlin, Germany, New York, USA and Amsterdam, The Netherlands: Morton.

Prior, L. (2003) *Using Documents in Social Research*. London, UK: Sage.

Raynor, D., Savage, I., Knapp, P. and Henley, J. (2004) 'We are the experts: People with asthma talk about their medicine information needs', *Patient Education and Counseling*, 53: 167–74.

Reese, S. D. (2003) Framing public life: A bridging model for media research, in S. D. Reese, O. H. Gandy, Jr. and A. E. Grant (eds) *Framing public life*, (pp. 7–31). Mahwah, NJ: Erlbaum.

Riessman, C. K. (1990) 'Strategic uses of narrative in the presentation of self and illness: A research note', *Social Science & Medicine*, 30: 1195–200.

Ribeiro, B. (1996) 'Conflict talk in a psychiatric discharge interview', in C. R. Caldas-Coulthard and M. Coulthard (eds) *Texts and Practices: Readings in Critical Discourse Analysis*. London, UK: Routledge.

Roberts, C. and Sarangi, S. (2003) 'Uptake of Discourse Research in Interprofessional Settings: Reporting from Medical Consultancy', *Applied Linguistics*, 24: 338–59.

Roberts, C., Moss, B., Wass, V., Sarangi, S. and Jones, R. (2005) 'Misunderstandings: a qualitative study of primary care consultations in multilingual settings, and educational implications', *Medical Education*, 39: 465–75.

Roos, I. (2003) 'Reacting to the diagnosis of prostate cancer: Patient learning in a community of practice', *Patient Education and Counseling*, 49: 219–24.

Rose, N. (1999) *Powers of Freedom: Reframing Political Thought*. Cambridge, UK. Cambridge University Press.

Rosenthal, D. and Moore, S. (1994) 'Stigma and ignorance: Young people's beliefs about STDs', *Venereology*, 7: 62–6.

Rowen, M. (1977) '"Do you always hear out your patients? I don't"', *Medical Economics*, 26: 82–86.

Royal College of General Practitioners (2004) *RCGP Information Sheet Number 3: General Practitioner Workload*. London, UK: Royal College of General Practitioners.

Royal National Institute of Blind People (2006) *See It Right: Making Information Accessible for People with Sight Problems*. London, UK: RNIB.

Rundblad, G., Chilton, P. and Hunter, P. (2006) 'An enquiry into scientific and media discourse in the MMR controversy: Authority and factuality', *Communication and Medicine* 3.1: 69–80.

Sacks, H., Schegloff, E. and Jefferson, G. (1974) 'A simplest systematics for the organizing of turn-taking for conversation', *Language 50*: 696–735.

Salvage, J. and Smith, R. (2000) 'Doctors and nurses: doing it differently', *British Medical Journal*, 320: 1019–20.

Salmon, P. and Hall, G. (2004) 'Patient empowerment or the emperor's new clothes', *Journal of the Royal Society of Medicine*, 97: 53–6.

Sarangi, S. and Roberts, C. (1999) 'The dynamics of interactional and institutional orders in work-related settings', in S. Sarangi and C. Roberts (eds) *Talk, Work and Institutional Order*. Berlin, Germany: Mouton de Gruyter.

Sarangi, S. (2004) 'Towards a communicative mentality in medical and healthcare practice', *Communication & Medicine*, 1: 1–11.

Schegloff, E. (1997) 'Whose text? Whose context', *Discourse & Society*, 8: 165–87.

Scott, M. (2004) *WordSmith Tool Help Manual*. (Version 4.0) Oxford, UK: Oxford University Press.

Scott, M. B. and Lyman, S. M. (1968) Accounts. *American Sociological Review*, 33: 46–62.

Seale, C. (2003) *Media and Health*. London, UK: Sage Publications.

Seale, C. (2006) 'Gender accommodation in online cancer support groups', *Health*, 10: 345–60

Seale, C., Boden, S., Williams, S., Lowe, P. and Steinberg, D. (2007) 'Media constructions of sleep and sleep disorders: A study of UK national newspapers', *Social Science & Medicine*, 65: 418–30.

Searle, J. (1969) *Speech Acts. An Essay in the Philosophy of Language*. Cambridge, UK: Cambridge University Press

Short, M. (1996) *Exploring the Language of Poems, Plays and Prose*. London, UK: Longman.

Silverman, D. (1987) *Communication and Medical Practice*. London, UK: Sage.

Skelton, J. and Hobbs, F. (1999a) 'Descriptive study of cooperative language in primary care consultations by male and female doctors', *British Medical Journal*, 318: 576–9.

Skelton, J. and Hobbs, F. (1999b) 'Concordancing: use of language-based research in medical communication', *Lancet*, 353: 108–11.

Slovic, P., Fischhoff, B. and Lichtenstein, S. (1979, July) 'Risk assessment: Technical and behavioral issues.' In *Risk/Benefit analysis in the legislative process*, 133–88. Washington, DC, USA: Government Printing Office.

Smith, B. (1999) 'The abyss: Exploring depression through a narrative of the self', *Qualitative Inquiry*, 5: 262–3.

Spears, R. and Lea, M. (1994) 'Panacea or Panopticon? The Hidden Power in Computer-mediated Communication', *Communication Research*, 21: 427–59.

Sperber, D. and Wilson, D. (1986) *Relevance: Communication and Cognition*. Oxford, UK: London.

Spielberg, A. (1999) 'Reply to Gurwitz', *Journal of the American Medical Association*, 282: 730.

Sproull, L. and Kiesler, S. (1986) 'Reducing social context cues: Electronic mail in organisation communication', *Management Science*, 32: 1492–512.

Steen, G. (2010) 'Researching and applying metaphor', TTWiA, vol (nr): 91–102.

Stommel, W. and T. Koole (2010) 'The online support group as a community: A micro-analysis of the interaction with a new member', *Discourse Studies*, 12: 357–78.

Strunk, W. and White, E. B. (2009) *The Elements of Style* (Fifth Edition). Boston, USA: Allyn and Bacon.

Stubbs, M. (1983) *Discourse Analysis: The Sociolinguistic Analysis of Natural Language*. Oxford, UK: Blackwell.

Stubbs, M. (1997) 'Whorf's children: critical comments on critical discourse analysis', in A. Wray and A. Ryan (eds) *Evolving Models of Language*. Clevedon, UK: Multilingual Matters.

Stubbs, M. (2005) 'Conrad in the computer: Examples of quantitative stylistic methods', *Language and Literature*, 14: 5–24.

Suler, J. (2004) 'The online disinhibition effect', *CyberPsychology & Behavior*, 7: 321–26.

Szasz, T. (1970) *Ideology and Insanity*. New York, USA: Anchor Books.

Taylor, B. (2005) 'The experiences of overseas nurses working in the NHS: results of a qualitative study', *Diversity in Health and Social Care*, 2: 17–27.

ten Have, P. (1989) 'The consultation as a genre', in B. Torode (ed.) *Text and Talk as Social Practice*. Dordrecht, The Netherlands and Providence, RI, USA: Foris Publications.

ten Have, P. (1991) 'Talk and institution: A reconsideration of the "asymmetry" of doctor–patient interaction'. In D. Boden and D. Zimmerman (eds) *Talk and Social Structure: Studies in Ethnomethodology and Conversation Analysis*. Cambridge, UK: Polity.

Terrence Higgins Trust (2007) *Understanding HIV Infection: HIV? AIDS?* (Fifth Edition) London, UK: Terence Higgins Trust.

Thomas, J. (2001) 'Cooperative principle', in R. Mesthrie (ed.) *Concise Enyclopedia of Sociolinguistics*. Oxford, UK. Elsevier.

Todd, A. (1989) *Intimate Adversaries: Cultural Conflicts between Doctors and Women Patients*. Philadelphia, USA: University of Pennsylvania Press.

Toogood, J. (1980) 'What do we mean by "usually"?', *Lancet*, 1: 1094–102.

Toolan, M. (2001) *Narrative: A Critical Linguistic Introduction*. (Second Edition) London: Routledge.

Treichler, P., Frankel, R., Kramarae, C., Zoppi, K. and Beckman, H. (1984) 'Problem and problems: power relationships in a medical encounter', in C. Kramarae, M. Schultz and W. O'Barr (eds) *Language and Power*. London, UK: Sage.

Triggle, C. (2010) 'NHS left with 34m stockpile of swine flu jabs' http://news.bbc.co.uk/1/hi/8606032.stm (accessed 19 April 2010).

United Nations Educational, Scientific and Cultural Organization (2006) *UNESCO Guidelines on Language and Content in HIV- and AIDS-Related Materials*. Paris, France: UNESCO.

Van Dijk, T. (1988) *News as Discourse*. Hillsdale, NJ, USA: Erlbaum.

Van Gorp, B. (2007) 'The constructionist approach to framing: Bringing culture back in', *Journal of Communication*, 57: 60–87.

Verschueren, J. (2001) 'Predicaments of criticism', *Critique of Anthropology*, 21: 59–81.

Wallis, P., Nerlich, B. and Larson, B. M. (2005) 'Metaphors and biorisks: the war on infectious diseases and invasive species', *Science communication*, 26: 243–268.

Walsh, S. (2011) *Exploring Classroom Discourse*. London, UK: Routledge.

Walstrom, M. K. (2000) ' "You know, who's the thinnest?": Combating surveillance and creating safety in coping with eating disorders online', *CyberPsychology & Behavior*, 3: 761–83.

Warshaw, C. (1989) 'Limitations of the medical model in the care of battered women', *Gender & Society*, 3: 506–17.

Warwick, I., Aggleton, P. and Homans, H. (1988) 'Young people's health beliefs and AIDS', in P. Aggleton and H. Homans (eds) *Social Aspects of AIDS*. Sussex, UK: Falmer Press.

Washer, P. and H. Joffe (2006) 'The hospital "superbug": Social representations of MRSA', *Social Science and Medicine* 63(8): 2141–52.

Watney, S. (1989) 'AIDS, language and the third world', in E. Carter and S. Watney (eds) *Taking Liberties: AIDS and Cultural Politics*. London, UK: Serpent's Tail.

Weijts, W., Houtkoop, H. and Mullen, P. (1993) 'Talking delicacy: Speaking about sexuality during gynaecological consultations', *Sociology of Health and Illness*, 15: 295–314.

Weiss, M. (1997) 'Signifying the pandemics: Metaphors of AIDS, cancer, and heart disease', *Medical Anthropology Quarterly*, 11: 456–76.

Wenger, E. (1998) *Communities of practice: learning meaning and identity*. Cambridge, UK: Cambridge University Press.

West, C. (1984) *Routine Complications: Troubles in Talk between Doctors and Patients*. Bloomington, USA: Indiana University Press.

Widdowson, H. (2000) 'On the limitations of linguistics applied', *Applied Linguistics*, 21: 3–25.

Wilkinson, A. (1992) 'Jargon and the Passive Voice: Prescriptions and Proscriptions for Scientific Writing', *Journal of Technical Writing and Communication*, 22: 319–25.

Williams, R. (1983) *Keywords*. London, UK: Fontana.

Williams, S. J., Seale, C., Boden, S., Lowe, P. and Steinberg, D. L. (2008) 'Medicalization and beyond: the social construction of insomnia and snoring in the news', *Health: Interdisciplinary Journal for the Social Study of Health, Illness & Medicine*, 12 (2), 251–68 (1363–4593).

Wilson, D. (1999) 'Relevance and relevance theory', in R. Wilson and F. Keil (eds) *MIT Encyclopedia of the Cognitive Sciences*. Cambridge, MA, USA: MIT Press.

Withers, J. and Snowball, J. (2003) 'Adapting to a new culture: A study of the expectations and experiences of Filipino nurses in the Oxford Radcliffe Hospitals NHS Trust', *Nursing Times Research*, 8: 278–90.

Wodak, R. (1997) 'Critical discourse analysis and the study of doctor–patient interaction', in B-L. Gunnarsson, P. Linell and B. Nordberg (eds) *The Construction of Professional Discourse*. London, UK: Longman.

Woodward, J. (2001) 'Are health care chaplains professionals?', in H. Orchard (ed.) *Spirituality in Healthcare Contexts*. London, UK and Philadelphia, USA: Jessica Kingsley Publishers.

Wooffitt, R. (1992) *Telling Tales of the Unexpected: Accounts of Paranormal Experiences*. Hemel Hempstead, UK: Harvester.

Woollett, A., Marshall, H. and Stenner, P. (1998) 'Young women's accounts of sexual reproduction and sexual reproductive health', *Journal of Health Psychology*, 3: 369–81.

Wright, P. (1999a) 'Writing and information design of healthcare materials', in C. Candlin and K. Hyland (eds) *Writing: Texts, Processes and Practices*. London, UK: Longman.

Wright, P. (1999b) 'Comprehension of printed instructions', in D. Wagner, R. Venezky and B. Street (eds) *Literacy: An International Handbook*. Boulder, CO, USA: Westview Press.

Zinken, J. (2003) 'Ideological imagination: Intertextual and correlational metaphors in political discourse', *Discourse & Society*, 14 (4), July: 507–23.

Zinken, J., Hellsten, I. and Nerlich, B. (2008) 'Discourse metaphors', in R. Frank, R. Dirven, T. Ziemke and E. Bernardez (eds) *Body, Language and Mind. Vol. 2: Sociocultural Situatedness*. Amsterdam, The Netherlands: John Benjamins.

Index